International Political Economy Series

General Editor: Timothy M. Shaw, Professor and Director, Institute of International Relations, The University of the West Indies, Trinidad & Tobago

Titles include:

Hans Abrahamsson
UNDERSTANDING WORLD ORDER AND STRUCTURAL CHANGE
Poverty, Conflict and the Global Arena

Morten Bøås, Marianne H. Marchand and Timothy Shaw (*editors*)
THE POLITICAL ECONOMY OF REGIONS AND REGIONALISM

Sandra Braman (*editor*)
THE EMERGENT GLOBAL INFORMATION POLICY REGIME

James Busumtwi-Sam and Laurent Dobuzinskis
TURBULENCE AND NEW DIRECTION IN GLOBAL POLITICAL ECONOMY

Elizabeth De Boer-Ashworth
THE GLOBAL POLITICAL ECONOMY AND POST-1989 CHANGE
The Place of the Central European Transition

Bill Dunn
GLOBAL RESTRUCTURING AND THE POWER OF LABOUR

Myron J. Frankman
WORLD DEMOCRATIC FEDERALISM
Peace and Justice Indivisible

Helen A. Garten
US FINANCIAL REGULATION AND THE LEVEL PLAYING FIELD

Barry K. Gills (*editor*)
GLOBALIZATION AND THE POLITICS OF RESISTANCE

Richard Grant and John Rennie Short (*editors*)
GLOBALIZATION AND THE MARGINS

Graham Harrison (*editor*)
GLOBAL ENCOUNTERS
International Political Economy, Development and Globalization

Patrick Hayden and Chamsy el-Ojeili (*editors*)
CONFRONTING GLOBALIZATION
Humanity, Justice and the Renewal of Politics

Axel Hülsemeyer (*editor*)
GLOBALIZATION IN THE TWENTY-FIRST CENTURY
Convergence or Divergence?

Helge Hveem and Kristen Nordhaug (*editors*)
PUBLIC POLICY IN THE AGE OF GLOBALIZATION
Responses to Environmental and Economic Crises

Takashi Inoguchi
GLOBAL CHANGE
A Japanese Perspective

Jomo K.S. and Shyamala Nagaraj (*editors*)
GLOBALIZATION VERSUS DEVELOPMENT

Adrian Kay and Owain David Williams (*editors*)
GLOBAL HEALTH GOVERNANCE
Crisis, Institutions and Political Economy

International Political Economy Series
Series Standing Order ISBN 978–0–333–71708–0 hardcover
Series Standing Order ISBN 978–0–333–71110–1 paperback

You can receive future titles in this series as they are published by placing a standing order. Please contact your bookseller or, in case of difficulty, write to us at the address below with your name and address, the title of the series and one of the ISBNs quoted above.

Customer Services Department, Macmillan Distribution Ltd, Houndmills, Basingstoke, Hampshire RG21 6XS, England

Sugar: Refined Power in a Global Regime

Ben Richardson

First published 2009 by
PALGRAVE MACMILLAN

Palgrave Macmillan in the UK is an imprint of Macmillan Publishers Limited, registered in England, company number 785998, of Houndmills, Basingstoke, Hampshire RG21 6XS.

Palgrave Macmillan in the US is a division of St Martin's Press LLC, 175 Fifth Avenue, New York, NY 10010.

Palgrave Macmillan is the global academic imprint of the above companies and has companies and representatives throughout the world.

Palgrave® and Macmillan® are registered trademarks in the United States, the United Kingdom, Europe and other countries

ISBN-13: 978-0-230-23220-4   hardback

This book is printed on paper suitable for recycling and made from fully managed and sustained forest sources. Logging, pulping and manufacturing processes are expected to conform to the environmental regulations of the country of origin.

A catalogue record for this book is available from the British Library.

A catalogue record for this book is available from the Library of Congress.

10   9   8   7   6   5   4   3   2   1
18   17   16   15   14   13   12   11   10   09

Printed and bound in Great Britain by
CPI Antony Rowe, Chippenham and Eastbourne

Contents

List of Figures and Tables

Figures

Tables

Acknowledgements

It is nice to think that in writing these acknowledgements there are so many people to thank. First, I would like to give heartfelt gratitude to my two PhD supervisors, Tony Payne and Tony Heron. I don't think I could have got a better combination of academics to guide me through the PhD (and the Master's and BA before that!) and it is thanks to their professionalism and friendliness that I managed to complete the thesis and translate it into this book. I hope in doing so, I have repaid some of the faith you have shown in me. While we're on the subject of academics, I would also like to thank all the people at Sheffield, and the many others I met along the way, who took the time to help me with my work. Those who spring to mind include Michael Billig, Brigid Gavin, Jean Grugel, John Hobson, Graham Harrison, Peter Jackson and Fiona Lewis... but I'm sure there were more. Thanks also to the fantastic administration staff at Sheffield, who made things run so smoothly, and to Tim Shaw, Alexandra Webster and Renée Takken at Palgrave Macmillan, who did likewise during the publishing stage. Gratitude too goes to the interviewees who generously gave up their time. I hope I have reflected your views and comments accurately, and done justice to the work that you do. As an extension of my PhD research, I would also like to thank the ESRC here for sponsoring my further studies, and my colleagues in the post-graduate department for their support, advice and general banter. It was an awesome four years. But most of all, I have to thank Katy for her unending support and affection. You've made these last few years happy ones and I hope we have many more together. Those are the people who helped me achieve something I'm really proud of. For even getting to this stage in the first place, I have my family to thank. It says so much that I don't often realise how lucky I've been growing up or think about all the sacrifices you must have made. I would like to dedicate this book to Mum and Dad, for everything I owe you.

List of Abbreviations

ACP	African, Caribbean and Pacific
ASEAN	Association of Southeast Nations
CAP	Common Agricultural Policy
CMO Sugar	Common Market Organisation of Sugar
COMECON	Council for Mutual Economic Assistance
CSA	Commonwealth Sugar Agreement
CSRC	Colonial Sugar Refining Company
DR-CAFTA	Dominican Republic-Central American Free Trade Agreement
DSB	Dispute Settlement Body
EBA	Everything But Arms
EC	European Community
ECLA	Economic Commission for Latin America
ECU	European Currency Unit
EPA	Economic Partnership Agreement
EU	European Union
FDA	Food and Drug Administration
FDI	Foreign Direct Investment
FTA	Free Trade Agreement
GATT	General Agreement on Trade and Tariffs
GDP	Gross Domestic Product
GM	Genetically Modified
GSP	Generalised System of Preferences
HFCS	High Fructose Corn Syrup
IMF	International Monetary Fund
IPE	International Political Economy
IR	International Relations
ISA	International Sugar Agreement
ISI	Import Substitution Industrialisation
ITO	International Trade Organisation
LDC	Least Developed Country
MST	Movimento dos Trabalhadores Rurais Sem Terra
MT	Million Tonnes
NAFTA	North American Free Trade Agreement
NAMA	Non-Agricultural Market Access
NGO	Non-Governmental Organisation

OECD	Organisation for Economic Co-operation and Development
OPEC	Organisation of the Petroleum Exporting Countries
POJ	Proefstatien Oost Java
RTA	Regional Trade Agreement
SCP	Sugar-Containing Product
SP	Special Product
SSM	Special Safeguard Mechanism
SSP	Sensitive Product
SUA	Sweetener Users Association
TRQ	Tariff Rate Quota
UNCTAD	United Nations Conference on Trade and Development
UNICA	Brazilian Sugarcane Industry Association
USDA	US Department of Agriculture
USTR	US Trade Representative
WTO	World Trade Organisation

The story of a lump of sugar is a whole lesson in political economy, politics, and morality.

– Auguste Cochin, cited in Scheper-Hughes (1992: 34)

1
Introduction

In 2005 sugar policy once again found its way into the headlines. This time the story revolved around the imminent reform of the Common Agricultural Policy of the European Union (EU) and the effects this could have on farmers and companies both in Europe and the group of mainly former colonial states known as the African, Caribbean and Pacific (ACP) countries. In essence, the stories had two angles: first, that the sugar industry in the EU was a bastion of protectionism and was long overdue reform, and second, that while this reform was necessary, the sugar exporting ACP countries dependent on these arrangements were likely to lose out. As the negotiations intensified around this esoteric piece of legislation, competing interests were increasingly set into relief and the timbre of dissension grew as the final verdict neared. In the end, the decision was taken in Brussels to substantially lower the price received by suppliers to the EU market, causing the biggest change to European sugar policy in over 30 years and substantial losses for the ACP. As the *Financial Times* later reported, the reforms would herald a new economic reality for sugar in which 'the days of preferences are over' and 'the era of competitiveness' underway (Hawkins 2008).

But there was also another dimension to these stories. It was the idea that these new economic realities, or the forces of globalisation as they are more commonly known, were an unstoppable and indispensable development. If this was the case, there seemed to be something missing from the journalists' reports, some discrepancies and oversights in the logic. For one, if these liberal reforms were unstoppable, why was the sugar policy of so many other countries still able to elude it? Did globalisation in fact have an incomplete reach? And for another, if these types of reform were indispensable, why was it that the poorer

1

sugar-exporting countries seemed to suffer most? Was globalisation actually hurting the people its defenders argued it was meant to help?

The reform of this single piece of sugar legislation opened the door onto these and many other questions besides. Having since immersed myself in the subject and read the introductions to many other publications about sugar, this unfolding of questions seems to be a common feature of the commodity. What starts with a single story or point of interest quickly escalates into a serial fascination, and what at first seems an innocuous, pure substance – the ubiquitous refined white sugar – quickly comes to embody a complex social relation and penetrating capitalist metaphor. In a way, sugar comes to represent the ultimate commodity: commonplace enough to seem totally banal yet integral to so many aspects of people's lives as to be totally vital. It is this obscured dimension of sugar, the story behind the sweetener, which we seek to explore in greater detail.

Why sugar as a topic?

So sugar makes for such an interesting topic because it is both ubiquitous and provocative. Slavery, degradation, obesity, poverty... the list is longer still. As such, the commodity can be studied from a number of perspectives, making its productive genesis, its environmental impact, its links to ill health, or even its cultural and symbolic attire a motivation for enquiry. Building on the questions generated by the story above, what we articulate here are two analytical puzzles that act as motivation for a study pertaining to sugar's international political economy.

The first puzzle is the fact many countries protect their domestic sugar farmers from trade, and have done for centuries, despite in most cases being able to import the product at much lower cost. Closer examination of the production chain of sugar detailed in Figure 1.1 helps clarify why so many people find this situation absurd.

The first thing to note is that the same product (white sugar) can be made from two different crops (sugar cane and sugar beet). This product is absolutely identical, even down to its chemical formula $C_{12}H_{22}O_{11}$ – the properties of pure sucrose. Given that cane grows in tropical climates and beet in temperate climates, it is therefore possible for sugar to be grown right across the globe. However, the efficiency with which the sucrose can be extracted in these different locations differs. At a *very* general level, and despite the extra stage of processing, it is more efficient to produce sugar from cane. Given that many developing countries are in tropical areas and thus suitable destinations for this crop, to obstruct this oppor-

Figure 1.1   The Transformation of Sugar Crops from Farm to Food

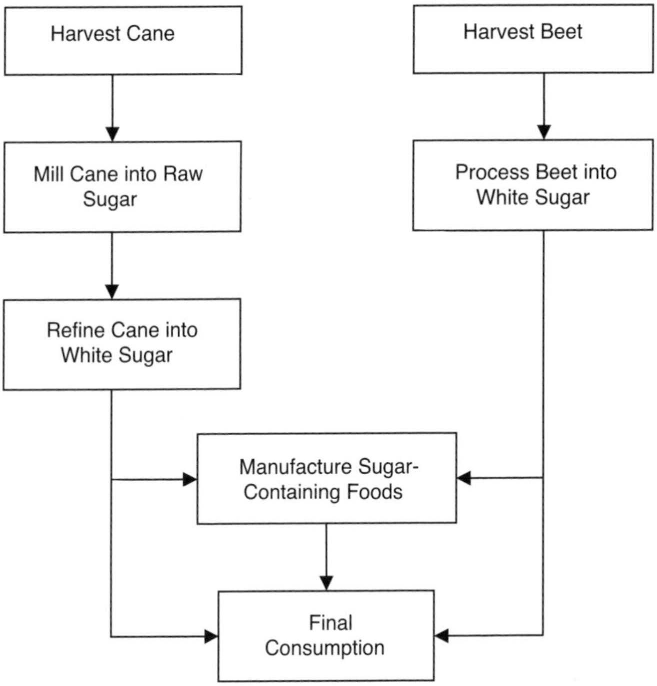

```
┌─────────────────────┐          ┌─────────────────────┐
│    Harvest Cane     │          │    Harvest Beet     │
└─────────────────────┘          └─────────────────────┘
          │                                 │
          ▼                                 ▼
┌─────────────────────┐          ┌─────────────────────┐
│  Mill Cane into Raw │          │   Process Beet into │
│        Sugar        │          │     White Sugar     │
└─────────────────────┘          └─────────────────────┘
          │                                 │
          ▼                                 │
┌─────────────────────┐                     │
│   Refine Cane into  │                     │
│     White Sugar     │                     │
└─────────────────────┘                     │
          │       ┌──────────────────────┐  │
          ├──────▶│  Manufacture Sugar-  │◀─┤
          │       │   Containing Foods   │  │
          │       └──────────────────────┘  │
          │             │                    │
          │             ▼                    │
          │       ┌──────────────────────┐  │
          └──────▶│        Final         │◀─┘
                  │     Consumption      │
                  └──────────────────────┘
```

Source: Author.

tunity through protectionism seems perverse to advocates of both international development and free trade. The second point to note at this stage is how refined sugar is bought by manufacturers for use in processed goods like confectionery and soft drinks, and by consumers directly, for use in home cooking and to sweeten drinks and cereals. By protecting domestic markets from trade and keeping the price of sugar higher than it would have otherwise been, these policies confer additional costs on these actors and create another set of losers. The size of these costs is staggering. Between 1999 and 2001, the OECD (2002: 56) reckoned more than *half the value* of sugar production in its member countries came from government support or transfers from consumers, totaling an average of $6.4 billion per year.

To add to what is typically seen as an inefficient and unjustifiable transfer of wealth to sugar producers in developed countries, these policies also act as a major sticking point in international trade negotiations, hindering the conclusion of free trade more generally. While all countries are expected to feel some pressure to defend liberalisation of 'sensitive' industries, meaning those in which there is a strategic or social exigency in protecting, sugar seems an unlikely candidate for such special treatment. The industry contributes a fraction of GDP in developed countries and employs dwindling numbers of farmers and workers, relative to both industrial and service sectors, and indeed the rest of agriculture. So for sugar to be protected in the first place, and then to hold up reciprocal liberalisation and greater welfare gains across the economy as a whole, appears to some as even more irrational. Taken together, these points comprise what we might refer to as the 'protectionist paradox', one of the central themes animating the political discourse on sugar.

A second puzzle, and again one that speaks directly to the discipline of international political economy, is the way in which sugar is associated both with rural development and with poverty. An implicit assumption in the arguments presented above was that if poor countries were able to export sugar to protected markets, employment rates, tax receipts and foreign exchange earnings in the industry would all increase and the lives of their citizens would thereby be enriched. An opposing view, and an unequivocal one at that, was summed up by the editor of the *New Internationalist* David Ransom, who wrote in a 2003 special on the commodity:

> Sugar has never enriched anyone but slave traders, local landlords, industrial farmers, sugar barons, speculators, food corporations, PR consultants and professional politicians. No-one has ever traded their way out of poverty with sugar, and there's no reason to suppose that they ever will.

This is what we might call the 'production paradox': how the existence of a sugar industry, with all its negative connotations, can still be seen as a boon for rural communities, even a necessity in those areas where it has long been established. Debates and decisions about this paradox are certainly no academic triviality. According to the International Labour Organisation (2005: 127), 75 per cent of the world's poor live in rural areas and in developing countries the agricultural sector accounts for 40 per cent of employment. Sugar is an important component in this make-up: worldwide, the industry accounts for approximately 15 million direct jobs in estate and factory work and in the region of 100 million indirect jobs in small-holder cultivation and temporary cane cutting (Better Sugarcane Initiative 2005: 8). The vast majority of these jobs are in developing countries.

Again the crop transformation diagram offers an initial insight into how this paradox emerges. Unlike fruit, vegetables or grains, sugar cane and beet is rarely eaten directly as it requires extensive processing to become edible. The juice must first be extracted, cleansed and crystallised, then finally purified through centrifugal force to leave refined white sugar. Moreover, as a supplement to diets rather than a staple, it is typically produced as a cash crop. Because of these features, production usually entails concerted capital investment and to ensure commercial viability is often large scale. From the beginning, sugar becomes predicated on hierarchical organisation and inequalities of ownership; the plantation economy being the best known manifestation. But, as one starts to scratch the surface, varying types and readings of production begin to appear. For example, commercial ventures they may be, but it is evident that many sugar producers provide essential services such as health care and community clubs and, furthermore, are often considered to be good employers (possibly even the only employers) in remote rural areas. In addition, despite the persistence of 'backward' and deplorable practices such as bondage slavery and child labour, it is often the case that the factories and their farm suppliers are highly advanced technologically, even seen in some quarters as the vanguard of economic growth in the countryside. In short, normative judgements about the poverty-reducing value of the sugar industry clearly cannot be made without first engaging with the complex, concrete realities of production.

Why a political economy approach?

The analytical problems highlighted above have been cited as motivations for an international political economy approach and will undoubtedly be already familiar to readers in some form. Debates about protection and production in sugar are centuries old, and in many cases, the outcomes of these debates, transformed into policy, have changed the course of history. Who would have thought that today, for example, New York might still have been New Amsterdam had the Dutch accepted the British offer in 1667 to keep the American port town in exchange for its sugar estates in Surinam? For our two paradoxes, the continued importance of their consequences has continued to generate a fresh flow of words debating them. So in effect, what we are really asking here is: why *this* book? In other words, what can a renewed look at the political economy of sugar tell us about the world of sugar that we cannot already read, or easily extrapolate, from existing literature? To answer this question, we now briefly review the leading academic books that address these issues and identify the shortcomings and gaps contained within them. The literature is divided according to the following typology: world history, world economy, agri-food geographies, and idiosyncratic commodity studies.

World history

World history refers to the writings that cover the spread of sugar production, typically cane production, as it made its way west from Southeast Asia to Europe and from then on to the Caribbean. The symbiosis of colonialism and cane forms a central theme as the unfolding of slavery, migration, land appropriation and even capitalism itself are all visible in the expansion of sugar production through the tropics. Standout texts in this category include Sidney Mintz's *Sweetness and Power* and Jock Galloway's *The Sugar Cane Industry*, both of which surpass simple colonial narratives to bring into focus the systemic international dimension of production; in Mintz's case highlighting the changing cultures of consumption that drove demand for sugar in Britain, and in Galloway's case highlighting the variegated forms that sugar production took and the multicultural societies it left in its wake. Cojoining these older histories are studies profiling the nationalisation and increasing unionisation in many sugar industries during the turn of the 20th century; Bill Albert and Adrian Graves' two-book edited collection *Crisis and Change, 1860–1914* and *War and Depression, 1914–1940* serving as the best example here.

While essential building blocks for contemporary analysis, the obvious drawback of this literature is exactly its historical focus. Even the more recent world histories, such as George C. Abbott's *Sugar* that presents a systematic look at the international commodity agreements between beet and cane producing states and the policies pursued within this framework, take us only as far as the 1980s. While such work is necessary to historicise the structures of the modern sugar economy, and while some of the analytical insights stand the test of time, serving as useful points of entry into contemporary debates, there have been enough recent changes in sugar production to warrant a renewed mapping of the issues and power struggles crystallising in the current era, with reference in particular to the phenomenon of globalisation.

World sugar economy

One set of literature that has kept abreast of recent developments has been work devoted to translating the world sugar economy. This refers to those studies which attempt to make sense of the plethora of data on production costs, trade flows, consumption drivers, etc. and piece them together in an intelligible whole, articulating the directions of individual national markets and how they scale up to influence the world market. Besides giving the 'bigger descriptive picture', as it were, this type of work also offers explanatory insights into the idiosyncrasies of national markets and the price volatility characteristic of the world market, centring on the effects of trade barriers and production regulations. Chief among this literature is *The World Sugar Market* by Sergey Gudoshnikov, Lindsay Jolly and Donald Spence, *Sugar and Related Sweetener Markets* edited by Andrew Schmitz, Thomas Spreen, William Messina Junior and Charles Moss, and *The Economics and Politics of World Sugar Markets* edited by Stephen Marks and Keith Maskus.

While this literature offers the advantage of being up to date and is always quantitatively insightful, it is found wanting in two crucial departments. The first is in its explanatory insights, which it generates almost exclusively from a position of overt economism. This is a perspective that seeks to explain price movements as the result of temporary disequilibria in self-regulating market mechanisms, or, where structural imbalances are detected, as largely the fault of government intervention. As a result, its political economy is essentially predicated on a description of how governments disrupt smooth functioning markets, or, more fundamentally, how politics gets in the way of economics. In this way, the analysis tends to a truncated view of politics, understood merely as the actions of states, and a facile view of the economy, understood as a universal and impersonal sphere of interaction. Related to this, the second limitation is that there is a strong normative thrust in the literature in favour of liberalisation and market rule, so much so that it tends to be overly preoccupied with predicting the gains from wholesale liberalisation. By way of example, in his paper entitled 'Alternative US and EU Trade Liberalization Policies' Won Koo believes a fundamental question to be 'what is going to happen in the US sugar industry if the US government eliminates the Sugar Program while other countries maintain their subsidies' (Koo 2002: 342). Notwithstanding the limited probability of this type of radical reform actually happening (and thus the practical relevance of such studies), these enquiries also direct attention away from other more pressing political economy questions, particularly about the relationship of sugar to equality and sustainability; questions which are typically marginalised, even maligned, within this approach.

Agri-food geographies

The literature that takes us closest to a contemporary and critical perspective on international sugar production can be found in what is commonly referred to as 'agri-food' studies. The epithet agri-food refers to the work of rural geographers who inscribed into their studies a consideration of how food processors and biotechnology companies were driving change in farm production. One strand of this work that is particularly relevant is the work on 'food regimes' that emerged in the 1980s associated with Harriet Friedmann and Philip McMichael, and since carried through by scholars such as Tony Weis. Their research agenda, grouped around a comparison of alternate world historical food regimes, showed how the mass production of standardised, durable and highly processed foods in the post-war era was born of two trends in the new international division of labour. First was the import substitution of tropical exports from the South by agri-food industries based in advanced capitalist countries, which created cheap competition to traditional cash crops, and second was the integration of agri-food sectors, also in the capitalist core, based on the emergence of food manufacturing as a transnational sphere of accumulation. Under this approach, valuable new insights were generated into the place of sugar in both the disintegration of the old colonial division of labour and the changing nature of the Fordist diet.

Undoubtedly, the food regimes scholarship gave studies about agriculture and the international food system a much-needed 'shot in the arm' with its Marxist-inspired political economy, and much can, and will, be taken here from this approach (Ward and Alma[o]s 1997). However, its tendency to centre analysis round a 'broad-brush' account of the transformation of capitalist agriculture has left it open to the criticism that it overlooks heterogeneity at the local level and is too quick to lump together disparate and divergent processes into grand epochal narratives (Whatmore 1994; Marsden and Arce 1995). Moreover, derived from this broad-brush analytical commitment it also has an empirical tendency to focus on the US and its traditional export sectors (grains and livestock), or, in more recent scholarship, the 'value-added' export sectors emerging in developing countries (seafood, fruits, etc). In exploring the issues idiosyncratic to sugar and which run counter to many of those happening in the rest of agriculture, a food regimes approach tends to leave a lot of unanswered questions or a 'residue of anomalies' connected to the commodity (Fine *et al.* 1996: 120).

Idiosyncratic commodity studies

Overcoming these drawbacks, a number of other writings have considered the political economy of sugar through alternative, more idiosyncratic theoretical lenses. Ian Drummond and Terry Marsden in their book *The Condition of Sustainability* compare the modes of sugar production in Australia and Barbados through the prism of an ecologically informed regulation theory; Michelle Harrison, in her book *King Sugar*, looks at the place of Jamaica in the regional and global sugar economy through an approach infused with commodity chain theory; and Ben Fine, Michael Heasman and Judith Wright consider in *Consumption in the Age of Affluence* the demand management of sugar in the UK through Fine's systems of provision analysis. Yet whilst they explore the intricacies of sugar in greater detail, in respect of our analytical problems they arguably go too far in the other direction, sidestepping explanation about the formation of global rules and international trends in favour of studying the environmental, social or consumer politics of sugar in largely national terms. It is this lacuna that the book will attempt to fill. Detailed more in the next chapter, it will suffice to say here that our 'regime' approach is intended to highlight the spatial, modal and contradictory nature of the rules and norms associated with a particular industry. In this way it will both decouple the regime in sugar from the prevailing food regime at large whilst also providing the platform to link changes in individual states to pressures emanating from systemic global forces.

Aims of the book

So far a rationale for studying the prevailing regime in sugar has been constructed out of desire to explore the paradoxes of protection and production that remain overlooked in existing literature. This general thrust will now be broken down into a set of specific research questions that details the points of entry into these debates and also suggests where the wider intellectual contribution of the book will lie. The first question asks: what are the terms of competition for sugar producers? This refers to the different regulatory environments that exist worldwide and the opportunities and constraints they confer on firms according to their locale. An exploration of these environments is expected to reveal the different international and intra-national advantages received by certain fractions of capital and labour at the expense of others. Implicitly, this question also enquires about the extent of globalisation in the sugar regime, understood as the entrenchment of a set of rules and norms that correspond to the free movement of goods, an opening of capital investment, a deregulation of state controlled prices and the homogeneity of tastes and technology. If globalisation is indeed occurring, we should expect to witness significant convergence among previously distinct regulatory environments to this standard.

The second question then asks: what are the ascendant strategies of accumulation within these terms of competition? Accumulation is understood here as the transformation of capital – encompassing finance, knowledge and social power – into privatised wealth, and strategies of accumulation as the ways in which this transformation manifests itself among the owners/managers of capital. The implicit interrogation here is of the relationship of sugar production to development, as it is only with reference to how businesses relate to labour and land within the environment set for them that their contribution to living standards can be concretely understood. Simply equating international development with increased export opportunities or decreased import competition is considered far too shallow a reading.

The third and final question asks: how are the terms of competition remade? This is directed to the preferences of state elites – it is maintained through the book that states continue to underpin the international trade and production in sugar – and how these are shaped by the demands of different industry actors, international negotiations, and general electoral and economic imperatives. In this respect, an implicit question is posed about reform in policy systems that have long been immune to change, and, upholding the critical stance we wish to take, the options for resistance by actors typically marginalised from the arenas of policy formation.

Tying the answers to these three questions together will also shed light on a more fundamental issue about how we should best conceptualise and critique the exercise of power in the international political economy. In particular, it will highlight the 'power to institutionalise' – which we refer to as 'refined' power in contrast to explicit forms of 'raw' power seen in prolific political donations or the use of forced labour, say – which condition outcomes seemingly without recourse to politics. In re-politicising the sugar regime this way, it is intended that the study will both correct the oversights of current literature highlighted above, and also encourage further debate on the causes and consequences of globalisation in the agri-food sector but this time with the 'anomalous' case of sugar more fully factored in.

To answer these questions, the book draws on country data included in four case studies – the EU and ACP, the US, Asia, and Brazil respectively – which were chosen for several sets of reasons. First, the case studies are geographically widespread and cover countries with different governing institutions and economic profiles. As such, they provided a litmus test as to whether the sugar regime is indeed in the process of globalisation, as we would expect in such an eventuality to witness uniform pressure across all these spatial and economic frames. Putting this in terms of our research questions, we were able to monitor whether the international and intra-national terms of competition were coalescing around a universal standard, and whether this was due to the same mechanisms of policy reform in all places.

Second, and related to the spread of countries chosen, the large range of case studies better allowed for the full spectrum of sugar politics to be interrogated. By avoiding the temptation to focus solely on the core countries of the world economy or the former colonies in the Caribbean, each of which make certain aspects of sugar politics more apparent than others, we both guarded against an ethnocentric bias *and* created the space in which to explore different contestations found in this multi-faceted industry. For example, while the chapter on the EU looks primarily at the relationships within the sugar-producing industry, the chapter on Asia looks at the relationships between the sugar-producing and sugar-using industries. Giving adequate space to these differing contests ensured that we could drill down into their respective minutiae, before tying them together in the concluding chapter and acknowledging the cumulative presence of these contestations, if only retrospectively, in all countries engaged in sugar production.

Last of all, the cases were chosen as they corresponded to the leading architects of international rules governing production and trade. Either because of broader economic and diplomatic weight (the US, EU and Japan) or because of moral and legal weight as developing countries and low cost sugar producers (India, Thailand and Brazil), these countries maintain the biggest influence over sugar policy and as such we can learn a lot about the sources of power within the sugar regime by delineating the linkages between their domestic and international preferences. Moreover, as the country most likely to benefit under trade liberalisation, the inclusion of Brazil and an interrogation of the social and political economy effects of increased exports is considered highly revealing of the purpose of power in the regime.

Shape of the book

Following on from this introductory chapter, Chapter 2 starts our theoretical overview by tracing the formation of the international political economy (IPE) discipline in its mainstream guise. In the narrative built around this branch of IPE the discipline is said to emerge in the 1970s as US scholars tried to account for the renewed importance of economic affairs in international relations. Central to these academic efforts was the concept of a 'regime', which referred to an international issue-area subject to interstate regulation. The battles between realists and liberals, and later on, constructivists, over the way in which regimes should be conceptualised helped map out the substantive and normative concerns of the IPE field. However, these theoretical frames harboured a regime concept that was weak on the sources of power and weak on critique, given that it focused mainly on state interactions and had a normative bias toward stability. Thus the second half of the chapter turns to critical IPE theory, particularly the work contributed from a 'post-states and markets' perspective, that followed in its wake, and which provide a more appropriate framework in which to re-embed the regime concept. Given the suitability of the core theoretical tenets of the regime to a study of global sugar production, we argue that this concept is also preferable to two common alternatives, global governance and global value chains. The chapter ends by providing three methodological imperatives – regulatory structures, strategic coalitions and economic identities – that together will help map out the evolution of the broad-set sugar regimes.

Chapter 3 takes up this challenge by charting the emergence of the commercial sugar trade and its apotheosis in the colonial sugar regime in the 18th century. It argues that the rules and practices constituting this regime drew Europe, Africa and the Americas together in the famous 'triangle trade' and, in the Caribbean in particular, inscribed a number of legacies which would fundamentally shape its future social and political economy development. But the regime also withheld a number of potent contradictions that were ultimately made manifest by liberal discourse, abolitionism, and war, and which led to the collapse of this regime and its replacement by the national sugar regime. Chapter 4 picks up the consolidation of the national sugar regime in the aftermath of World War II and argues that the trade regulation, domestic coalitions and processed food consumerism that characterised the latter half of the 20th century in sugar were essentially inherited from the pre-war era. The only major dislocation was caused by the geo-politics of the Cold War, but, once the regime had been pressed and fitted into this foreign policy orientation, relative stability was resumed. This was shaken by the food crisis of the 1970s, which again can be seen as a result of inherent contradictions in the way production and trade was controlled, and again created the momentum for wholesale regime change. The inauguration of the World Trade Organisation in 1994 and the inclusion of sugar within the multilateral process suggested that the globalisation of previously nationally-ordered regimes would be the most likely outcome.

Chapters 5, 6, 7 and 8 cover the contemporary, empirical section of the book and examine how the anticipated globalisation of the sugar regime has been played out in different sugar-producing countries. Chapter 5 begins by focusing on the EU and its erstwhile preferential trade agreements with the ACP. When the EU reformed its long-standing protectionist policy in the wake of a WTO challenge by Australia, Brazil and Thailand, the case was hailed as a victory for liberalism and evidence of the strength now entrenched in international rules on trade. The main point raised in this chapter is to argue that, despite defeat at the WTO, dominant capital in the EU sugar industry has continued to prosper after reform while divestment in the ex-colonies has left producers in the ACP facing difficulties of adjustment far in excess of plain terms of trade losses. Further, it also reveals why EU reform was not solely a response to WTO legislation but, rather, because of the relationship of sugar to wider economic fortunes, resulted from an assiduous attempt by the EU Trade Commission to press the sector into a WTO-compatible Common Agricultural Policy.

Chapter 6 considers the evolution of the national regime in the US, especially in light of the free trade agreement in sugar now in force with Mexico. Even though imports are still under tight control, this and other trade agreements have sharply reduced the ability of the US industry to relieve domestic pressure by manipulating imports and have thereby intensified the threats to one of the most important world markets. The chapter then makes the more novel argument that imports are only one source of competition to US sugar producers. Declining real prices have forced significant restructuring on the industry and spawned a number of interesting evolutionary developments. The first has been the attempts by sugar producers to manipulate government policy to bolster consumer demand in both sugar and sugar-based ethanol, while the second has been the weakening of the traditional alliance between the sugar industry and the corn industry. Together they suggest new institutional opportunities and challenges to the mechanisms that have traditionally protected US sugar.

Chapter 7 turns attention away from the core economies of the North and instead toward the Asian region. It opens with an account of the prevailing system of trade relations in Asia, defined as a bilateralism that has liberalised export-oriented sectors whilst protecting import-sensitive sectors, with sugar firmly in the latter category. Nonetheless, as in the previous chapter, it is argued that regulatory pressure stemming from the trade environment has not been the sole factor conditioning strategies of accumulation in the sugar industry. In this case, it is the volatile conditions of domestic price instability and credit shortages that have led to severe agrarian hardship. In addition, the 'nutrition transition' in Asia toward diets with higher sugar content is also depicted as a likely stimulus for change or, at the very least, a source of endemic contradiction, as pressures are placed on states in the form of growing health risks and increasing opportunities to benefit from the processed food trade that cannot be avoided simply by abiding to a protectionist policy orientation.

Chapter 8 completes the core research section of the book by returning to the recently inaugurated global trade architecture, tracing the evolution of agricultural policy negotiations under the WTO. It argues that the ascendance of the G20 coalition of developing countries has ended the reign of the EU and US duopoly but that the prospects this holds for pro-development regulation are less than sanguine. Taking examples from the negotiations over agriculture, it is noted that consensus around the Doha Round text has been thwarted by the split over further preference erosion in the EU, which has pitted the ACP against Brazil and Thailand, and that confidence in the notion of progressive liberalisation has been undermined by the constant renewal of state-support in agriculture, as governments find loopholes in, create policies compatible with, or exclude commodities from, WTO regulation. The chapter then looks in detail at Brazil, the country expected to gain most from a global, liberal regime. Based on the growth in the industry since 2000, it finds that under the export-led agricultural model being promoted by the country's elites, rural development in the country is bifurcating, with some fractions of labour gaining better employment terms but many more losing job opportunities and access to land.

Chapter 9 offers some final conclusions on the nature of the incipient global regime in sugar. It addresses, first, the terms of competition that characterise the current regime, finding them to have the spatial and legal scope to ensure WTO legislation is adhered to but still lacking the social scope to expose farmers, especially those in the more powerful countries, to institutionalised price volatility. It then looks at the predominant strategies of accumulation and finds dominant capital in the industry breaking the 'national envelope' of investment as well as moving into ethanol and niche sweeteners in order to insulate themselves from price competition. This is encouraging the further bifurcation of labour and the reconstitution of farmers as the industry becomes dependent on a slimmed down and increasingly technocratic workforce. Finally, it details the existence of bottom-up resistance to ever intensified agro-industrial production in the consumer movements in the North and farmer and landless protests in the South, but argues that, ultimately, the greatest form of agency is likely to be a corporate and path dependent one, as sugar processors in developed countries expand in such a way as to undercut their own support base and rationale for protectionism.

2
Conceptualising Power in the World Economy: Reviving Regimes in IPE Theory

The two paradoxes detailed in the introduction pointed the way toward an analysis led by some sort of international political economy approach. We say 'some sort' because there are manifold orientations and cleavages that mark out the theoretical terrain of IPE, nearly all of which could be used to garner some understanding of the issues surrounding protection and production in sugar, though each asking different questions and providing different results. It is necessary at this juncture therefore to define the type of IPE we intend to use and, within this, the exact meaning of the regime concept that will animate our analysis. Fortunately, this task is made a little easier insofar as the concept of a regime has to a significant degree marked out the formation of the IPE discipline in its mainstream guise, allowing us to trace one within the other.

The task of this chapter, then, is to trace the rise (and eventual decline) of the regime concept within IPE in chronological fashion and make the case for its resurrection, albeit in a different theoretical attire. It considers first the emergence of the discipline itself in the 1970s, forged through the dominant theories of realism and liberalism, before then examining the contributions and challenges made to these 'neo-utilitarian' theories by the constructivist literature, which also utilised the concept of regimes to reflect on international organisation but did so in manner that emphasised the role of knowledge, identity formation and history in their function. From this point we turn to the theoretical tradition recalled and recovered by the self-proclaimed 'critical IPE' scholars and chart their contributions to the state-market debate. It was through this debate that concepts such as global governance and global value chains would ultimately arise, all but replacing the concept of an 'international regime' in the discipline which was now

16

felt to be analytically restrictive in its privileging of the nation-state and the *status quo*. Sections three and four of the chapter then suggest why these new approaches are inappropriate ways in which to approach a study of power in the global production of sugar, and what a revived conceptualisation of an 'industrial regime' can offer in their stead.

A genealogy of regimes

The predominant story of the emergence of IPE within the social sciences is a well recounted one and will be dealt with quickly (see Denemark and O'Brien 1997; Murphy and Nelson 2001; Watson 2005; Cohen 2008). It begins in the 1970s and the challenges made to the prevailing orthodoxy in International Relations (IR) theory, realism. Realism was a theory based on the primacy of the state and its national military security and so seemed incapable of addressing the pre-eminent concerns surrounding the 'triple crisis': the devaluation of the dollar and the breaking of the fixed exchange rate system, the rise in protectionism, and the hikes in oil prices engendered by the OPEC cartel. Yet by drawing on Robert Gilpin's (1971) mercantilist work that situated patterns of economic activity within the global balance of power and Charles Kindleberger's (1973) theory that proposed public goods such as open trade and finance systems were in fact underpinned by a hegemonic state, realists were able reorientate their empirical outlook and bring economic security to centre stage. Based on the liberal tradition in IR, an alternative account of the change in world politics was offered by Robert Keohane and Joseph Nye (1977) in their book *Power and Interdependence*. Interdependence referred to how states and their societies were linked through (among other factors) the interactions and structures of the market, which was used as an opposing ideal-type to the realist's power politics scenario.

The concept of a regime, meanwhile, had been brought into the purview of IR literature in the mid-1970s from the legal discipline and was intended to give form to the collective practices in international politics that existed beyond the workings of international organisations and which contributed to a semblance of order (Haas 1975; Ruggie 1975; Young 1980). The collective and thus intersubjective dimension of regimes became closely bound up with the growing literature on hegemonic stability and interdependence in world politics and in this way found its way into both realist and liberal scholarship. In the case of hegemonic stability theory, the public goods of open trade and financial flows became reconceptualised as regimes that guided state behaviour through the carrot and stick policies of the predominant world power, the United

States. In the case of interdependence theory, regimes were cast as intervening variables shaping international affairs, as each issue-area along the continuum would have its own set of collective practices that influenced who participated and what instruments were at play. As the triple crisis unfolded, the regime concept thus became increasingly pervasive within (and to a degree synonymous with) the emergent field of IPE.

Seeking some rigour for this popular new concept, in his edited collection called *International Regimes* the avowed realist Stephen Krasner (1983a: 3) offered what would become the standard definition for the discipline:

> Regimes can be defined as sets of implicit or explicit principles, norms, rules and decision-making procedures around which actors' expectations converge in a given area of international relations. Principles are beliefs of fact, causation, and rectitude. Norms are standards of behaviour defined in terms of rights and obligations. Rules are specific prescriptions or proscriptions for action. Decision-making procedures are prevailing practices for making and implementing collective choice.

The essence of regimes was thus considered to revolve around the injunctive dimension of norms, rules and decision-making procedures that regulated behaviour and produced a predictability that was conducive to cooperation, and how this in turn affected state interaction and the undisputed principle of self-help.

In contrast to the definitional unity advanced by Krasner, the contributors to *International Regimes* adapted and applied the concept to a surprisingly diverse range of theoretical positions. In his chapter, Keohane (1983: 141–172) advanced a theory of regime formation that drew a microeconomic analogy with market failure and suggested that, by providing information, monitoring compliance, increasing iterations and facilitating issue linkages, regimes made cooperative agreements easier to strike and harder to break. Regimes were therefore 'in demand' by states as a rational means to correct political market failure. For Keohane, this explained the apparent contradiction between the onset of the triple crisis and the fact that the fundamental outcomes permitted by the liberal economic order had continued unabated. Drawing attention to the sustained unity of the world market and expansion of transnational capital, he argued that hegemonic stability theory was incongruous with real world events as a decline in hegemony had not been followed by a definitive outbreak of 'beggar thy neighbour' policies; the reason being the injunctions provided by extant international regimes.

John Gerard Ruggie (1983: 195–232), meanwhile, advanced a historicised account of regimes, linking the *type* of international regime to the compromise of intra-state social relations in the dominant state. Thus he questioned the extent to which hegemony in itself was sufficient for liberal multilateralism given that states with different social relations would produce different types of regimes. By way of example, he argued that it was less the fact of American *hegemony* that accounted for the post-war order than the fact that it was *American* hegemony. Had Nazi Germany, the Soviet Union or even Britain emerged hegemonic from World War II, for example, a very different world order would have been constructed. For his part, Krasner (1983b: 355–368) took a sceptical view of regimes, seeing them as epiphenomenal and having autonomy only in those situations where realist power differentials attenuate and states defer to regimes out of custom or uncertainty. Likewise, Susan Strange (1983: 337–354) also struck a circumspect tone about regimes, sceptical of their durability and how they detracted from the real sources of power. Based on a very different account of power to Krasner's, however, Strange's chapter, titled '*Cave! Hic dragones*' (Beware! Here be dragons) went much further. She warned that an excessive focus on regimes risked overlooking the determining factors of technology and markets in international agreements, implied an exaggerated measure of stability in the international system, and contained a value bias in presuming that what everyone wanted was more and better regimes. Thus in her account of hegemonic stability theory and regime breakdown, Strange argued that, while the relational power of the US may have waned, its power to control outcomes in the international system had been maintained via its ability to determine the structural context in which interstate bargaining and processes of capital accumulation took place.

Building on his contribution to *International Regimes* and sceptical of Krasner's own approach to regimes, Keohane again propelled the field of IPE through his 1984 book *After Hegemony*. As the title suggests, Keohane moved the starting point of inquiry and rather than asking, 'why do regimes emerge?', as most had done before, instead asked, 'what accounts for the persistence of regimes in the absence of a hegemon to enforce them?'. The answer was the magnitude of the resources that had to be invested in their establishment (Keohane 1984: 101). Drawing on the transaction costs thesis of new institutional economics, Keohane proposed that as the 'sunk costs' of reputation could not be recouped if a regime was broken, and due to the cooperative inducements that they helped facilitate anyway, states were given a greater stake in maintaining their success. This meant it was the evolution of regimes, rather than their construction and deconstruction, that was more likely in practice; an evolution that was the result of states rationally responding to the shifting cooperative payoffs engendered by exogenous forces like technological change or population growth. The term neo-liberal institutionalism was thus coined to capture the essence of Keohane's expanded theory: 'neo-liberal' as it drew upon the idea of welfare-enhancing exchange through the prism of rational actor modelling; 'institutionalism' as it saw regimes as both robust realities of the world and the necessary mechanisms to achieve this cooperation.

In retrospect, the triumph of Keohane's argument was to show that cooperation could be achieved in the international arena, even by purely rational, self-interested governments unmoved by idealistic concern for the common good. Crucially, this conclusion was derived by proceeding logically from the core assumptions of neo-realism and thus enabled a certain rapprochement between the two heavyweight approaches of international relations theory. These assumptions were, first, that states follow self-help, *the* salient behavioural guideline in a non-hierarchical system, and second, that this can be modified through regimes away from a 'myopic self-interest' toward an 'enlightened self-interest' in which states pursue mutual long-term goals achieved through cooperative behaviour. In this way, international regimes became seen as instrumental creations by states, designed specifically to help them articulate and realise their goals. All accepted that the competition for survival would compel states to swiftly adjust political bargains and their attendant regimes to exogenous changes in interests and resources – the only remaining questions were in what circumstances and to what degree this would happen (March and Olsen 1998). The upshot of this neo-neo synthesis was that it took a fundamental challenge to one of the core assumptions of neo-realism to inject new life back into the regimes literature.

This challenge came from the social constructivist school, associated with the work of Alexander Wendt (1992), Nicholas Onuf (1989) and Friedrich Kratochwil (1989) among others. In contrast to the neo-neo scholars, who viewed states as rational actors seeking to maximise utility by calculating their preferences and following the most effective course of action, these constructivists conceptualised the international realm as a society containing normative and ideational structures that conditioned the identities and interests of actors. By ignoring the social context in which policy was formed, the neo-neo theory – henceforth grouped together as neo-utilitarianism – was criticised for leaving open the way in which actors defined their interests in response to under-lying structural conditions. As Thomas Risse-Kappen has argued (2004: 539) egocentric utility maximisation can be rationalised as a reason for action and prevailing interests, but only after the event. In respect to international regimes then, neo-utilitarian explanations not only overlooked why specific norms, rules and decision-making procedures were adopted and not others, but also deemed the question itself unnecessary.

As with the theoretical alterations wrought by the triple crisis in the 1970s, real world events shook many neo-utilitarian scholars into taking the role of ideas in preference formation seriously. The unforeseen dissolution of the Cold War and the seemingly normatively driven interest in human rights and the environment that followed in its wake led some scholars to think of ideas as variables that affected the solutions to state negotiations. For example Emanuel Adler and Peter Haas (1992) argued that knowledge could impact on regimes by serving as normative and analytic 'road maps', guiding states toward suitable destinations out of the universe of possible actions in the absence of a unique equilibrium. Further, once embedded in international regimes, knowledge could serve to perpetuate those arrangements by constraining public policy as long as the prevailing ideas remained effectively uncontested by new scientific discoveries or normative shifts. The relationship between knowledge/ideas and regimes did not just run one way, though. Regimes were also treated as an independent variable that could exert an influence on the production of ideas, in the sense that they induced change in bureaucratic operating procedures, provided new coalition and access opportunities, and created new policy spaces through formal meetings. What were originally dubbed 'feedback' mechanisms by Krasner (1983b: 362) were now understood as facilitating debate and learning among state elites, mutating state self-interest prior to the outcomes perceived in negotiation 'games'.

Such contributions thereby added two key propositions to the neo-neo synthesis – knowledge can change and knowledge has consequence – and thus functioned as an 'add on' to the neo-utilitarian framework. For this reason it can be dubbed 'thin constructivism', explaining the sources of state interests whilst adhering to the neo-neo positivist epistemology and view of regime engagement by states as strategic interest satisfaction (Hasenclever *et al.* 1997: 154). In contrast, proponents of 'thick' constructivism argued that the institutionalised norms that shape actors' identities not only helped define their interests but also their strategic rationality. To study the institutionalisation of regimes in the international system, it was felt necessary by these scholars to stop conceding to neo-utilitarians the assumption of strategic interaction and embrace a more holistic, sociological perspective of state behaviour that asked whether states understood the 'rules' in the same way and whether they assigned the same payoffs to outcomes. In short, the epistemological assumptions in the neo-utilitarian framework were said to have bequeathed theories that had a truncated picture of institutions that failed to take into account the full repercussions of institutionalised practices on actors' behaviour.

This broader view of institutions was one that emphasised the slow, sporadic and uncertain pace of institutional adaptation to environmental change. Dovetailing with the political science literature on historical institutionalism, this position pointed to the constraints placed on actors by the incentive structures that reproduced and magnified particular patterns of power distribution, leading actors to unintentionally adopt strategies reflecting and reinforcing this institutional logic (Hall and Taylor 1996; Thelen 1999; Schmidt 2005). Revisiting the regime concept with this alternative approach in place, thick constructivists offered three new perspectives on its usage. First it was argued that neo-utilitarian based approaches recognised only regulative rules in channelling behaviour (e.g. prohibiting export subsidisation or enforcing tariff reductions) and had no space in their ontology for constitutive rules, which made such affairs possible in the first place. In this light, regimes were understood as social structures that enabled intelligibility and an acceptability of actions, and also conferred legitimacy upon their member constituents (Ruggie 1998: 85; Young 1999: 94). Second, the existence and strength of a regime was to be established counterfactually. Less emphasis was placed on defining a threshold of compliance separating a regime from a non-regime situation and more on understanding how actors' self-perceptions were formed and transformed within the institutional setting (Kratochwil 1989: 62). Third, the fundamental coherence and instrumentality that neo-utilitarians perceived between principles, norms, rules and decision-making procedures were criticised as unrealistic. Instead, regimes were seen as subject to incremental adjustment and prone to path dependencies in which the trajectory of development up to a certain point constrained that trajectory afterward. Processes of change were thus accounted for by critical junctures, created by endogenous developments or exogenous shocks in which an opening occurred for different political visions to alter the nature of an institution, with the change itself understood as contingent rather than inevitable or deducible fact (Thelen 1999: 384). As a result, thick constructivists saw institutions as historical entities, situated within a bounded evolution that could lock in *prima facie* irrational policies and produce outcomes that did not necessarily maximise the gains to be had from state interaction.

Despite these differences, however, the *type* of IPE to which the constructivists put the regime concept differed little from its predecessors. Encapsulating this point, Lisa Martin and Beth Simmons (1998) have argued that in its embryonic form, the regimes literature concerned itself with the outcomes of wealth, power and autonomy, reckoned in terms of the distributive consequences of the behaviour of a myriad of producers, distributors, and consumers, and in a minor way, of international organisations and state bureaucracies. However, further research moved thinking in three important directions:

> First, distributive consequences fell from the centre of consideration as research began to focus on how international regimes are created and transformed in the first place, as well as the behavioural consequences of norms or rules. Second, attention to the normative aspects of international regimes led naturally to consideration of the subjective meaning of such norms and a research paradigm that was in sympathy with developments in the constructivist school of thought. Third, explanations of international regimes became intertwined with explanations of international cooperation more generally (Martin and Simmons 1998: 737–738).

This analytical route can be nicely illustrated with reference to the IPE literature on food and agriculture. For instance, published in 1979 the aim of Raymond Hopkins and Donald Puchala's edited book *The Global Political Economy of Food* was to explore 'the effects of the contemporary international relations of food upon human welfare'. This critical angle addressed problems such as food shortages, price instability and malnutrition and was supported by a holistic conception of those regime participants who 'make decisions about production, distribution and consumption that accord with commonly accepted and widely prevailing norms which lend legitimacy to certain practices and declare others illegitimate' (Hopkins and Puchala 1979: 19–20). Domestic coalitions and bureaucratic departments of the United States, multinational agribusiness, and the World Bank, International Monetary Fund and a plethora of United Nations food organisations were thus all implicated into the exercise of power. As mentioned in the introductory chapter, regimes also found their way into the work of Harriet Friedmann and Philip McMichael (a point overlooked by Martin and Simmons), who used the concept to link the international relations of food production and consumption to the national regimes of accumulation identified by the Regulation School. Subsequent regime-type analyses of agriculture and food within IPE sadly lacked such breadth. They were railroaded down the 'neo-neo' corridor and became subject to a more formal set of questions. Chief among these were: the preconditions needed to form regimes, such as International Commodity Agreements; the procedural structure of the regime architecture; and the extent to which regime injunctions enabled states to transcend unilateralism and agree to mutual action in the shape of cartelisation, liberalisation or a coherent policy agenda (see Rothstein 1984; Zacher 1987). In short, the regime concept became fleshed out within neo-utilitarian and constructivist frameworks that continued to give precedence to questions about interstate cooperation and consequently lacked an integrated economic dimension.

This analytical paucity in fact stemmed from another ontological presupposition of neo-utilitarian theories, the notion that 'states' and 'markets' interact in the production of world order, with the conceptual categories of both 'state' and 'market' taken as givens (Watson 2005: 92). An example of this dichotomous underpinning can be found in Robert Gilpin's book *The Political Economy of International Relations* (1987: 8–11) in which he asserted:

> The parallel existence and mutual interaction of 'state' and 'market' in the modern world create 'political economy'...In the absence of the state, the price mechanism and market forces would determine the outcome of economic activities; this would be the pure world of the economist. In the absence of markets, the state...would allocate economic resources; this would be the pure world of the political scientist.

The underlying approach in IPE was one of 'add economics and stir', with economics simply understood as the trade and finance relations that exist between states. Thus, whilst ostensibly bringing the realm of economics into its ambit, the IPE theory that developed through the 1980s actually reduced notions of power and the 'political' to the activities, arenas and authority of states with little consideration for how markets were constituted and how market actors operated. IPE was, in effect, merely a sub-field of IR (Watson 2005: 14).

As will be argued shortly, the regime concept, particularly as adapted by the thick constructivists, offers many appealing entry points for an analysis of the global production of sugar, not least its insights into path dependent change. Yet dressed in the analytical attire of what subsequently became known as 'mainstream IPE', we must acknowledge the force of Strange's initial critique back in 1983 and dismiss the concept as unsuitable for the task in hand. However, we maintain that the concept is not beyond recovery and that its core tenets can and should be salvaged. To make this case, we now turn to the 'critical IPE' school that arose to challenge mainstream IPE and examine the state-market debate which has characterised much of its efforts to generate new questions about, approaches to, and visions of, the existence of power in the world economy.

Critical IPE and the state-market debate

With the end of the Cold War and the new multilateralism that appeared in its wake – manifest in agreements such as the Uruguay Round of the General Agreement on Trade and Tariffs (GATT), the Plaza Accord on exchange rate stability, and the Kyoto Protocol on climate change – we saw how some mainstream IPE scholars turned to the ideational 'add on' offered by thin constructivists in an attempt to account for the scientific and intellectual consensus appearing among state elites. For the scholars who would form the backbone of the critical IPE movement, however, it was the concept of globalisation that formed the watchword for debates about the changing nature of production, trade and finance in the new world order. Dubbed 'British School' scholars by Murphy and Nelson (2001), in contrast to the American School scholars associated with mainstream IPE, this literature on globalisation built on the early British School responses to the triple crisis and was directed to questions about state autonomy as power was conferred upon, and seized by, the growing global market (Payne 2005: 28). It was through this line of inquiry that perspectives on the state-market relationship began to be reworked, most notably in the work of Robert Cox.

The starting point for Cox was his break from the systemic and state-centric theorising common to much IPE at the time and his adoption of Antonio Gramsci's conception of hegemony, which was reworked by Cox to suggest that global authority in fact derived from the international expansion of the dominant *social class* of the dominant state or group of states (a similar argument to that made in early work by Ruggie). His neo-Gramscian approach thus sought to move beyond the domestic-international dichotomy to suggest how states played an 'intermediate though autonomous role between the global structure of social forces and local configurations of social forces within particular countries' (Cox 1981: 141). To account for the changes visible in world order, Cox argued that it was the 'internationalistion of the state' that accounted for a growing homogeneity in policy as it moved from acting as buffer between the national and global economy to acting as a 'transmission belt', adjusting and harmonising policy to the exigencies of the global economy and neo-liberal ideology. Accompanying this was the 'internationalisation of production' in which production was fragmented globally by low-cost transnational sourcing, supported by unregulated networks of capital that assessed investment risks and allocated finance accordingly (Cox 1993: 259–260).

In contrast to Cox's interpretation, in which the state formed the middle part of a 'layer cake' of authority that changed as a whole, Susan Strange instead differentiated state authority according to the function in question. She drew attention to the 'pyramid' of security, production, finance and knowledge structures which together comprised our social needs, and within which mutable combinations of power were exercised by state and non-state actors (Strange 1988: 26). Nevertheless, for both scholars what stood at the vanguard of these developments was an emergent 'transnational managerial class' or 'international business civilisation', present in the major private banks and global corporations, and allied with the politicians of the US and other leading capitalist states as well as the bureaucrats of the major international financial institutions. These social forces and their attendant discourse were seen by many critical theorists, such as Stephen Gill and Kees van der Pijl, to constitute a new, transnational historic bloc and hegemonic order, giving rise to a 'disciplinary' neo-liberalism which restrained the democratic control of public and private economic organisation and institutions (van der Pijl 1984; Gill 1990).

These perspectives on globalisation were supplemented in more popular literature by the business school writings of authors like Theodore Levitt (1983) and Kenichi Ohmae (1990) who triumphantly predicted the End of the State and a new frontier of borderless capitalist accumulation. If we crudely lump these critical and business writings together as the 'globalist' position, a reactionary wave could henceforth be seen in work coming from an 'internationalist' position, which argued in turn that far from a borderless world or even a transnational business class, globalisation was essentially about heightened interconnectedness between states. Internationalists maintained that control over globalisation was still held by the state as production was home-state orientated rather than de-territorialised, and technological and business developments were a function of national institutional and social arrangements rather than happening beyond them (Hirst and Thompson 1996; Zysman 1996; Weiss 1998). While these globalist and internationalist perspectives introduced new sites, sources and uses of power that challenged the basic Westphalian state model operationalised in mainstream IPE, they ultimately remained wedded to the conception of politics as states and economics as markets, particularly in their more simplistic formulations. Indeed, Cox's own, sophisticated account received criticism along these lines, namely, for giving the state a passive role in the dissemination of global neo-liberalism and assuming a transformational conformity to globalising pressures whereby all states respond in a likewise fashion to become 'Western-states-in-training' (Ling 1996). In short, the globalisation debate in critical IPE heralded a zero-sum battle between two separate spheres of activity.

Seeking to move beyond the 'states versus markets' perspective evident in the opening salvos of the globalisation debate, scholars such as Michael Mann (1997) reiterated that, while the state did remain an important locus of power in world order, globalisation was undoubtedly having a restructuring effect on the nature of political power, though its exact form was an historically open question. In lieu of such claims, the meeting of nation state and global market became conceptualised less as a zero-sum battle and more as a reciprocal engagement between alternate centres of social organisation. Phil Cerny's (1993) model of the 'competition state', for example, recognised non-state actors as providing governance functions within a more complex, multilevel international political economy, and acknowledged the existence of mutual benefits from the interplay of state and market power. But again, despite efforts to engage with the wealth-generating function of states, politics and economics continued to be understood as separate activities, albeit activities that had a fundamental reliance on one another. This shortcoming could in part be attributed to the problematic taken by critical scholars. What was sought was an understanding of the convergence in state forms that the economic 'logic' of globalisation engendered; too little attempt was made to genuinely integrate the two spheres or allow for comparative difference (Phillips 2005a: 100).

One further attempt at state-market integration made from within the critical IPE camp, and one we approve of here, was by Geoffrey Underhill (2000). The thrust of his argument was the need to reject the idea of states as the concrete realisation of politics and of markets as the concrete realisation of economics. On politics for instance, Underhill posited that 'the private interests of market agents are integrated into the state, asymmetrically in accordance with their structural power and organisational capacity, through their close relationship to state institutions in the policy-decision process and in the continuing pattern of regulatory governance of market society'. Likewise, on economics, it was claimed that 'the structures of the market are constituted as much and simultaneously by the political processes of the state and the political resources of the various constituencies involved in the policy process as by the process of economic competition itself' (Underhill 2000: 821). Recalling the work of Karl Polanyi in *The Great Transformation* (1944) what was necessary, then, was to abandon the 'interdependent-yet-dichotomous' state-market conceptualisation and to adopt instead a 'state-market condominium' model in which these two abstract identities would be understood as a joint or concurrent dominion. Importantly, the state-market condominium was not a distinctly national phenomenon that functioned discreetly in different societies but rather a relationship that *inherently* crossed political (i.e. state) borders. It was arguments such as these that set an imperative for IPE to become 'post-states and markets' (see also Phillips 2005b; Watson 2005).

As Benjamin Cohen (2008: 117) has noted though, while broad theoretical perspectives with ontologies that transcend dichotomies and abstract from complexity may be appealing to the imagination, they do leave us 'uncertain about precisely who or what actually exercises authority, and how it is done'. In other words, though the space to ask questions about the forms and ways in which power is exercised is opened within this state-market condominium, as scholars we may still be unsure where to look for it. This is the point at which heuristic concepts need to be reintroduced to orientate analysis and narrow down, within the parameters of a post-states and markets IPE, the types of structural and agential power that we seek to explore. After an initial period of malleability, we saw how the regime concept crystallised within IR-inspired frameworks and was deployed predominantly to answer questions about the robustness of international order. Coming from a perspective that positioned itself in opposition to mainstream IPE, scholars subscribing to critical IPE premises have thus largely ignored regimes and in the conceptual space left by its atrophy have instead turned to new alternatives. For our purposes in investigating the terms of competition and strategies of accumulation characterising the production of sugar, two of these alternatives are particularly good candidates: global governance and global value chains. But the final two sections argue why, the strengths of these approaches notwithstanding, the general abandonment of regimes in this case is *neither* desirable *nor* necessary.

Rejecting global governance and global value chains

Arguably the most influential scholar in bringing the concept of global governance into IPE has been James Rosenau (1992, 1997). In the advent of contemporary globalisation and the accelerating trends in social organisation, Rosenau argued that certain 'spheres of authority' in world politics could be minimally dependent on hierarchical, command-based arrangements. As such, decentralised systems of rule or 'steering mechanisms' could be maintained even in the absence of established legal or political authority – i.e. the state (Rosenau 1997: 146–147). Out of Rosenau's work thus grew the notion of global governance; a new form of order understood not as a superstructure responding to the interests of an already differentiated global ruling class, but rather as a site, one of many sites, in which struggles over wealth, power, and knowledge would take place (Murphy 2002: xiv). A number of perspectives have been offered on how best to conceptualise the fount of these new 'spheres of authority'. Most prominent have been the reorientation of individuals' political horizons (Rosenau 1992), the weaving of a global civil society (Lipschutz 1992; O'Brien *et al.* 2000), the rising power of globalising elites (van der Pijl 1984; Cox 1987), and the emergence of global informational elites (Comor 1994; Hewson and Sinclair 1999), all accredited as the source of decentralised political rule. Rolled in with these analytical features has been the normative positioning of the global governance literature which in similar fashion to much of the regimes literature, has often proposed, either explicitly or implicitly, that what we need is more and better global governance (Held and McGrew 2002: 8). This proposition takes two forms. On the one hand, the thrust of thinking is biased towards the provision of a technocratic fix to political problems and the concomitant strengthening of world organisations (United Nations Commission for Global Governance 1995). On the other hand, it is often suggested that the 'legitimacy deficit' perceived in the major world organisations be corrected by the pluralist input of different societal groups, usually non-governmental organisations (NGOs). What unites these strands is that both processes are encouraged to occur unmediated by the state, in order that the dissipating democratic link between effective authority at the apex of political organisation and political representation at the bottom is successfully restored.

Following on from this definition we can stylise the routes that literature adopting this approach – and relevant to our study – has taken. First, the study of governance has not been confined to a single sphere of endeavour but rather has referred to the conflicts and resolutions that emerge when alternative governance systems come into contact with each other, focusing particularly on the triumph of market-based institutions in such instances. In respect of trade, attention has in particular been drawn to the neo-liberal ideology of the World Trade Organisation (WTO), witnessed in the priority given to comparative advantage in deciding trade flows and the burden placed on governments to construct the conditions that will best enable this competitive game to be played out, even to the detriment of public health or environmental concerns (Wilkinson 2000; Williams 2001). Second, focus has been devoted to the major international economic organisations like the WTO or the World Intellectual Property Organisation, the power transferred to these, and the role of their respective staff in agenda setting and policy-making. In matters of trade and production, this has led to expositions of the 'unfair' policy processes structured by the architecture of the WTO consisting of consensus decision-making predicated on informal, club-like meetings among the 'big players' and the coercion of developing countries during formal stages of negotiation (Narlikar 2003; Jawara and Kwa 2004). Third, charting the role played by non-state actors has increased the focus on emergent political forces such as transnational corporations, global civil society or informational elites as a means of directing opinions and delivering services that are no longer the sole preserve of the state. In the case of regulating production, this has included the 'dialogues' held with corporate and NGO representatives in interstate agreements (Clapp 2003), the jurisprudence of the WTO Appellate Body and its attendant, unelected advisors (Smith 2004) and the transformation of state institutions themselves through concerted industry lobbying (Sell 2002).

While this serves as a valid and valuable theoretical platform, it also deflects attention (as any theory must) from other phenomena that would render an account of the 'global governance of sugar' somewhat deficient. The first problem is that it would replicate the danger found in the food regimes literature and insert a study of sugar too firmly within the global agricultural negotiations underway at the WTO and regional trade bodies to the detriment of the idiosyncratic politics of sugar production. The second problem relates to the internal functions of the state, which 'governists' tend to overlook yet which in fact create the universalising social and economic space for the very agencies and moments of 'transnational consciousness' that are seen as essential to contemporary global governance (Latham 1999). And thirdly, the global governance concept not only implies that resistance must be excluded from governance, but, further, that it is something that should effectively be overcome *by* governance. For example, Adam David Morton (2006) has argued that, in advocating NGO-participation in the institutions of global governance, the concept in fact effaces the conditions of capitalist *un*freedom and exploitation central to critical theory and instead replaces them with an orientation toward liberal pluralist idealism. Similarly Susanne Soederberg (2006) has argued that an insufficiently critical adoption of the concept legitimises the power relations associated with the dominant US state, supports an inclusive agenda of engagement for the Global South, and relegates progressive struggles to the confined spaces of the Internet or the ring-fence outside closed governance summits. The point is not simply that this type of resistance may be inadequate in some sense, but that the exclusive focus on this political action risks overlooking other forms of resistance such as organised labour movements or peasant revolt that exist below the rarefied air of global civil society and supranational organisations.

Turning now to the option offered by global value chains, we can trace the introduction of this concept to IPE through the pioneering work of Gary Gereffi and his colleagues (1994, 2005). According to Gereffi and his colleagues, the attractiveness of the commodity chain approach is derived from its rejection of conventional spatial categories such as inter-state or core-periphery trade in favour of focusing specifically on the various stages of production that constitute particular industries. This is considered necessary given that contemporary capitalism is characterised by densely networked firms operating across national boundaries but at the same time remains both place specific and socially embedded within local institutions (Gereffi *et al.* 1994: 1–2). Ultimately, this led proponents of the concept to take a 'firm-centric' and organisational approach to capital accumulation and focus on the value adding capacities of individual firms and enterprises located at each sequential stage of the commodity chain, e.g. raw materials, design, manufacture, marketing and sales (Raikes *et al.* 2000; Gereffi *et al.* 2005). And it was through this vision of productive linkages that the notion of governance was also deployed, though understood here as the means by which corporations organise economic activity 'with the purpose of achieving a certain functional division of labour... resulting in specific allocations of resources and distributions of gains' (Ponte and Gibbon 2005: 3).

A number of studies pertaining to agriculture have since arisen from the global value chains field and in the same manner as above, we now stylise their mode of analysis. First, attention is paid to the 'lead firms' within a given chain, the kind of activities they control, and what type of market structure this gives rise to. For example, in his account of the global cocoa-chocolate industry, Niels Fold (2002) identified dominant transnational firms in the segments of cocoa grinding and manufacturing and branding chocolate, which together created a 'turn-key' industry shaped by the 'bi-polar' buyer-driven chain. Other prominent lead firms to have emerged in agri-food value chains literature are international trading houses and supermarkets, which despite not owning farms or processing facilities are still able to dictate to – and therefore define – chain suppliers given their monopoly over procurement or control over consumer demand (Dolan *et al.* 1999; Gibbon 2001). Closely following this, the second step in value chains analysis is precisely that: to identify the market value of each stage of production in the chain and who is able to benefit from this (Fitter and Kaplinsky 2001). In the case of vegetables sold in supermarket-led chains, for example, it is noted how the requirements specified by the retailers for cost, quality, delivery, product variety and food safety act as an effective barrier to participation in the chain by small exporters and, to some extent, small producers, but by the same token, for those firms that can participate, the rewards through taking on extra functions can be considerable (Dolan *et al.* 1999). Finally, strategies by which firms in poorer countries might maintain and improve their position ('upgrade') within the chain are considered, in some cases through public action (Gibbon 2001) but more often by moving into more complex processing and logistic activities or by playing a more effective role in product innovation.

The likely drawbacks of attempting to examine the 'global value chains of sugar' would be, first, the difficulty in placing the commodity at the centre of analysis. Compared to other agricultural products such as cocoa, coffee or cut flowers, sugar is used in a wide range of final products and in each case is usually one among many inputs. Moreover, it is notable that sugar is produced in nearly every country in the world, defying the straightforward selection of specific production locales that often mark out other agricultural products. Thus core chains of final-end buyers and producers do not really distinguish the sugar industry and attempts to bring these manifold chains together would unduly complicate the picture. Second, assuming we did pick up on a set number of chains, perhaps examining the slice of wealth afforded to producers just in different Asian countries, we would likely be struck by how much regulation and rewards are marked by comparative political space. This is because the state has remained so involved in managing the production of sugar, often establishing price floors, thereby mitigating to a significant degree the encroachment of power asymmetry based on market structures that value chains are so useful in revealing (cf. Talbot 2004 on reclaiming the institutional determinants of value chains). Third and finally, the focus on vertical relationships within the production-consumption chain shifts our attention away from the horizontal processes of coordination and competition among actors (Ponte and Gibbon 2005: 4). For instance, the constraints for farmers in switching crops or the opportunities for sugar processors to diversify profit streams by investing outside the commodity chain, in ethanol production say, may be overlooked. Related to this some of the more economistic/policy-orientated value chain research also has a tendency to overlook resistance to chain governance, and, in similar fashion to the global governance literature, considers predominantly how businesses can be integrated into its prevailing order (Bair 2005).

Reviving regimes: an industrial regimes approach

The preceding critique has suggested that it may not be desirable to deploy the global governance or global value chains concept in this instance, but, if the regime concept remains inevitably restrained by its mainstream straitjacket, then, desirable or not, using one of them may still be preferable. This section illustrates why this is not the case. As Fred Gale (1998) noted in his article *'Cave! 'Cave! Hic dragones'* (i.e. beware of Susan Strange's critique) and as illustrated through our genealogy of regimes literature, the concept can, and has been, employed flexibly within IPE. As such, it is argued here that the regime concept found within mainstream IPE theory can be stripped of its heritage and embedded within a critical framework without doing damage to its conceptual essence. In short, there is nothing inherent in the concept of a regime that prevents its deployment in a post-states and markets theoretical framework.

The core tenet, or conceptual essence, of regimes is simply a meta-theoretical orientation that takes institutionalised behaviour seriously – think of an exercise or dietary regime in your personal life. As Oran Young (1999: 20) put it, 'institutions play a constitutive role in shaping the identities of their members and, to be more specific, [influence] the way in which these actors define their interests'. In his reconstruction of regimes, Fred Gale explained how international regimes could thus be considered as instances of institutionalised hegemony in the neo-Gramscian vein, something that Hasenclever *et al.* also proposed when mapping out the application of the concept in IR. Yet, while theoretically tenable, this conceptualisation misses an opportunity to suggest a more concrete alternative to global governance (which, in fairness, was not something any of the authors set out to do).

To provide this alternative, we begin by shifting the analytical focus of regimes from an *international* to an *industrial* one, thereby replacing an avowed attention to the interactions of states with a perspective that privileges a given realm of production and includes states only inasmuch as they influence this. From this point, the nature of inquiry becomes an examination of how control is exerted over this social process of production, which begins with how the terms and spaces of competition are set within a given industry. This concerns commonplace factors such as private ownership and market exchange but also moves beyond them to include things such as the manipulation of consumer wants, inter-firm collusion, the erection of entry barriers, and the influence of producers over government policy, intellectual property rights, and international organisations (Nitzan and Bichler 2000: 80). In this way, the state can (and usually should) be fundamentally inscribed into market activity though the point here is not the extent to which states should be in or out of the picture but rather *what kinds of state activity* are evident, how this relates to their broad social functions, and how such purpose is decided.

As for the process of institutionalisation within this complex of market rules and norms, two significant insights can be discerned. First, it is argued that it is only to the degree that institutionalisation sets in that dominant capital is able to retain and augment its exclusive power against lesser capitals (meaning existing or potential competitors). In pointing to the contradictions that lurk beneath seemingly unified efforts, such as the market dominance of a particular group of firms, a regime analysis illustrates how it is necessary for these latent conflicts to be sublimated in the pursuit of profit, and how the institutionalisation of these terms of competition – be it through regulatory rules or behavioural norms – serves to naturalise the extant creation and distribution of wealth. Second, by looking at the day-to-day recurrence of patterns of accumulation within a regime, we can also reveal how these internal dynamics make the regime something more than a simple derivative of the wider neo-liberal economic order. By exposing the institutionalisation of actors within given organisational networks and ways of working, we can gain a greater understanding of the differentiated rationalities and preferences to emerge and how these reproduce (different) regimes over time, rather than privileging external forces like the logic of capital as the explanation for change.

It is this attentiveness towards the historical and discreet processes of politics – as opposed to some of the more functional and apolitical theory supporting the emergence of global governance or value chain 'steering mechanisms' – that helps reveal the asymmetrical and embedded nature of different forms of power through which production takes place, and ultimately, how this relates to the perpetuation and extension of contemporary arenas of capitalism. Having spelt out the alternative foundations for an industrial regimes analysis, we now flesh out the concept by suggesting three methodological imperatives that will help to map out the institutionalisation of behaviour across the international sugar industry, that is to say, the spatial extension of productive control inherent in a regime situation. These imperatives are: regulatory structures, strategic coalitions, and economic identities.

Regulatory structures

The *sine qua non* of a critical approach to regimes would be to recognise that institutions and the patterns of accumulation they support are not a consensual expression of the preferences of affected groups, but are constructed by certain actors that favour certain interests. What follows from this is that we ask not just whose interests and what interests dominate institutions, but why certain interests are able to do this and what the distributive outcomes are. As Nicola Phillips (2005b: 262) maintained, we need to discern and interrogate those structures in the international political economy that sustain dominant interests in certain types of inequality and ask how these are reproduced.

Certainly some of the most important structures for sugar descend from the decisions made at WTO and Linda Weiss (2005: 724) has illustrated to good effect how the extension of WTO discipline has reproduced a structural inequality in economic power. While the more economically advanced countries are able to align national growth goals with support for industry, technology and exports through newer, supposed non-trade distorting policy (namely research, environmental and redistributive subsidies) the older investment and subsidy measures sought by developing countries to promote labour- and capital-intensive industries are by contrast heavily circumscribed. Regulatory discrimination is also evident across institutions, most notably the option faced by many developing countries in pursuing trade policy through the WTO or through Regional

Trade Agreements (RTAs). As Kenneth Shadlen has argued, RTAs typically offer developing countries increased market access at the cost of deeper concessions on inward investment, intellectual property and the 'Singapore issues', thereby spelling further curtailment in state activism. Thus when analysing contemporary development strategies the most useful contrast is not between the alternatives that countries now have under the WTO and the alternatives that countries once had in the past, but between a constraining multilateral environment and an even more constraining regional-bilateral environment (Shadlen 2005: 775).

In addition to the structural inequality found in trade legislation, a critical regime perspective should also consider the terms of trade that exist between countries and how this is shaped by domestic and international industry regulation. A trademark of much literature on international commodity production is that its critical angle, to the extent that it has one, is based on *procedural* justice, proposing that if the inequalities present at the moment of international negotiation, past and present, could be eliminated, then the essence of fairness would result.[1] Drawing on Marxist political economy, we need to ask whether voluntarism and diplomatic equality in trade agreements alone would endow the international trading system with justice, or whether barriers surrounding the value accorded to different productive tasks also determines wealth distribution. One perspective on this debate was offered by dependency theory, which examined the disproportionate rate at which export portfolios of core (developed) and peripheral (developing) economies equalised (Cardoso 1972; Sunkel 1972). Through this prism a *deserts*-based justice was brought to light, that is, a view of production that asked how equal labour-effort could result in unequal labour-reward. Key to this process of unequal exchange were the structures that operated outside trade agreements, namely, a higher rate-of-return on capital-led innovation compared to globally available commodity staples and the existence of unorganised, surplus labour maintained for poorly remunerated production. Though a full exposition of dependency will not be attempted here, it suffices to say that the search for the 'transnationalisation' of classes and the delineation of inequality along a social, as well as a territorial dimension, (and we should add to this a racial and gendered dimension also), needs to remain a central concern (cf. Peterson 2003).

Strategic coalitions

Turning now to the social forces that come together to mould the preferences of states and, through them, the shape of international and domestic regulation in sugar, we briefly outline the predominant approaches in mainstream IPE to show the ways in which our regime approach differs. One popular approach in this canon is the factoral model, which posits that the preference for liberalisation or protectionism will be dependent on the international comparative advantage of the sector (Rogowski 1989), industry (Gourevitch 1986) or firm (Milner 1988) in question. The logic of these arguments is to link the interaction between changes in relative prices in the international economy and how this favours the producers' assets, on the one hand, with changes in the domestic policy preferences of those same actors and the coalitions they form to advance them, on the other. This is frequently overlaid with another widespread approach, the collective action model, which 'adds in' a political dimension by examining how the preferences of these different groups are weighed in the policy process (Garrett and Lange 1996). The general assumption drawn from this factoral-collective action approach is that intensified international competition encourages import sensitive producers to lobby harder for protection, and that, in the absence of a unified voice representing consumers and a wide range of export-oriented producers, such protection is likely to be awarded given the importance of securing votes from geographically concentrated under-threat industries.

While these structural approaches offer parsimonious, first-cut accounts of the internal preference-formation process in states, they have been criticised extensively for their inability to account for the timing and content of policy and their heroic assumptions about the individual as a rational actor. It is necessary to consider instead the ways in which policies become embedded rather than smoothly adjusting to changing competitive capacities and material incentives (Heron and Richardson 2008). One such perspective can be found in Judith Goldstein's (1989) historical account of post-war US farm support, which argues that the source of the regulation lay with the successful politicisation of agriculture in the 1920s and the ideas generated at the time that were later seized on and utilised by politically powerful individuals. Consequently, these acts then spawned attendant institutions that embedded the necessity of farm support for interest groups and so despite its comparative advantage held in almost all aspects of agricultural production, the US never considered opting for a liberalisation of agriculture throughout the lifespan of the GATT.

Another way in which policy favouring certain economic activities can become embedded is through the active manipulation of state elites. For example David Coen and Wyn Grant (2005) have drawn attention to how specific fractions of capital can create an 'imprisoned zone' of policy-making through their deployment of informational and financial assets. Typically these efforts draw together a number of powerful stakeholders within a given industry, building a coalition that helps to shape policy conducive to the continued growth and protection of the industry as a whole, even if the coalition members consider themselves competitors within that industry. Potential conflicts are thereby mitigated and individual firms given a stake in maintaining the policy *status quo*. But this is not to suggest that every regime is able to sublimate conflict. Indeed, it is intended that focusing on the institutionalisation of practices within an industry will help highlight the distributional effects underpinned by a given regime, namely, how they empower some actors whilst disarticulating and/or marginalising others – particularly the ideas of those likely to oppose the orthodoxy and challenge institutional legitimacy. Philip McMichael's (2006) account of the transnational peasant movement *Via Campesina* has highlighted how, despite the mass enclosure programmes and encroaching industrialisation of production typical to the agricultural sector in the South, antithetical movements are (in the Polanyian sense) inescapable and reinforces the notion that extant patterns of accumulation are only able to continue to the extent that such reactions are mollified.

Economic identities

So far we have focused on how actors implicated into a certain industry operate across and through states to affect the environment within which their agendas are then institutionalised in rules and norms. To infuse this largely material reading of the state-market condominium we conclude by introducing the role of economic identities and suggest how these come to shape the patterns of preferences and policies. Frank Trentmann's (1998) analysis of Britain's repeal of the Corn Laws serves as an excellent starting point here. Recognising that ideas can be seen as formative of interests, Trentmann argues that unilateral liberalisation was less the result of sectoral lobbying and more the result of political culture and the ideological construction of British national identity, moral virtue, and the low wage consumer. Each of these suggested the merit of free trade and together created a convergence of ideas sufficient to generate collective allegiance and action. This process of interpellation – appealing to people in a certain way which encourages them to interpret events from a particular standpoint – in turn encourages us to make evident the discursive framing of issues amongst both the public and industry elites in the formation of policy preferences. While the prevailing mode of interpellation is often conditioned by engagement with extant institutions, and thus will replay itself over time, this must be considered a fundamentally contingent outcome. We maintain throughout that it is possible for actors to uproot the institutionalisation of 'commonsense views' and de-naturalise certain patterns of economic activity.

A contemporary example of changing identities and preferences can be seen in the fair trade movement, which has bucked the 'logic' of market forces by re-spatialising the distance between producers and consumers. By revealing the working conditions and income that farmers receive under the fair trade label (implicitly contrasting it with the fortunes of those producing for brand name suppliers) consumers have been willing to pay more for their products and have created a worldwide market worth over $1bn, arguably supporting a more sustainable and equal mode of production (Fairtrade 2007). Likewise, the so-called 'quality' turn in consumption has addressed the environmental exploitation resultant from mass produced food commodities. The emergence of organic production, social cooperatives, quality assurance schemes and the territorial valorisation of products can all be seen as responses to the placeless and artificial nature of the convenience food panorama. In 2007 the organic market alone was worth close to $40bn (Organic Monitor 2007). What both these consumer movements present is a formidable challenge to, and contradiction within, the capitalist industrial food system, and, as such, insist that we make product demand endogenous to the economy. Rather than thinking of demand as an abstract price response by commodity fetishistic consumers, it is more productive to think of consumption as part of a regime; a profoundly intersubjective and institutionalised act open to moral and habitual persuasion as well as market manipulation.

Conclusion

This chapter has narrated the genesis of mainstream IPE and the key role played by regimes within this literature. Despite the insights offered by some proponents of the concept (notably Ruggie and Young) we found that the discipline at large was too state-centric, too concerned with the international relations of economic activity, and too biased toward stability, and so set out to see how these overarching theoretical deficiencies could be overcome. This project first involved mapping the terrain of critical IPE, focusing in particular on the neo-Gramscianism of Robert Cox and the scholarly developments made in the wake of the globalisation debate. The new and germane concepts of global governance and global value chains that have arisen through this debate were then discussed but dismissed as inappropriate for the nature of our study. So, with a critical research agenda and post-states and markets IPE theory in hand, we set about reconstructing the conceptual vehicle of a regime. The rationale for this reconstruction was that, in order to better understand the nature of power at work within the sugar industry, we needed to identify how the institutionalisation of economic activity sets in, how this privileges certain fractions of capital and labour, and how these patterns are reproduced to create seemingly sealed and path dependent trajectories. The core tenets of the regime concept were deemed apt for this job. By identifying three methodological imperatives out of this concept – locating the regulatory structures, strategic coalitions, and economic identities that condition patterns of accumulation in sugar production – an industrial regimes approach was thus articulated and our mode of analysis defined.

Turning now to the application of our conceptual vehicle, the emphasis that the regime places on tracing processes of institutionalisation demands that a historicised account of the contemporary situation is paramount. Not only does this provide us with explanations of where current policy came from, and the coalitions and identities that were needed to bring it into being, it also offers examples of what kinds of events cause change and how these are internalised by extant actors. This task will be taken up in the next two chapters, which detail the emergence and exigencies of broad-set and stylised regimes as they have arisen in the sugar industry. To begin this challenge, we first consider how the production of sugar spread across the globe, focusing on the period covering the 16th century to the early 20th century and depict the rules and norms that structured this journey, echoes of which can still be heard today.

3
From a Colonial to a National Regime, 1500–1945

To begin our historical journey through the previous incarnations of the sugar regime this chapter traces the evolution of the commercial trade in sugar from its beginnings in the Atlantic in the 16th century through to its circumnavigation of the globe in the 20th century. It is marked in the main by the rise and fall of the colonial regime, the legacies of which were then inscribed into the putative national regime that began to take shape from the mid-19th century onward. Key in these transitions was the trade regulation of the dominant trading powers, which played a critical, though not always successful, role in assisting the process of aggrandisement and assuaging the contradictions that accompanied it. Tracing this changing policy thus provides both an explanatory variable for the nature of power and purpose in the sugar regime and a monitor on its spatial ascent.

The chapter is divided into three sections. The first examines the Westward expansion of sugar cane under European colonialism and the famous 'triangle trade' that arose in which slaves, sugar and manufactured goods traversed the Atlantic Ocean. In parallel with this it also raises a number of features often marginalised in historical accounts of the early plantation system in the Caribbean, namely, the consumption dynamics in industrialising countries that underpinned the demand for colonial sugar, and the trade that existed between Asian nations on the other side of the world. The second section details the emergence of the sugar beet industry in Europe and the end of slavery in the Caribbean, and how these compromised the cane industry and instigated a new set of problems to resolve. It then details how the answer to these problems was found in a new form of state interaction – international commodity agreements – and how these arose out of state-society conflict and processes of institutionalisation rather than simple rational responses by states to market management. The third section interrogates the transformation of sugar toward mass production in the early 20th century, both geographically in its global spread, and economically in the concentration and modernisation of ownership, concluding with the international structures of inequality that came to pass into the modern era of sugar production.

Colonialism and cane

The sugar cane plant is believed to be native to New Guinea and is thought to have first spread among the Southeast Asian islands over 2,000 years ago. From there it found its way to India, China, and the Middle East, where refining techniques were developed to turn the extracted juice of the cane into sugary solids that were used in cooking (Abbott 1990: 11). Sugar making then spread to the Mediterranean basin after the Arab conquest (630–710 AD) and continued under Christian rule, notably in southern Spain and Sicily. Individual entrepreneurs in the Iberian Peninsula were later encouraged to establish sugar cane plantations on the Atlantic Islands to produce sugar for the home and European markets and to safeguard the extension of Portuguese trading routes. From this point cane was carried by Columbus from the Spanish Canaries to the New World in 1493, from whence it went to the Caribbean and then Brazil. By 1625, the Portuguese were supplying nearly all of Europe with sugar from Brazil, through refining centres in Lisbon, Antwerp and Amsterdam (Mintz 1985: 29).[1]

Under Spanish control, early sugar production in the Greater Antilles (Cuba, Puerto Rico, Jamaica, and Hispaniola) represented a transitional stage in the evolution of cane farming. While estate size began to rise, the small-scale planting and milling techniques were essentially no different from those inherited from the Arabs (Galloway 1989: 69). It was not until 1650 that the Caribbean began to produce significant amounts of sugar for export, due primarily to English planting, first in Barbados and later Jamaica, and French planting in Saint Domingue (Mintz 1985: 38). Barbados emerged as an attractive location for sugar cane cultivation both because of its military and political economy security. Not only was the island safe from attacks by Indians, pirates and the Spanish, but prior to the arrival of the English, some Barbadians had already established estates through farm building and the profitable export of cotton and tobacco. The properties and established reputations of the indigenous entrepreneurs provided planters in the West Indies with the confidence to engage in risky investments; a proposition borne out by the frequency with which English merchants became partners with pre-existing, resident growers (McCusker and Menard 2004: 289). As investment continued and the concentration of land-ownership began to increase, indigenous and newly domiciled capital and labour began to decline. Planters became predominantly investors rather than growers (many returning to England and leaving the plantation in the hands of overseers), and servant labour faded in importance as slavery, now organised into gang labour, was increased to intensify output. A fundamental and contingent transition had occurred – from extensive agriculture to intensive monoculture – and thereafter spread throughout the Caribbean. In this sense, sugar did not revolutionise Barbados; rather, Barbados revolutionised sugar (McCusker and Menard 2004: 303).

One effect of the shift to monoculture was that it became increasingly prudent for Caribbean elites to import food for domestic consumption from North America, Bermuda and Ireland rather than to produce it locally in smallholdings worked by slaves (Smith 1991: 138). Not only did this increase profitability, as the extra sugar produced through increased man-hours could be exchanged for greater amounts of food than could be produced domestically, it also had a political advantage in that it avoided the dangers inherent in giving an exploited class the means to provide sustenance for itself. In this respect, it is evident how the early patterns in international agricultural trade arose out of carefully staged decisions rather than unfolding under comparative advantage between natural trading partners. Another result of sugar monoculture was that it created the way for production to intensify and the division of labour to fragment through the introduction of the plantation system. For Sidney Mintz (1985: 51) these early experiments should be considered as instigating a partial industrial revolution, despite the existence of forced labour that is antithetical to modern-day notions of organised industry. The combination of agriculture and processing under one disciplinary authority, the organisation of the labour force into skilled and unskilled parts separate from their tools, and the regulation of working hours shifted to the rhythms of the factory all marked significant divergence from established economic organisation. What had emerged within intensive monoculture was a *proto-type* of industrial capitalism, a system that, according to Robin Blackburn (1997: 19) was:

> A hybrid mixing ancient and modern, European business and African husbandry, American-Eastern plants and processes, elements of traditional patrimonialism with up-to-date bookkeeping and individual ownership... These borrowings necessarily involved innovation and

adaptation, as new social institutions and practices, as well as new crops and techniques of cultivation, were arranged in new ensembles.

In short, commercial sugar production represented a capitalist frontier, but not one that emerged fully formed from the Old World in Europe and which in turn developed the New. Rather the experiments and accidents of colonial sugar production took place *outside* the heartlands of Europe, *before* the revolutions that would refine and extend colonial industrialism, and firmly *in conjunction with* indigenous and African manpower. The composite and vanguard sugar economy was born.

The Atlantic trade circuit

From the beginning, then, the colonial production of sugar was embedded in the 'triangle trade' exchange relations that linked Europe to Africa and to the New World and which generated novel and frequently violent encounters. Finished goods were sold to Africa, African slaves were shipped to the Americas, and American tropical commodities were sent back to their respective mother country. This Atlantic circuit was tightly orchestrated by the political elites of the Old World who attempted to confer national monopoly status on those engaged in the trade. Under the 1651 English Navigation Act, for instance, planters in the English colonies were compelled to ship their raw sugar to British ports and to buy their slaves from English merchants.[2] Subsequently, further legislation also required that sugar from foreign sources be taxed at double the import duty levied on home colonial sugar, and that higher duties be placed on refined sugar than raw sugar (Polopolus 2002: 5). Following suit from the English, in 1664 the French Finance Minister Jean-Baptiste Colbert passed a similar tariff act to attract the sugar of the French Caribbean islands exclusively to French ports and exclude market entry of Dutch refined sugar, overlaying the Anglo-triangle with its Gallic counterpart (Stols 2004: 271).

The foundations of these policies can be located in the predominant ideology of the time, mercantilism, according to which European states sought to maximise balances of trade and bullion accumulation by encouraging the re-export rather than domestic consumption of colonial goods such as sugar (Thomas and McCloskey 1981). Underpinning these prerogatives was the received economic wisdom which held demand to be a constant for any person or country. Under such conditions, the pursuit of 'economic efficiency' was futile as lowered prices could only mean lowered profits given the absence of compensation in the form of increased sales. Indeed, so firmly did people believe in static markets that the adoption by the masses of the fashion and consumption habits of their social superiors was received as a symptom of moral economic disorder, believed to drain the state of its treasure (Austen and Smith 1990).

For Mintz (1985: 46) the importance of mercantilist dogma to Britain's development and the story of sugar was fourfold: it promoted a constant supply of tropical products and profits made from processing and re-exporting them; it secured a large overseas market for finished British goods; it supported the growth of civil and military marine; and it provided money to the Treasury. A popular anecdote of the time reveals the privileged position of the 'sugar aristocracy' and is telling of their relationship to the policy-makers of the day. As Peter Macinnis (2002: 105) has it:

> Around 1780, King George III was riding in a carriage with the then Prime Minister, Pitt the Elder, when he saw a carriage far outclassing his own. He asked who the owner was, and learned that it belonged to a West Indian planter, to which he replied, 'Sugar, sugar, eh? All that sugar. How are the duties, eh, Pitt, how are the duties?'

Seeking to protect their conspicuous wealth, these sugar importers and plantation owners took an active though theoretically inconsistent part in the politics of mercantilism. On the one hand, they supported protection from foreign imports, whilst, on the other hand, they opposed the idea that widespread consumerism endangered society and the economy. Ironically, this latter position later contributed to the positive-sum view of consumerism as advanced in Adam Smith's *Wealth of Nations* and would ultimately undermine the rationality of the closed trading circuit on which the West Indian plantations were dependent (Austen and Smith 1990). But, for the time being, as sugar demand in Britain grew so the Atlantic trade grew too. From 1660 onward, the value of sugar imports to England exceeded its imports of *all other colonial produce combined* (Mintz 1985: 44).

This seemingly boundless demand for sugar encouraged the establishment of new plantations across the Caribbean, the commercialisation of sugar by-products such as molasses and rum, and the rising importance of London as a refining centre.[3] As the sugar trade became ever more lucrative, fissures began to appear in the triangle system. Most notably, distilleries in New England began to import molasses to make rum themselves and sell into British markets. In fact, the 1764 ruling that forced New Englanders to terminate this trade and import the drink exclusively from Britain sparked the systematic boycott of British goods, which in turn bolstered the 'No Taxation without Representation' independence movement and ultimately ruptured the oversees rule of North America. Nevertheless, the Atlantic circuit remained prosperous well into the 18th century as the Caribbean – and British Jamaica and French Saint Domingue in particular – became responsible for producing more than 80 per cent of the world's sugar. The dark side to this prosperity was that these islands were also the destination for more than 80 per cent of the world trade in slaves (Coote 1987: 21). In a hundred year period around the 17th century, Barbados received 252,500 slaves, Jamaica 662,400, and Saint Domingue 864,000 (Mintz 1985: 53; Galloway 1989: 115). Meanwhile, in Brazil, roughly one million slaves were acquired purely for work in the sugar industry between 1770 and 1852 (Hannah 2000: 5). This marked the beginning of the Africanisation of the Caribbean and Latin America and the transformation of cultural geography in the region.

It was males that predominated in the Atlantic slave trade, though compared to other branches of pre-19th century migration (both coerced and free) females and children were well represented, creating the opportunities for miscegenation on the plantations.[4] Males were generally favoured, in part because of the nature of the work, which in its most labour-demanding form required a cane-cutting workforce able to swing heavy machetes at high repetition. But the preponderance of males was also conditioned by the political economy of the African slave trade. In domestic African slave markets, women could be sold for more than men, whereas men commanded higher prices in markets supplying the Atlantic. In this way, African conceptions of gender thus helped shape the structure of the Atlantic slave trade, a structure that favoured the continual import of slave labour rather than its reproduction (Nwokeji 2001: 47).

Population density in the Americas also shifted in rhythm with the sugar factories, as the industry supported the greatest concentrations of rural peoples in the continent. During the last years of the 18th century, over much of the Americas there were no more than one or two people per square kilometre. By contrast, Saint Domingue had 19, Jamaica had 25, and Barbados had 181 people per square kilometre, respectively (Galloway 1989: 113). This distribution of labour and its attendant capacities for wealth creation help explain why, in the 1667 Anglo-Dutch Treaty of Breda, the Dutch declined to trade New York (née New Amsterdam) for its strongholds on the coast of Surinam, and why in 1763

France abandoned claims to Canada in exchange for British recognition of French sovereignty over Guadeloupe. In short, the New World represented a vast and uncompromising political venture against which the sugar estates on its fringe stood as relative havens of fortune. But, as Creole communities emerged in the estates, the demography of these 'havens of fortune' changed and planned social resistance began to ferment, particularly through the racially intermixed mulatto population. The social relations of sugar had begun to evolve independently of European designs and the scene was set for the very first wave of decolonisation.

Counterparts to Atlantic colonialism: consumerism in Britain and trade in Asia

From a starting point in the Caribbean, many historical narratives of the Atlantic trade in sugar retain their focus on the region, charting the conditions of exploitation and the economic developments outlined above in much greater detail (see Carrington 2002; Sheridan 2000). Consonant with our comparative methodology, this section will instead explore some of the spatial counterparts to the colonial system of production, beginning with the rising consumption of sugar in Britain and the institutional transformations that supported this. It is notable that up until the end of the 17th century sugar remained the monopoly of a privileged minority, and was used not as a basic foodstuff but as a medicine, a spice, or a decorative display substance (Mintz 1985: 44). Yet while many accounts have put the emergence of a mass market in sugar down to falling prices, assuming the existence of a latent demand for the commodity as a food, in doing so they ignore the paradox of why demand continued to grow long after the trend of prices took an upward turn in the 1730s. To explain this puzzle, we again draw here on the work of Sidney Mintz and consider the transformation that took place in the *social value* of sugar – from curiosity to necessity.

Focusing on the English diet in particular, Mintz argued that enthusiastic sugar consumption was driven by demand from the working classes. Eschewing the teleological and essentialist explanations that socially inferior groups imitate their superiors or that the English have an innate 'sweet tooth', he looked instead at the diet of workers at the time, which was both inadequate in calories and monotonous in taste. Sugar found a ready home here – as did other colonial produce such as alcohol, tobacco, coffee, chocolate and tea – as a 'drug food'; foods which provided respite from reality, deadened hunger pangs, gave stimulus and calories, and improved the attractiveness of substances they were mixed with (Mintz 1985: 44). Crucial in this uptake was the way in which the sugar 'drug' was sold to and made acceptable to society. The marketing of sugar followed an oft-neglected development in gendered culture and morality, centred on women as the main purchasers, providers and participants in 'sugar rituals' (Austen and Smith 1990). These rituals involved the bourgeois pastime of using sugar to conserve fruits and to make jam, and also the consumption of sugar with tea, an activity which signified a particularly Victorian respectability (it was both a more modest way of consuming sugar compared to the fanciful sugared decorations of the aristocracy, and, as a popular substitute for alcoholic drink, a morally decent way also). Furthermore, female-authored cookery books were also formidable advocates of sugar, proposing its increased use in breads, cakes and even salads (Galloway 1989: 8). Aided by the increasing social prestige attached to sugar consumption, by the mid-1700s sugar had overtaken grain as the world's most valuable traded commodity (Polopolus 2002: 3).

A second counterpart to the colonial expansion of sugar onto the American seaboard was the existence of another network of trade flows separate to the colonial regime; an Asian circuit centred round China and India. Sugar cane had long been cultivated commercially outside Europe and an intra-Asia trade developed as early as the 16th century: Japan and Southeast Asia supplied by Chinese merchants with sugar from south China, Vietnam and Siam; and south Asian markets supplied by the Bengali producers of India (Mazumdar 1998: 71). After the Dutch East India Company was chartered in 1600, sugar passing through these intra-Asian markets then became linked to the world market. To put the two sugar circuits in some context, in 1630 Brazil produced 45 million pounds of sugar, supporting virtually the entire European demand, while China, even after catering for its own internal market, still exported 15 million pounds, mainly to the refining centres in the Netherlands (Mazumdar 1998: 2). Buoyed by growing Asian-European trade, when the Dutch took over trading posts in the 17th century they sought out the voluminous Chinese export and also began to produce sugar themselves in Taiwan and Java. The notion of Dutch production, though, is something of a misnomer. While the *trading* was monopolised by the Dutch, the factory ownership and technology was firmly in the hands of Chinese entrepreneurs.

For many authors, including such esteemed scholars as Fernand Braudel (1981) the failure of Asia to 'progress' into monoculture and the decline of European trade in 1660 in the face of restrictive British tariffs on East Indies sugar spelt the end of the commodity in the East.

In actuality, the intra-Asian sugar trade continued to flourish. Given the internal demand for sugar and the distance to European markets, most South and East Asian sugar was sold in regional markets. For example, in 1710 there were 131 mills in Java producing 8.8 million pounds of sugar, exported largely to Japan and Persia. And, in China, sugar remained the third most important export, after silk and tea, right up until the end of the 19th century (Mazumdar 1998: 89). Further, approaching the Asian sugar circuit from a non-Eurocentric perspective, we can locate reasons for the absence of monoculture internally to the region and forgo the oft-cited argument that plantations never arose simply because of 'Eastern backwardness'. In Taiwan, for instance, subsequent to its conquest by China in 1683 the colony was never subjected to plantation agriculture, despite the fact that China had considerable demand for sugar – indeed, per capita consumption was probably higher there than in Europe until the 19th century. According to Kenneth Pomeranz and Stephen Topik (1999: 135) the absence of monoculture in Taiwan was because the Qing elites were more concerned about exile rebellion and challenges to empire than they were in boosting production. Hence the Chinese maintained Taiwan's diversified agricultural landscape and extensive wooded areas so as to deter concentrations of wealth amassing among landowners and to provide the opportunity for indigenous peasant strongholds to survive. Recounting such a narrative of the Asian trade circuit is not only necessary as historical corrective, it will also aid us later in explaining why the global regime evident today has such variegated differences between regions.

A colonial regime in sugar, 1640s–1830s

The opening of this chapter has attempted to sketch out the practices that came to constitute the colonial regime of the Atlantic in order to trace the legacies it would bequeath to the subsequent national regime. These practices revolved around an intensified agro-industrial mode of production that harnessed the slave labour of antiquity and the scientific and social techniques of modernity, and which led to a fragmented division of labor and the imposition of racialised hierarchies under hybrid forms of capitalism. Once this system had settled, capital accumulation was maintained through the use of extra land and labour rather than the continued adoption of new technologies, which could have raised output per worker or per hectare. In this respect, the support of the British and French imperial powers under the discursive imperatives of mercantilism was crucial in securing the land, sea-lanes and domestic market opportunities necessary for risky investments abroad, but, by the same token, also contributed to the fixed path of accumulation by limiting production to raw sugar only as refining centres continued to be held in the metropole.

The liberal political economy of Adam Smith and others was crucial in exposing the contradictions upon which this system laid. By setting into relief the multiple interests that existed within the state, given that consumers benefited from cheaper domestic prices while those supplying the market benefited from monopoly and the higher prices therein, liberals made evident that the British governments had faced the choice of promoting one group of domestic interests or another: consumers of sugar and the sugar-using industries, on the one hand, and West Indies planters and refiners, on the other. Thus, far from there being one single and over-riding 'national interest' embedded in the colonial regime, trade discourse and policy had simply been constructed to make it appear as such. As Thomas and McCloskey (1981: 99) have noted, 'British mercantilism during the eighteenth century was not a consistent national policy designed to maximise the wealth of Britain; nor was it a preview of the alleged enrichment of capitalist nations by nineteenth century empires. It was instead…a means to provide revenue to the government and a device to enrich special interest groups'.

To the beet surrender: the demise of the colonial regime

The contradictions of mercantilism and the possibility of cheaper sugar for consumers increased as European grown sugar beet began to emerge as a viable alternative to cane. In 1747 German chemist Andreas Marggraf had discovered a process for extracting sugar from beet, a small beetroot-like vegetable that grew in temperate, northern climates and which produced a final product indistinguishable from that of sugar cane. Hugely inefficient at the outset, the embryonic European sugar beet industry was given the aid it needed during the Napoleonic Wars (1803–1815) when Britain's blockade of Europe interrupted the supply of Caribbean sugar cane to the continent, leading governments to encourage mass production through subsidisation. Following the end of the blockade and the return of cane imports, the commercial development of the beet industry collapsed, but was soon resurrected by the establishment of drawback systems across the continent. The drawback had initially allowed European refiners of cane sugar to receive repayment of their duties on raw sugar imports once the refined sugar was exported, but was extended to beet sugar exporters as the composition of sugar supply shifted.

Allied to the duty drawbacks were other developments favouring the beet industry, namely, the abolition of slavery and British trade liberalism that together broke the monopoly hold of the English planters over the biggest sugar importing market. Even as late as the end of the 19th century, at 1.58mt Britain still imported ten times as much sugar as the next largest European importer, France (Pigman 1997: 193). The upshot was that European beet producers were able to export into Britain at below the cost of production and beet sugar production grew through the 19th century from virtually nothing at the beginning to 5.5mt by the end, accounting for 65 per cent of world sugar production (Earley and Westfall 1996: 3). To put this in context, by the 1890s Belgium was producing as much sugar as the British West Indies, and Germany more than the entire Caribbean (Mahler 1981: 474). Figure 3.1 illustrates the growing importance of beet in the composition of world production throughout the latter half of the 19th century.

Slave emancipation and the replacement indentured labour

The abolition of slavery, which would be so important in the changing nature of sugar production, had a long and troubled gestation in the Caribbean. In all the sugar colonies slaves had tried to escape, though

Figure 3.1   World Sugar Production, 1840–1899

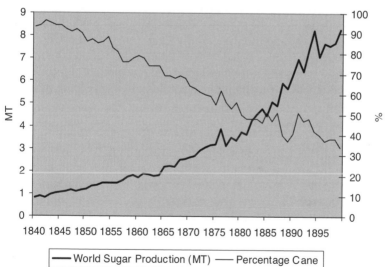

Source: Tony Hannah (2000) 'Early History', in Jonathon Kingsman (ed.) *Sugar Trading Manual* (Cambridge: Woodhead Publishing Limited), pp. 9–10.

the prospects for runaways – known as maroons – were hindered by the geography of having to survive in small, densely populated islands. Maroons thus became part of the frontier of plantation society, occupying land that was either unsuited to sugar cane cultivation or that in time would be absorbed by the expanding sugar industry. They became smallholders and peasant cultivators, contributing to the formation of many local villages and arguably West Indian peasant society itself (Galloway 1989: 117). In some instances, however, revolt took precedence over running. The most famous of these was the rebellion of Saint Domingue beginning in 1791, which dismantled the sugar industry and commercial agriculture, forcing virtually all members of the planter class into exile. The rebellion, which ultimately became a revolution, established the first independent black republic outside Africa under the name of Haiti (cf. James 1938).

In tandem with this resistance, by the 18th century criticism of slavery in Europe had gained enough momentum to make abolitionism a serious political force. As the biggest export from the colonies sugar was particularly redolent for the movement, and its protagonists sought to connect consumption of the commodity to the act of cannibalism. This political project was highly gendered, effected both by the cultural imperatives of femininity and sympathy advanced by religious groups such as the Quakers and poets such as Percy Shelley, and, in a more material sense, by women refusing to buy colonial products for the home, an act which was likened to purchasing the flesh of slaves (Sussman 2000: ch. 4–5). The first success of the abolitionists was the Slave Trade Act of 1807 (quickly followed by the US Slave Trade Act of 1808), which ended the Atlantic shipment of slaves and introduced fines and punishments for continued traffic, though, as slavery itself remained, a fugitive slave trade was quick to emerge.

The end of slavery, what William Green (1976) has called the 'Great Experiment', was finally brought about due to the intense political activism of the Anti-Slavery Society, galvanised in 1831 by the slave rebellion in Jamaica and buttressed by the economic critique, associated with Smith and the French physiocrats, which maintained that the self-interest of owners and workers should coincide for 'enlightened' and beneficent wealth creation to be sustained. This argument formed part of a wider attack on the West India trade more generally, led by the free traders and 'Manchester men' who advocated abandonment of protectionist policy wholesale, and was supplemented by the sectional interest of the East India Company that stood to gain from an end to slave-grown sugar. These ideational and material persuasions were then given institutional support by the 1832 Electoral Reform Act that widened the franchise and revised parliamentary districts, virtually divesting the House of Commons of West Indian planters (Green 1976: 114). Consequently, in 1833 the Slavery Abolition Act was passed and the West Indies became a testing ground for the notion that free labour could produce tropical staples at lower cost, with greater efficiency, and under more civilised conditions than could slave labour. While global emancipation was not immediately forthcoming – in the British colonies a compromise was added to the final bill that required a term of apprenticeship for slaves, and within other European powers slavery persisted for a number of decades – by the late 1880s bondage labour had been universally abolished.

The political struggle between the metropolitan capitalist classes and the colonial planters over abolition was partly eased by recourse to external but politically accessible pools of indentured labour. In fact, the defeat of abolition for West Indian sugar planters was accompanied by a victory in regard to labour importation as funds were provided to promote immigration (Mintz 1985: 70). It is remarkable to consider the amount of compensation granted by the British government to the planters in this respect: £2,000,000 in 1833, equivalent to an astonishing 5 per cent of national GDP at the time. This recompense helped fund the transfer of indentured labourers, who were contracted for around five years on pittance wages, and by 1916 over 500,000 Indians had made the journey to the Caribbean, though only 100,000 returned home (Harrison 2001: 109). Similarly, over 100,000 Chinese were channelled to Cuba, with more going to Peru. This 'coolie' trade was hardly more respectable than the slave trade. Jock Galloway has commented how 'few of them could have understood the nature of the indenture they had entered into', given that recruitment by the Chinese and Indian crimp gangs often involved debt bondage and reprehensible practices such as kidnapping and the purchase of prisoners taken in local wars. Moreover, 'the ships were overcrowded, the Chinese badly fed and brutally treated, and the death rate on the voyages high, about 15 per cent' (Galloway 1989: 128). In short, the formal freedoms instituted by abolition were compromised by substantive unfreedoms contained in migrant labour recruitment.

Within the Caribbean, meanwhile, the freed slaves, like maroons before them, sought out the marginal land that existed beyond the plantation, many heading for the hilly interior of Jamaica. Here they reconstituted themselves as a peasantry that by 1900 stood in possession of over 100,000 smallholdings (Galloway 1989: 149). For those ex-slaves unable or unwilling to turn to subsistence farming, seasonal cane cutting remained the only viable alternative and so they joined indentured labourers in working on the bulging plantations of Cuba, the Dominican Republic and Puerto Rico. This practice of short-term contracting initiated a second shift in cultural geography in the region, establishing patterns of 'sojourning' in the Caribbean and an intermingling of island cultures that still reverberate today.

British hegemony and the first international commodity agreement

As mentioned before, intertwined with abolitionism in the downturn of fortunes for the colonial planters was Britain's changing trade policy, which was slowly coming into line with the philosophy of the free traders. Passed the same year as another free trade act, the famous Corn Law repeal, the 1846 Sugar Duties Act dealt another blow to the planters by equalising duties on cane and beet sugar, thus ending the preferential treatment long accorded to the Caribbean in the British market. Planters were furious that the British government should deal the colonies another blow so soon after the abolition of slavery and the Abolitionists too were angered about the policy; some feeling that it would encourage sugar imports from Brazil and Cuba which still used slave labour, others feeling that any support for colonialism was immoral and that the Caribbean should be encouraged to develop autonomously of the West. Yet the Duties Act was ultimately passed in the interests of free trade and cheap food, resulting in a massive influx of refined European sugar into Britain and the degeneration of production in the Caribbean. This was followed in 1849 by the repeal of the Navigation Acts that had restricted the shipping of sugar to British merchants, making the message even clearer: the era of mercantilism had passed and a new age of liberalism had begun.

For many countries, though, even those supposedly benefiting from the new market regulation, this resulted in an untenable situation. Continental European governments were incurring serious costs in supporting inefficient infant industries, while in Britain concern was rife about the deterioration of supplies from the West Indies and its effects on the political stability of the colonies more generally. What followed next was unique in the domestic management of British trade policy, which was by now tightly configured to unilateral liberalism, and indeed a first in world trade more generally. A formal, international commodity agreement was struck between governments by which to regulate the terms of trade in sugar.

In 1864 Belgium, France and the Netherlands joined Britain in becoming signatories to the Paris Sugar Convention under which the parties agreed to suppress protective duties and export subsidies so as to put production and trade in beet and cane on an equal footing. As with the 'First International of Working-Men', which in the same year drew leftist political groups and trade unions together to work for international socialism, the Paris Convention represented a recognition that certain problems could only be solved through cooperation, and that this had to take place at the international level. Despite the novelty of this solution, or perhaps because of it, the Convention failed to achieve its goals. Determined to capture market share, the major European beet exporters continued their aggressive national economic export policy and subsequent conventions designed in the 1870s and 1880s went unratified. For its part, Britain also failed to endorse the agreements owing to opposition from the sugar-using industries that benefited from cheap European imports. By the late 1880s, world sugar prices were below the cost of production, leaving the burden of export subsidies in national accounts weighing heavier than ever (Polopolus 2002: 7). To remedy this problem, the 1902 Brussels Convention was struck. This aimed at a more comprehensive equalisation between the beet and cane industries by committing the principal signatory producers to eliminate *all* subsidies and limit surtaxes (the difference between foreign and domestic applied taxes). Crucially, it would also be enforced by a mandatory penal clause whereby imports from countries that operated subsidy incentives would either be refused entry or made subject to special duties. As the largest sugar importer, this was essentially a compliance mechanism to be enforced at British behest. While the Convention did not lead to a significant increase in world prices, it did end the more pernicious Treasury-draining effects of subsidised continental exports and stemmed the decline of cane exports and so in this respect it was a success. Thus it was only with the outbreak of World War I in 1914 that the Brussels Convention was drawn to a close.

In analysing the interstate politics of this period, it is tempting to characterise the early sugar agreements as classic examples of hegemonic power and the utility of international regimes. In the vein of mainstream IPE theory, we could argue the case that the European states remained fallible to their short-term interest of capturing market share at any cost until they submitted to regimes with sufficient enforcement mechanisms. From this point beet producing states were able to achieve their wider interests in reducing subsidy expenditure and Britain was able to embed its hegemonic position by spreading the gains of liberalisation evenly and preventing its biggest political and economic rival Germany from pushing all others out of the continental market. This section ends by historicising this collective action problem and offering a more nuanced take on the construction of the international sugar agreements.

Beginning with Geoffrey Allen Pigman's (1997) assessment, we note that Britain systematically if sporadically broke its taboo against commercial diplomacy in the late 19th century not because of a rational intermittent pursuit of international hegemony but rather because of ideological oscillation over how to achieve the broad goal of liberal international trade. The bastions of unilateralism during the period of pax Britannica were the Liberal Party, in particular the industrialist Richard Cobden and, later, Prime Minister Henry Campbell-Bannerman (1905–1908). Notably, it was the Liberal Party that was in power when the Paris Convention treaties were left unratified. This stood in stark contrast to the multilateralism of the Conservative Party, as embodied by Prime Ministers' Lord Salisbury (1895–1902) and Arthur Balfour (1902–1905), which was much more willing to engage in negotiation with other countries and to use British market power for retaliatory means. That these preferences came to the fore particularly in negotiations over sugar was no doubt encouraged by the lobbying of Joseph Chamberlain, Secretary of State for the Colonies at the time of negotiation of the Brussels Convention (and himself a one time investor in the West Indies), who strongly advocated an end to continental subsidies. Unsurprisingly, it was the Conservative party that was in power when the Brussels Convention was signed, much to the chagrin of the Cobden Club of unilateral free traders. In this way, the Conservative Party was able to achieve its long-standing goal of halting non-liberal trade practices (Pigman 1997: 202).

Whilst not denying the central role played by the threat of British import-suspension in the Brussels Convention, teasing out this account, three additional insights can be offered into the early international commodity agreements and the abstract problem of collective action. First, the interests of the state are not pre-defined and should instead be considered a product of state-society conflict. In this sense we return to Ruggie's notion that the type of regime that arises stands as a reflection of the domestic social relations in the dominant state. Though we may take the successes of the Brussels Convention as evidence of a rational British 'food diplomacy' – where trade policy is used to influence a series of food and non-food goals – as Pigman (1997: 207) has suggested, the institutional dynamics of sugar trade owed more to domestic ideology than they did to any grand British strategy to construct international hegemony.

Second, and related to this, we saw the political malleability of the free trade concept as both Liberals and Conservatives appealed to its authority, but did so meaning different things and serving different ends. This further suggests that just because a liberal international trade agreement is successful it cannot be considered unambiguously beneficial. By achieving liberalisation through commodity agreements, i.e. reducing subsidisation abroad rather than simply opening the domestic market to any type of sugar, certain interests were favoured. The extensive sugar-using industry in jam, marmalade, confectionery and sweet biscuits that had been building in Britain was denied the cheapest sugar possible, while the domestic refining industry and the colonies were given respite from foreign competition. In this respect, we might also consider the neo-Gramscian argument that a function of international organisations is to placate potential antagonists to the extant regime of accumulation (Murphy 1994). By delivering a modicum of market opportunity to cane producers and diverting the colonies from social upheaval, the Brussels Convention had the (largely unintended) benefit of also prolonging the British imperial system.

Third, rather than taking the collective action problem as a given, it should be acknowledged in this instance as an active construction built on political decisions to create extensive market competition through under-pricing. This practice established a divide between the continental European and colonial sugar producers (to re-emerge in the 20th century as a North-South divide over the use of protectionism) that was neither inevitable nor irreparable. But once the collective action problem had been recognised as such and the framework established to deal with it, elites seeking regulation of sugar benefited from the institutional memory of previous Conventions. This refers less to the neo-liberal institutional idea of sunk costs encouraging the persistence of regimes, but rather to the constructivist idea of social learning, as states created a new arena and dialogue for interaction that would be ready to call upon whenever domestic factors provided the appropriate context to strike another international commodity agreement.

Security in sugar: the rise of the national regime

Interwoven with the continental-colonial divide was another division that affected who gained what from the production and trade of sugar. The arrival of high industrialism in Europe and the transfer of new machinery and large-scale factory plants to the production of cane sugar in the late 19th century began to cleave producers apart in terms of cost efficiency and competitiveness rather than simply who had recourse to the most powerful government intervention. Importantly, this was not just happening *between* producers of different countries, but between producers *within* countries, and was driven by changes in the owner-ship of production: from the planter class to corporate capital. This shift was pioneered in Cuba, which based on its plentiful virgin land, late abolition of slavery and wealthy landowning class, was targeted as a source of supply for the growing US sugar market. In a new twist to monoculture expansion, refiners and industrial consumers began to buy land and factories in Cuba themselves, some, such as the chocolate manufacturer Hershey's, becoming leading sugar suppliers in their own right. These food processors were joined by financiers who formed enterprises such as the Cuba Company – the largest single investor in Cuba between 1900 and 1920 – that developed infrastructure for the export industry and which channelled further corporate and pri-vate investment into the industry (Santamarina 2000). By the end of the World War I Cuba was producing about 4mt of sugar annually, of which the lion's share was US bound (Galloway 1989: 168).

This trade relationship was complicated by the emergence of the domestic US sugar industry. Though early experiments in cane produc-tion in the southern states of Louisiana, Mississippi, South Carolina and Florida had been hindered by unfavourable climate and geography, they were eventually overcome by flood controls, swamp drainage and irri-gation projects that allowed the crop to take hold. These nascent sugar-growing states were soon joined by beet farmers in the US West and Mid-West, putting the US in the unique position of growing both types of sugar and importing raw cane sugar. The need to secure evermore quan-tities of raw sugar to feed its refineries, however, led to continued overseas investment as US sugar interests were recast across a dispersed geograph-ical area. Military force, preferential trade policy and strong commercial penetration functioned reciprocally to lock a whole raft of producers – the Dominican Republic, Hawaii, Puerto Rico and the Philippines among them – into the US sugar economy. In the case of Hawaii it even resulted in annexation following the deployment of US troops to protect the properties of American citizens threatened by the monarchy's bid to seize power. As the New York newspaper *The Nation* (1898) charged at the time, this annexation was 'of sugar, for sugar, and by sugar'. If proof were needed, by 1899, the commodity accounted for 96 per cent of the total value of Hawaii's exports (Tate 1968: 121).

The corporate takeover of sugar was not just confined to the coun-tries and colonies complicit in the traditional Atlantic trade circuit. As happened in the West, industrialisation in Japan led to an increase in the per capita consumption of sugar – from 5 to 12 pounds between

1888 and 1903 – which domestic production could only partially meet. As a Japanese colony after 1895 and with a long history of sugar production, Taiwan was thus targeted as a supplier. Changing barriers to agro-industrial manufacture by fiat and providing sugar exporters with a preferential customs tariff, Japan was able to quickly advance Taiwan to the status of major producer in Asia (Mazumdar 1998: 370–376). Moreover, indigenous Taiwanese participation in sugar was rapidly reduced to small-scale cane growing and, by 1915, 13 Japanese companies dominated the industry (Galloway 1989: 209). Elsewhere in Asia, important shifts were underway as China became a net importer of sugar, a commodity it had previously exported and, by the mid-1920s, was purchasing between 0.5mt and 0.7mt a year (Mazumdar 1998: 385). This stimulated production in the Philippines, whose exports increased from about 15,000 tons in 1830 to 236,000 tons by 1914, and most of all Java, whose exports leapt from 222,000 tons in 1880 to 1.6mt by 1920, based largely on growth in the intra-Asian trade circuit (Galloway 1989: 212–216).

Finally, it was during this period that sugar completed its circumnavigation of the globe as producers in the Pacific came to compete in international export markets. Fiji, Mauritius and Natal, each manned with large swathes of indentured Indian labour, began to export sugar in significant amounts (around 100,000 tons each) by the late 19th century, whilst in Queensland, Australia, the Colonial Sugar Refining Company (CSRC) established a near monopoly on the burgeoning national industry. Indeed it is in Australia that we can see in microcosm the broader patterns in the shift from entrepreneurial and hybrid planter capitalism to an expansionist and integrated corporate capitalism. The CSRC centralised productive control by bringing under its ambit tenant and freehold estates, private and cooperatively owned central factories, and the cane refineries. This was all done with state approval as the industry was seen as the means by which a strong nation-state could be created, in terms of turning land into productive factors, creating an internationally competitive economy, and marginalising the alternate nationality claims of indigenous people. In fact, the idea of nationality was so central to the expansion of the industry that once it had consolidated itself in the 1900s, immigrant workers were abruptly deported under 'White Australia' racist policy (Galloway 1989: 231). Meanwhile, present in Fiji's sugar industry from the start, the CSRC began taking advantage of economies of scale and the opportunity of vertical integration with its refineries in Australia. By 1926 it had bought all domestic mills and assumed control of the entire Fijian industry (Moynagh 1973: 22–34).

Productive revolution and agrarian backlash

A key theme of this chapter has been to ground the otherwise anodyne descriptions of trade flows and productive capacity in the agency of particular actors. To pick this thread up, we now consider in greater depth the causes and consequences of the productive revolution in sugar. As already mentioned, in the late 19th century the mechanisation that spearheaded the beet industry in Europe began to spread through colonial conduits to the capital-intensive stage of processing and the labour-intensive stage of planting, harvesting and transporting. Table 3.1 illustrates the technical advances achieved in processing that enabled cane to be transformed with greater capacity and with more efficiency into sugar.

The increased appetite of the modern factories in turn called for greater and fresher amounts of cane to be sent to the mill, which in many cases led to increased land acquisitions by millers to give them greater control of their cane supply and an extension of state power to underwrite investment. In Java, for example, this involved passing laws allowing the government to claim uncultivated 'waste land' for lease to private plantations and permitted the Javanese peasantry to rent, but not to sell, land to foreigners for the establishment of plantations. Two points are of note in this respect. First, that the state was an active agent and moderator of the penetration of capital into the countryside. As Galloway (1989: 212) has suggested of the Javanese case, in language reminiscent of Polanyi, this was nothing more than a 'tactical means of protecting the basis of village society while opening up land to commercial interests'. Second, while contemporary analyses of sugar production often draw a divide between beet and cane – with beet constituting an artificial interference in the 'natural' South-North sugar trade – taking the example of Florida, Queensland and Java, we have

Table 3.1   The Productivity of Sugar Cane Factories, 1917

	Primitive Plant	Modern Factory
Tons cane crushed per hour	1.25	227.00
Extraction of sugar from cane (%)	65.00	95.30
Tons cane per ton commercial sugar	12.00	8.30

Source: Jock Galloway (1989) *The Sugar Cane Industry* (Cambridge: Cambridge University Press), p. 140.

seen how cane also required huge investment, both political and financial, to become economically viable.

Staying with Java, in the late 19th century another aspect of the productive revolution manifested itself: biotechnology. The cane plant reproduces asexually (new plants grow from existing segments of the plant) and prior to 1887 growers had no way of altering the genetic structure of any of the wild varieties to increase yields. It was the agricultural experiment station in Java – the Proefstatien Oost Java (POJ) – that first established the fertility of the cane and the sexual reproduction of seedlings and was therefore able to produce new high yielding and disease-resistance varieties. By 1929, 400,000 acres of POJ cane were in production in Java with an estimated 30 per cent yield increase due to this breeding (Evenson 1974: 60–63). The professionalisation of sugar agronomy and the epistemic links fostered among these groups of scientists in different experiment stations, mainly among the former colonies, soon enabled this new technology to be planted in every cane-producing country in the world. It helped to increase the yield of sugar per acre ten-fold between 1850 and 1950, an increase unmatched by any other crop (Mazumdar 1998: 382). This was certainly an impressive feat, but one which highlighted the limits of improving terms of trade through higher yields: as temporary advantages over rivals they were a bonus, but as long-term barriers to entry and guarantors of higher revenues they were ineffectual.

Thus it became that the demise of cane production was saved by processes of agro-industrial centralisation and technological advance, engendered by partnership between the colonial state and both domestic and foreign capital. Inevitably, this modernisation conflicted with small-scale peasant farming, often with violent recourse. This was the case in Mexico, where the Revolution of 1910 witnessed the sugar industry in Morelos being swept away – mills, mansions and all. Agrarian land reform negotiated between the government and the Zapatista movement that followed made it impossible for the sugar industry to re-emerge in its old estate form, as peasants returned to the fields and *ejidos* (farming collectives) arose in their stead (Crespo 1988). Within plantation economies, meanwhile, out of the social upheaval wrought by strikes at Tate & Lyle's factories in 1930s Jamaica, the Bustamante Industrial Trade Union emerged to negotiate the first labour contract. Following this, the National Workers Union under the leadership of Norman Manley gained full bargaining rights for sugar workers. These two unions spawned the Jamaican Labour Party and the People's National Party respectively, which to this day remain at the centre of the country's political processes

(Harrison 2001). And, finally, in Cuba, labour dissent against wage restraint and unemployment, which began among the sugar workers, spread throughout the island and resulted ultimately in the 1933 Batista military coup (Balfour 1995: 16). Consequently, Cuban nationals captured a significant share of productive capacity in sugar as protective state regulations encouraged the resumption of small-scale milling that had ceased during the Great Depression and the purchase of mills owned by US capital.[5] Each of these cases illuminates the political potential of the peasantry and suggests that, although we have painted the productive revolution in sugar in a broad-brush manner, the reality is that it had a variety of manifestations and prompted a variety of responses.

The volatile world market meets national farm support

With cane production soaring and beet production beginning to recover after World War I and Russian revolution, attention in Europe soon turned back toward the low price of sugar, which had plummeted from 9.4 cents per pound in 1920 to 2.4 cents per pound in 1925 (Abbott 1990: 180). Unable to prevent falling prices – the Brussels Convention having fallen into abeyance with the onset of war – many sugar producers began to feel the squeeze. Cuban producers in particular faced severe financial losses due to the heavy capital investment in the country's industry, but their attempts to tighten production unilaterally were dented by US sugar refiners who at the time still owned mills in Cuba and wished to continue exports to satisfy their domestic processors. The jolt of the Great Depression, however, was enough to push both the Cuban and US parties to breaking point as the import market in the US contracted in the face of the 160 per cent *ad valorem* tariff placed on sugar by the Hawley-Smoot bill and all parties involved in the trade stood to lose out. The result was the 1930 Chadbourne Agreement, negotiated between US sugar representatives and Cuban sugar growers – thus more a 'Gentlemen's Agreement' than an international commercial treaty – under which the US was to limit domestic production and imports from third countries, while Cuba was to limit exports to America to 2.8mt, rising in line with US domestic demand (Pollitt 1988: 101).

Cuba, meanwhile, continued diplomatic efforts to stabilise the market price of sugar and it was out of the conference held under Cuban auspices in 1931 that the International Sugar Agreement (ISA) was born, a true successor to the Paris and Brussels Conventions. Signed between nine of the major sugar exporters, which together accounted for 50 per cent of world sugar production and 94 per cent of world market trade, the ISA was intended to restrict production and work off stocks, thereby pulling up prices and reducing uncertainty.[6] Importantly for Cuba, its US trade negotiated under Chadbourne was excluded from its national export quota in the ISA. Like the Paris Convention before it, however, the 1931 ISA failed to stem production, only this time it was not due to signatories breaking the terms of the agreement but because of the practice of 'free-riding' by non-signatories. Over the first two years, the ISA members reduced their output by 7.2mt yet output in non-member states increased by 5.2mt (Brazil, the Dominican Republic and Japan being the primary culprits). Consequently, by 1934, the ISA members had seen their share of total world production halved, with world price averaging less than 1 cent per pound for most of the agreement's life-span, and in 1935 the ISA expired to the mutual relief of all its members (Abbott 1990: 182). Figure 3.2 indicates how only global depression and world war could stem the indefatigable production of sugar.

The failure of the ISA meant low prices continued to characterise the world market in sugar. In response, another set of trade negotiations began, concluding with a successor to the ISA in 1937. This agreement differed from its predecessor in that it included exporters *and* importers, and thus its membership constituted a bigger share of world production. Exporters were again required to restrict production to the free market, but the decision over export quotas was now to be handled by the

Figure 3.2   World Sugar Production, 1900–1950

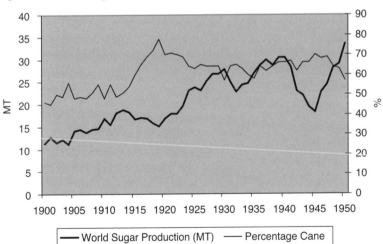

Source: Tony Hannah (2000) 'Early History', in Jonathon Kingsman (ed.) *Sugar Trading Manual* (Cambridge: Woodhead Publishing Limited), pp. 9–10.

International Sugar Council, a bureaucratic body administered in London, in the hope that this would depoliticise the quota decisions. For their part, importers, principally the US and UK, were to meet a minimum proportion of their consumption through imports and thus prevent further shrinkage in the world market. The emphasis laid on the world market is instructive, for, as in the initial ISA its successor also drew the same distinction between preferential trade and free trade. The 1937 ISA therefore excluded: 1) bilaterally agreed exports to the US; 2) all sugar traded between metropolitan powers and their overseas territories (i.e. Britain and France); and 3) sugar exported from Russia to adjoining territories (Abbott 1990: 183). A process of multilevel institutionalisation had been ushered into the national sugar trade regime, leaving international agreements covering the most volatile (and least valuable) part of the market. However, the time in which the 1937 ISA had to demonstrate the efficacy of these concessions was short-lived; in 1939 another international agreement on sugar was again abandoned in the face of war.

The effects of two world wars on national sugar policy were much more significant than the abandonment of international agreements. Mass dislocation reconfigured state-society relations at such a fundamental level as to totally reshape the broad-set sugar regime, replacing the brief interregnum of *fin de siecle* liberalism with a hardened (institutionalised) national protectionism. The instability and economic convulsions brought on by war and depression had placed a premium on food security, and, given the value accorded to the commodity in the public's perception of dietary requirements, sugar found its way on to the list of national necessities. As George Abbott (1990: 214) has written with respect to British policy-makers, the lessons of war could not be clearer:

> First, free trade had not paid off, and had to be abandoned. Second, it was dangerous to rely on a single source of supply or to make British sugar policy dependent on arrangements with another country. Third, domestic refining capacity had to be increased, and, finally, and perhaps most importantly, Britain needed its own beet sugar industry.

To guarantee supply, therefore, in 1919 imperial preferences for colonial sugar were reinstated – a commitment which continued right up to the end of World War II – while in 1925 a system of subsidies was created to support domestic beet growers and in 1936 the British

Sugar Corporation was established to process the beets from licensed acreages (Abbott 1990: 214). In the US, similar processes were at work. Per capita consumption had doubled between 1890 and 1930 from 54 to 110 pounds, making the commodity a national priority. Passed in conjunction with New Deal farm policy on other crops, the Jones-Costigan Act of 1934 tackled the problem of food security in sugar by providing remunerative prices but with strict supply controls to favoured producers. Sugar supply was thus divided among domestic firms (28 per cent) and foreign countries (Cuba 29 per cent, Philippines 15 per cent, Hawaii 15 per cent and Peurto Rico 13 per cent). In the maelstrom of negotiation over Jones-Costigan, refiners in the US were also able to work in their idea for guaranteed provisions on domestically refined sugars. Consequently, the overseas producers had to content themselves with exporting mainly raw sugar into the US under the agreement (Farley 1935: 177). Meanwhile in Asia, major sugar consumers also began to close their markets. In India, peasant-produced gur – an unrefined, hardened sugar cane juice – and refined sugar from Java had long dominated the national market, but, as modern, indigenously owned factories came on stream, the 1932 Sugar Protection Act was passed to offer complete protection from imports to India's nascent white sugar industry. Within two years, India was self-sufficient in refined sugar, production rising from 0.1mt in 1930 to 0.87mt in 1934 (Kaplinsky 1983: 31). In Japan, development of cane-production in its Taiwanese colony saw production outstrip consumption in the empire for the first time in 1929, supported by increasing tariffs on both raw and refined sugar throughout the 1930s (Farley 1935: 174). And, in China also, tariff walls were erected in the early 1930s in an attempt to revive the traditional Guangdong industry and capture the 1.0mt domestic market (Farley 1935: 173).

The desire for supply stability forged by war and depression helps in part to explain the economic irrationality of many countries promoting self-sufficiency in sugar, given that such policies were established and/or continued during periods in the early 20th century when the commodity could have been imported from the world market at extremely low prices. But of course, not all countries were expected to import sugar and the outcome of national farm support policies for these 'natural exporters' was devastating. In the most prominent case, on top of restricting production under the terms of the 1931 ISA, the closing of the Asian markets saw exports from Java shrink more than half between 1928 and 1934. This downward spiral continued, with the result that, despite being one of the lowest-cost and largest producers in the world at the time, by

World War II the Javanese sugar industry was a mere shadow of its former self (Boomgaard 1988: 167).

Conclusion

In 2,000 years sugar cane had come full circle, travelling westward from New Guinea through Asia and the Americas and right back round to Australia. In this time, the way the crop was cultivated, processed and consumed had changed immensely, even to the point that an identical product (refined sugar) could now be made using an entirely different input (beet). As the colonial regime unravelled due to abolitionism and free trade, a putative national regime came into being which satisfied the demand for adequate food supplies through a combination of domestic production and preferential trade with historic colonial suppliers, and under which the state became progressively more involved in micro-managing sugar. At the same time, corporate influence over trade policy mutated, caught between the colonial grouping of refiners, sugar-using industries and foreign sugar interests, on the one hand, and the newer national grouping of domestic cane and/or beet growers on the other. Typically, each of these groups was able to extract some concessions from the extensive government legislation that was enacted during this period, to the expense of consumers, who were assured regular supplies but at higher prices, and former/existing colonies, which were confined to exporting raw sugar only.

The effect of this was that, by the end of the 1940s, just 10 per cent of sugar produced was traded though the world market (Albert and Graves 1988: 7). Trade regulation within the national regime thus revolved round the power of the major sugar-importing nations and their adherence mechanisms of high preferential prices and latent military force. By comparison, regulation of the world market was weak. Exposed by free riders and diminished incentives for the major importers to promote stable trade, the 1931 ISA was unable to control output and prices effectively. But the two markets could not be totally bifurcated as the over-supply and low prices characteristic of the world market had the 'rebound' effect of threatening the viability of colonial/developing country exports *and* the expensive farm support programmes of industrial countries. This tension between preferential and free trade was carried on into the post-war era and, as the next chapter discusses, was one of the factors that contributed to the unravelling of the sugar regime in its national guise.

4
Imminent Crisis and the Embryonic Global Regime, 1945–1994

As the development economist Arthur Lewis (1970: 19) once commented, 'sugar cane was the only tropical crop to experience a scientific revolution before World War I'. As the previous chapter illustrated, this productive revolution was intimately tied to the extension of state regulation and corporate finance into sugar production. Moreover, the industrial structure and market conditions that this incipient national regime supported created a highly uneven distributive system, prompting Lewis (1955: 281) to remark on another occasion that 'cane sugar is an industry in which productivity is extremely high by any biological standard...Yet workers in the cane sugar industry continue to walk barefooted and live in shacks, while workers in the wheat industry enjoy among the highest living standards in the world'. More tellingly, Lewis might have contrasted the fortunes of the sugar cane workers in the former colonies with those of sugar beet workers in Europe and America. As the previous chapter also showed, while the institutions characteristic of the national regime were replicated across an ever-growing number of states, the terms brought to bear on the various countries and classes implicated in this transformation differed markedly.

This chapter picks up this narrative in the post-war era and begins by making the case that the sugar policy that emerged in the aftermath of World War II was not radically different from the pre-war era, but was rather a consolidation of state-led forms of national agrarian development and non-liberal forms of international trade agreements. The second section describes how the mounting contradictions within this regime were openly exposed during the 1970s 'food crisis', causing extreme market uncertainty, instability in preferential trade agreements and, perhaps most strikingly, the death of the ISA. Two sets of explanations are advanced for this: an economistic account, which points to interminable market forces and abstract notions of collective asymmetry as the reasons for price volatility, and an alternative critical account, which points to the political forces that became institutionalised in the regime and structured production in such a way as to instil instability into the world market. To conclude, the third section depicts the emergence of a global sugar regime under the auspices of the WTO, which according to its proponents would both liberalise trade and strengthen the rules governing it. Teasing out our historical account, we finish by questioning the supposed global credentials of this regime; in particular the ways in which the most powerful states were able to create 'exceptions to the rules' when it came to sugar.

Consolidating the national regime

Following Philip McMichael (1996: 53) the policies enacted by national governments in the aftermath of World War II can be heuristically grouped together as the Development Project. The objective of this project was to emulate Western living standards and the international norms that came to guide it were: 1) a national framework for economic growth; 2) a growth strategy based on urbanisation and industrialisation; 3) an international framework of aid that tied developing countries to the developed; and 4) central state initiatives to mobilise multi-class coalitions into the developmentalist alliance. The co-option of sugar into this project can be illustrated with reference to two trends – the growth of the industrialised food system and the provision of food security – both of which represented continuation and consolidation in the national sugar regime.

The growth of the industrialised food system refers to the expansion and cheapening of the range of durable products, which promised convenience and cultural association for a new generation of mainly urban consumers. With respect to sugar, these covered such goods as soft drinks, confectionery, bakery products and tinned fruit and vegetables, and promoted a culinary lifestyle that shifted preparation time from the home to the factory. This trajectory bore a strong legacy from the war, particularly in the US in which the consumer revolution in durable foods was spearheaded. The large number of women taken into factories, the preference given to commercial rather than home users in sugar rations, and the lobbying of the military by Hershey's and Coca-Cola among others to equip soldiers with chocolate and sugared drinks on account of their calorific and moral-boosting value, all served to encourage the ubiquitous and 'hidden' consumption of sugar through industrially processed foods and beverages. The outcome would be profound: in 1909 most sugar in the US was consumed directly, by 1997 less than a quarter was (Putnam and Allshouse 1999).

In matters of food security, meanwhile, the imperative of state policy was still firmly in domestic supply management. Contrary to the factoral and collective action models described in Chapter 2, the nature and manifestation of this imperative owed much to institutional memory, a claim borne out by the renewal of pre-war legislation across a number of countries. In the US, for example, while the 1934 Jones-Costigan Act was believed by officials at the time to be simply a temporary solution to low world prices, as soon as war and *de facto* state control ended, US sugar producers immediately called for its reintroduction. According to David Price (1971) it was the experience of existing within this system that had allowed farm and factory representatives to establish close links with their respective members of Congress and enough awareness of their collective predicament to put aside their differences and put their faith in a highly politicised regulatory framework. The 1948 Sugar Act that resulted was thus erected squarely on the design of its predecessor. Similarly in India, the 1955 Essential Commodities Act, which established a wide range of policy instruments to control the storage, trade, and prices of food crops including sugar, was built on the edifice of the 1939 Defence of India Act. The legislation supported a different system to that of the US – an industry composed of widely dispersed cooperative-owned sugar mills supplied by a large number of subsidised cane-growing smallholders – but highlights the intimate role played by governments across national sugar industries. To be sure, the trend was one of nationalism rather than nationalisation. In Britain for example, in 1949 when the Labour government planned to nationalise the sugar industry, Tate & Lyle fought back, even sending sugar out in bags labelled 'Tate Not State' (Macinnis 2002: 174). Nevertheless, the underlying orientation was clear: governments and farmers would survive in symbiosis.

To guarantee domestic supply through high prices, it was necessary to prevent cheap imports from entering the market and depressing prices. In this regard, it is of central importance that the institutionalisation of farm support, in compact with the Development Project, took root in the US, which emerging hegemonic from the war was able to shape the international environment in a manner conducive to this system. At the Bretton Woods Conference in 1944, the US and Britain signed an agreement that provided the blueprint for the post-war economy centred on three organisations: the International Bank for Reconstruction and Development (World Bank), the International Monetary Fund (IMF), and the International Trade Organisation (ITO). While the World Bank and IMF came into force almost immediately, the ITO was stillborn. Despite the leading role of the US in the genesis and evolution of the idea, it was unable to ratify the 1948 draft agreement (Wilkinson 2001: 401–402). The ITO thus joined the ill-fated World Food Board Proposal in the institutional mortuary and in its stead the provisional General Agreement on Trade and Tariffs became the pre-eminent source of international trade regulation. However, the GATT was explicitly written to accommodate the import tariffs, export subsidies, and later, the trade remedies such as absolute quota limits, of the US agricultural sector, and so, from its very inception, effective agricultural measures were excluded from its ambit (Hathaway 1987: 109; Josling *et al.* 1996: 21). In the regulatory lacunae left by the GATT in sugar, pre-war preferential trade agreements were duly resurrected. Britain formalised its imperial preferences through the 1951 Commonwealth Sugar Agreement (CSA), conducted with agencies representing dominant sugar producers such as Tate & Lyle, the Queensland Sugar Board and the Colonial Sugar Refining Company and which created a guaranteed market of 1.55mt of raw sugar in the UK at 'reasonably renumerative' prices (Abbott 1990: 214). The largest quotas went to the West Indies and Guyana (0.64mt), Mauritius (0.34mt), Australia (0.3mt), South Africa (0.15mt) and Fiji (0.12mt). Likewise in the US, the original foreign suppliers that made up the import allocation under the Jones-Costigan Act were reinstated with similar quotas under the Sugar Act, joined by a number of other politically favoured countries such as Brazil, Mexico and Peru.

Striking the right balance between domestic and foreign supply under these protective systems was not without its conflicts. Most prominently, sugar growers and processors in the US began to increase their capacity and pushed for production quotas to be reallocated to the mainland, to the detriment of US refiners and other quota holders such as Cuba. Already by 1955 a quarter of a million sugar workers had come out on strike in Cuba after their wages had fallen 23 per cent following a drop in export volumes and under mounting pressure from the tightening of the US market, the situation deteriorated. It was in this maelstrom that Fidel Castro was able to garner support from the country's labourers *and* sugar barons for his campaign for national regeneration and, by 1959, had led the country to revolution (Balfour 1995: 58). In response, the US immediately severed the 3.0mt Cuban sugar import and placed an embargo on all trade with the island. For its part Cuba turned to the USSR, which agreed to import 2.7mt of Cuban sugar at favourable prices. Thus despite the convulsions wrought by revolution and blockade in the world's biggest producer and importer, as illustrated in Table 4.1, the profile of

Table 4.1   International Net Sugar Trade, 1955–1965

Largest Exporters, MT			Largest Importers, MT		
1955	1960	1965	1955	1960	1965
Cuba	Cuba	Cuba	USA	USA	USA
4.65	5.63	5.32	3.66	4.63	3.65
West Indies	Dom. Rep.	Australia	UK	UK	UK
0.93	1.1	1.21	1.55	1.87	1.92
Philippines	Philippines	Philippines	Japan	USSR	USSR
0.91	1.1	1.1	0.99	1.45	1.49
Australia	Taiwan	Brazil	USSR	Japan	Japan
0.63	0.91	0.82	0.77	1.25	1.47
Taiwan	Brazil	Taiwan	Canada	Canada	Canada
0.59	0.85	0.81	0.65	0.61	0.86

Source: A. C. Hannah and Donald Spence (1997) *The International Sugar Trade* (Cambridge: Woodhead Publishing), pp. 93–94.

the world sugar market remained largely unchanged throughout the birth of the Cold War.

Yet while the profile of world trade maintained a degree of predictability, world prices were anything but. Facing low but relatively stable prices in the 1950s, major sugar exporters had again responded by reviving a pre-war institution, this time the International Sugar Agreement. Inheriting the basic format of its predecessors, the weaknesses of the ISA were cruelly exposed by the Cuban crisis and the surge of sugar moving from the preferential to the world market and back again. Prices were significantly bid up during the early 1960s as the US turned to the world market for its import requirement but once its own producers and remaining preferential suppliers successfully increased production, and as the USSR did not have a big enough internal market to consume all its Cuban imports and so refined and diverted a proportion back on to the world market, prices quickly bottomed out again. Lacking the efficacy to address these market trends, efforts to renew the 1958 ISA floundered, leaving the world market unregulated and unstable throughout the mid-1960s.

Capturing the gains from trade: the cuban, cartel and class perspective

During the 1960s, despite their best efforts to export commodities such as sugar to international markets, with prices frequently in the doldrums many poorer countries seemed to be failing at development 'catch up'. As such, the role of trade in development theory gained increasing prominence, most notably in the work of Hans Singer (1949) and Raul Prebisch (1950). These two scholars argued that the classical theory of international trade was inapplicable to poorer countries and that, far from acting as an automatic engine of growth, trade had in fact hindered development. The central premise was that primary exports faced declining terms of trade, meaning that successively more agricultural, forestry and fishing produce (concentrated in the developing countries) had to be exported to pay for the same amount of industrial imports (produced in the developed countries). Given the income inelasticity and competitive world markets of primary products, developing countries could not expect their terms to trade ever to improve in the long run. So, on the advice of Prebisch and, under his guidance, the United Nations Economic Commission for Latin America (ECLA) more generally, the policy prescription was for rapid industrialisation and entry into the monopolistic-priced manufactures markets, based on a strategy of import substitution industrialisation (ISI).

The relationship between ECLA thinking and sugar policy was uneven: though its discourse was widely imbibed, its influence on policy was sporadic. This is well illustrated in the case of Cuba, whose post-revolutionary strategy was at first influenced not by prevailing socialist development models (despite US claims to the contrary) but by the nationalist programmes of ISI developed by Prebisch. However, limited endowment of raw materials and the emigration of a large swathe of its business-owning middle class quickly made ambitious industrial programmes in Cuba highly expensive and import intensive. Further, this development strategy detracted resources from sugar, Cuba's main export, creating an acute balance of payments problem. It was in this context that Cuba – and in particular its sugar industry – became integrated into the Soviet 'socialist division of labour', as Castro put aside his early ISI programme in 1963 favour of the recovery and expansion of sugar production. The idea was that larger and better-priced sugar exports could then finance a renewed, but more selective, investment programme. As Ernesto Guevara, then Ministry of Industry, commented at the time:

> The entire economic history of Cuba has demonstrated that no other agricultural activity would give such returns as those yielded by the cultivation of the sugar cane. At the outset of the Revolution many of us were not aware of this basic economic fact, because a fetishistic idea connected sugar with our dependence on imperialism and with the misery in the rural areas, without analysing the

real causes: the relation to the unequal balance of trade (Pollitt 2004: 323).

A hugely ambitious target was thus set for 1970: to harvest a bumper crop of 10mt, twice the size of a typical annual crop. Further, contrary to the ECLA method of economic rationalism, the 10mt campaign was born not of sound economic planning but of a spirit of nationalism, the apotheosis of Castro's politics of mobilisation. In a speech in 1969 Castro declared that 'the ten million ton harvest represents far more than tons of sugar, far more than an economic victory; it is a test, a moral commitment for this country. And precisely because it is a test and a moral commitment we cannot fall short even by a single gram of these ten million tons' (Balfour 1995: 96). In the event, though, the campaign did fall short. Though the sugar harvest reached a record level of 8.5mt, the shortfall was a terrible defeat for the Castro leadership. Perhaps more importantly, in diverting much needed resources to the campaign, including half a million non-agricultural workers to cut cane, other sectors of the economy were severely dislocated. Over 21 per cent of industrial and agricultural goods and more than 41 per cent of forestry products registered their lowest output since the Revolution (Pollitt 2004: 330).

Disillusioned at the failure of those countries that embraced ISI to reduce their foreign exchange gap and stimulate satisfactory growth, Prebisch began to question not what was traded *per se* but rather the regulatory structure surrounding trade. Among the reforms he proposed were regional trade agreements among primary product exporters, non-reciprocal tariff cuts by developed countries on imports from developing countries, and measures to ensure equitable and stable commodity prices – policies that would later form the centrepiece of the work of the United Nations Conference on Trade and Development (UNCTAD), a Third World dominated forum to which Prebisch was appointed Secretary-General. UNCTAD subsequently initiated international commodity agreements in a variety of primary commodities and, under its supervision, the 1968 International Sugar Agreement was signed. This ISA differed from previous agreements by introducing limits on the amount of sugar that members could import from non-member states and requiring exporting members to release large proportions of their stocks to prevent prices rising above the upper value of the allotted price range. However, the efficacy of the first mechanism was dented by the absence of two of the largest importers of sugar, the US, which objected to Cuban participation, and the European Community (EC), which was dissatisfied with the size of its own production quotas having recently brought sugar into its Common Agricultural Policy. The efficacy of the second mechanism, meanwhile, had at first proved resilient, mitigating the increased prices faced by importers during the early 1970s, but was ultimately shattered by the next supply shock to follow the Cuban Revolution, the unprecedented USSR import beginning in 1973.

ECLA School theory had illuminated the relationship between primary commodity trade and inequality principally on a national level but this relationship also cut across another dimension, namely class. In promoting cash crop exports like sugar, many poor countries exposed themselves not only to the vagaries of geo-politics and world markets, but also exposed the poorest people within their borders to malnutrition. As Cheryl Christensen (1978) noted during this era, agricultural export commodities bound for export were typically supplements to Western diets and could not substitute for domestic dietary requirements. So when developing countries produced more sugar, it was often to the detriment of local food security as the revenue associated with export commodities was imperfectly or inadequately translated into wages for essential items. Moreover, the land and resources devoted to export crops frequently came at the expense of peasant-grown staple foods for personal consumption. In 1975 in Barbados, Belize, the Dominican Republic, Guadeloupe, Mauritius and Reunion, less than one third of arable land was assigned to basic food production and the majority was for sugar (Christensen 1978: 757). In addition, in developing countries in the 1970s it was typically the richer city dwellers that were driving demand, for example, by moving from a breakfast of staple foods such as maize, yams or cassava to cereal products that not only had sugar sprinkled over them but also contained it as an ingredient (Dinham 1983: 77). In this respect, the decision to produce more sugar, even if bound for domestic markets, could exclude the poor twice over: the commodity could damage self-sufficient food provision yet, even with the extra supply, still remain too expensive for the rural poor to purchase in the cash economy and boost their calorific intake. Whilst not a topic at the forefront of the pro-industrialisation agenda of the ECLA, the class dimension of hunger was likely to be the foremost struggle for those it affected.

The national regime in crisis

Through ECLA theory and its omissions, we attempted in the first section to map the uneven contours of beneficiaries of the national sugar regime and highlight the difficulties in equalising the gains from trade. This regime was one largely inherited from the pre-war era, with domestic and international institutions pressed and fitted into the Cold War order and the rules of the game challenged but not fundamentally changed. All this was thrown into flux from 1973 onward, when prices and trading patterns across a whole range of commodities became unstable and shortages became a recurrent possibility, a phenomenon referred to as the 'food crisis' (George 1976; Hopkins and Puchala 1979; Friedmann 1982). The spark that ignited the food crisis was held to be the adverse weather conditions that afflicted production in a number of countries and the price rises that followed the record sale of grains from the US to the USSR made possible by détente. In the case of sugar, changing trading patterns were also caused by a crack in the Cold War division as the USSR, following poor crops domestically and in its preferential supplier Cuba, imported an unprecedented volume of sugar from the world market, leading the price to spike in 1974; a phenomenon that then reoccurred in 1980. Figure 4.1 illustrates more clearly the historical precedence of these movements.

The volatility of prices was of concern to all major sugar-consuming nations, even those that had reduced their dependency on the world market through domestic production and preferential trade agreements, as the world price rose above the preferential price and caused supplies to

Figure 4.1   World Market Price of Sugar, 1945–1995

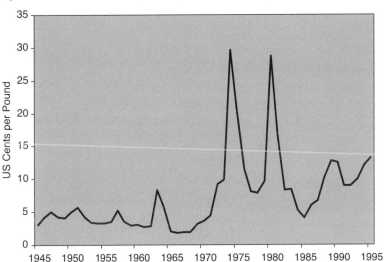

Source: F. O. Lichts *International Sugar and Sweetener Report*. Various years.

be diverted to the highest bidder. The rules that had governed international trade were suddenly abrogated and looming domestic shortages rapidly raised the incentives to renegotiate them. It was fortuitous for US policy-makers, then, that just at the time when sugar prices were climbing to historic highs, the US Sugar Program was scheduled for review. Long-standing opponents to protectionism in sugar were presented with the perfect opportunity to press for its abolition, given that US producers were essentially competitive at such high prices and that a programme extension would raise consumer prices to politically unpopular levels. As it happened, it was an unusual coalition of free-market Republicans and consumer-minded Democrats that defeated renewal of the Sugar Act in Congress, leaving the 1975 and 1976 American sugar crops without any support (though they would be reinstated in 1977 in response to the subsequent nosedive in prices). As the majority of the international trade in sugar had passed through preferential agreements, the abandonment of the US Sugar Act in 1975 represented a watershed moment. At a stroke, the world market nearly doubled in size as the US removed quotas, excise taxes and other restrictions on domestic production and imports and bought 5.2mt of sugar from the world market, 33 per cent of that year's trade, thereby further fuelling the spiralling prices (Hannah and Spence 1997: 143).

World market conditions also influenced domestic sugar policy in the EC, particularly the incorporation of the CSA into European legislation, which Britain insisted would have to carry on when it joined the Community in 1973. The European Commission initially proposed that a 1.4mt Commonwealth quota be accepted and a certain amount of quota production by domestic producers cut in order to make the area a net importer. However, Belgium, France, Germany and Italy were unwilling to accept cutbacks in favour of outside interests and suggested that, if extra sugar were needed, they could simply increase domestic production (Stevens and Webb 1983: 325). Among the ex-colonial exporters, meanwhile, uncertainty over their remunerative sugar market was significantly reshaping national politics. In newly independent Mauritius, the Indo-Mauritian middle class oversaw a coalition government between Francophile representatives of sugar and the domestic Labour Party, which guaranteed Mauritius membership of France's post-colonial welfare institutions and an influential place in the forthcoming EC sugar negotiations (Houbert 1981: 89–91). And in Jamaica, the 'Great Sugar Debate' saw the government and university academics do battle as to whether preferences were necessary to national welfare or would only serve to perpetuate dependency and long run immiseration (Harrison 2001: 54).

The case made against preferences was that not only did they lock in a concentrated export portfolio but also that the 'remunerative price' received only seemed so attractive because it was compared to prices on the world market; prices depressed by the excess production of the EC in which the Caribbean quota holders were complicit.

In the face of political deadlock, the rocketing price of sugar experienced during the food crisis in fact presented the Commission with a *deus ex machina*. Extant market conditions enabled the Commonwealth cane exporters and the European Sugar Beet Confederation to agree to the other's demand as both incorporation of the Commonwealth quota *and* the expansion of beet production were plausible. The Lomé Convention was thus signed in 1975, with Mauritius (0.49mt), Fiji (0.16mt), Guyana (0.16mt) and Swaziland (0.12mt) receiving the bulk of the final 1.3mt quota allocation; while, in the EC, domestic production quotas and prices were duly raised (Mitchell 2004: 31). The novel set of circumstances surrounding the 'Europeanisation' of British colonial history thereby initiated one of the defining path dependencies in the post-war sugar regime. The EC would henceforth act as one of the world's biggest importers *and* biggest exporters of sugar, intertwining the fortunes of the post-colonial quota holders and CAP beneficiaries in the process. Table 4.2 shows how the bloc moved from a net importer in 1975 to a net exporter in 1980, notwithstanding the 1.5mt it routinely imported during this period.

Table 4.2   International Net Sugar Trade, 1970–1980

Largest Exporters, million tonnes			Largest Importers, million tonnes		
1970	1975	1980	1970	1975	1980
Cuba	Cuba	Cuba	USA	USA	USSR
6.91	5.74	6.19	4.80	3.31	4.82
Australia	Australia	EC	Japan	USSR	USA
1.64	1.83	2.89	2.48	3.18	3.21
Philippines	Brazil	Brazil	USSR	Japan	Japan
1.18	1.73	2.66	1.49	2.44	2.31
Brazil	India	Australia	EC	EC	Canada
1.13	1.05	2.44	1.04	1.45	0.89
Dom Rep	Philippines	Philippines	Canada	Canada	Iran
0.79	1.00	1.79	0.98	0.95	0.78

Source: A. C. Hannah and Donald Spence (1997) *The International Sugar Trade* (Cambridge: Woodhead Publishing), pp. 93–94.

In the mid-1970s negotiations began on yet another ISA. As neo-Marxist approaches to dependency began to supersede ECLA thinking, the intellectual climate surrounding these negotiations became more radical. It was argued that the relationship between imperialism and underdevelopment did not take the form of *external* dependency between national economies due to declining terms of trade (as in the ECLA model), but rather an *internal* dependency that resulted from mono-poly capitalism and which altered the mode of production in such a way as to neuter growth or transfer the benefits abroad (Roxborough 1979: 43). This analysis gained some credence in Third World policy circles, notably in demands for a 'New International Economic Order' in UNCTAD which stipulated non-reciprocal non-discriminatory tariff preferences in trade, integrated cartels across a range of commodities, nationalisation of property, and technology transfer (Leys 1997: 47). Within the sugar regime, its agenda was reflected in the national-isation of foreign-owned plantations in Peru, Trinidad, Belize, Jamaica and Guyana at the turn of the 1970s, but, short of rhetoric, its influence on the 1977 ISA was negligible. Integration of the ISA with other commodity agreements was fudged and the only real difference to emerge was an emergency buffer stock of 2.5mt, fin-anced by a levy of 0.28 cents per pound on world market trade, designed to prevent against further spikes in prices (Mahler 1981: 720).

Despite its numerous technicalities, over the seven years that the 1977 ISA was in existence there was only one year where prices remained within the permitted range. The world market fluctuated between a high of 43.10 cents per pound (November 1980) and a low of 4.05 cents per pound (August 1984) and for most of the time prices gravitated toward the low end of that scale. In the end, it was upon the EC that the failure of the final ISA was resolutely pinned. Having abjured from its renewal in 1981, the EC became a free rider on the higher market price garnered by the ISA (a practice, it will be recalled, which put paid to the very first ISA in 1931). For example, in 1981 the largest export quota under the ISA was the 2.5mt granted to Cuba; by contrast, that same year EC exported 4.0mt *net* of the 1.3mt imported under Lomé (Mahler 1981: 726). In such a climate it was impossible to manage the world market and the agree-ment lapsed at the end of 1984. The grand institution of the ISA withered away, to be replaced by the International Sugar Organ-isation, an apolitical body in charge of gathering and disseminating statistics.

Advocating the market medicine: an economistic analysis of the food crisis

In terms of simple causality, it was undeniably the large USSR import that led to the two price spikes in 1974 and 1980. The question that preoccupied most commentators, though, was why the price jumped so much and why it returned to levels that were among the lowest real prices ever recorded (Harris 1987: 139). In short, an answer was sought as to why the world market did not adjust smoothly and why volatility seemed endemic. Given that the growth rate in world demand was essentially static, analysts coming from an economistic perspective concerned themselves with the ups and downs of world supply, focusing in particular on those countries that had a potentially large effect on trade flows. It was known during the period of the food crisis that production of sugar had increased in many countries, understandable during the times when world supply was tightening and prices were expected to rise but what was mysterious was why production failed to decrease when prices fell back down again.

To explain this incongruous behaviour, some pointed to the perennial nature of the sugar cane crop, which takes seven years to move from plantation to yield, meaning that prices could vary widely by the time the crop is released. Moreover, it was argued that the heavy capital investment that comes with agro-industrial expansion in sugar had created a high ratio of fixed to variable costs, meaning the marginal revenue was likely to exceed the marginal cost of production and so sugar would be supplied even at very low price levels (Hannah and Spence 1997: 126–127). Shifting the focus to contemporary events, others pointed to the appreciation of the dollar during the 1970s in aiding the huge expansion in domestic EC sugar production given that export revenue was a reflection of both current world price and the exchange rate between local currency and dollars. In the case of the EC, while world commodity prices in US dollars were falling between 1980 and 1985, in pounds sterling they rose by 65 per cent, in deutsche marks by 42 per cent, and in French francs by 86 per cent. So, at the peak of the dollar *vis-à-vis* the European Currency Unit in 1985, the internal prices of agricultural products under the CAP were only moderately above world dollar prices, reducing export subsidies without a reduction in internal prices and thus enabling cheaper promotion of exports (Hathaway 1987: 14). These agronomic and market explanations were typically supplemented by accounts that pointed out the distorting effects of political interference by farmers in the protected developed country markets, namely, the US, EC and Japan. The argument ran that low world prices were unable to exert a greater effect on inefficient producers because the sugar industry was able to gain government protection by virtue of its concentration in particular constituencies (that collective action logic again!). More precisely, sugar producers in the developed world were deemed capable of pushing for coherent and favourable policy reform in response to high world prices *and* resisting policy reversals when the world supply moved back into surplus and production should ideally decrease to equalise the market (Borrell and Duncan 1990: 5).

Tied together, these arguments presented the fundamental premise that volatility and persistent low prices in sugar existed because supply was more price elastic in the upward than the downward direction and trade was conducted through a residual world market. A market is said to be residual or 'thin' where only a small proportion of total production is cleared through it, meaning sudden export to, or, as happened in sugar, sudden imports from that market will have a proportionately greater impact on price. It was no surprise to some, therefore, that the two greatest price spikes in the post-war era came at a time when the world market in sugar was decidedly limited by policies that bypassed free trade in favour of domestic protection and preferential trade (Gilbert 1996).

While the practices that conjured up this scenario of oversupply and thin markets were deemed problematic to the world sugar economy, it is interesting to note that their rationality as such was never doubted. From an economistic perspective, market fundamentals inevitably trump normative obligations and so efforts to construct an effective ISA and restrain price volatility politically were doomed to failure. More sugar will be grown and placed on the world market as long as producers face price incentives, and oversupply will continue as long as the aforementioned agronomic, market and electoral conditions remain in place. To believe that states could overcome the tendency of each party to favour the lowest possible production quotas for everyone else but the highest possible production quotas for itself, be it inside or outside the cartel, was sheer naïveté. Given this analysis, the advice for governments was simple: rational political regulation of markets is futile, prone to vested interest at both the national and international level, and only economic *self*-regulation, through submission to free trade, is workable (World Bank 1986). Once implemented, liberalisation would ensure a greater percentage of production was traded and was done so through the free market, and would therefore reduce volatility and raise prices as inefficient producers in the EC,

US and Japan – and also in many traditional exporters – would be forced out of business (Borrell and Duncan 1990; Jabara and Valdés 1993).

Exploring power in production: a critical take on the food crisis

The economistic account as we have described it here has a certain merit. In a given context imperturbable market forces are hard to deny, and the collective action problems at the international and domestic level, abstract as they are, clearly existed. What this results in analytically, however, is an account in which the outcomes are seen as inevitable and its final solution as irrevocable. Contingency and broader types of political action are sidelined, making 'market forces' appear unassailable and in turn the de-politicisation of the world sugar economy seem both possible and desirable. In short, such an account fails to ask where political economy action originates and why it takes the form it does. As such, we examine how contradictions within the national sugar regime itself, namely, the trends of corporate penetration and modernisation, on the one hand, and domestic supply management, on the other, gave rise to additional political structures conditioning the crisis in sugar, and which thereby reveal the incompleteness of the economistic accounts.

The previous chapter concluded with the observation that the major economies undermined their own protected markets as capital investment in foreign sugar production rebounded as over-supply and low prives. Turning to Africa, we can see how this process continued into the post-colonial era, at a time when a number of countries looked to bolster their domestic sugar industries in the face of growing import costs and dwindling foreign exchange.[1] Under the norms of the national development model, these sugar industries were designed to be state-owned projects but lacking the requisite experience and knowledge, many countries sought out the guidance of foreign companies. As part of their strategic reorientation from ownership and investment to advisory work and futures trading, during the 1970s two British companies, Tate & Lyle and Booker McConnell, advised on over 55 sugar projects in 11 African countries. These commercial services were no less lucrative than the old plantation business: not only did the companies receive government fees for feasibility studies, management consultancy, technical services, and so on, but both Tate & Lyle and Bookers had UK-based engineering subsidiaries which were obviously well placed to prosper from the contracts awarded to design and construct the new sugar factories (Stevens and Webb 1983: 328). The upshot was that many countries ended up investing in expensive sugar projects that created relatively few jobs. This pattern was repeated across the continent, many arrangements following colonial ties and by 1978, of the 66 projects in Africa to increase sugar production, 44 were supported financially by banks or firms from the European Community (Dinham 1983: 83–85). Corporate Europe's involvement in agro-industrial planning was further reinforced by the preference of the World Bank and the UN Food and Agricultural Organisation for transnational consultancy. As Barbara Dinham (1983: 82) ultimately concluded, the state-led development of sugar industries hardly reduced the dependency of African countries on the West but replicated the large-scale capital-intensive model of the corporate estate and generated alternate forms of dependency not related to ownership.[2] The particular relevance of this for our argument is that production in the developing world played its part too in global over-production, and that this was not the result of domestic farm lobby pressure but of political decisions taken by trans-national networks of state elites, international organisations and foreign corporations.

The counterpart to over-production in developing countries was the process of substitution in developed countries, experienced across a number of commodities such as cotton (substituted by synthetic fibres) and palm oil (substituted by soy and canola oils). In the case of sugar, just as the high price of colonial sugar in the mid-19th century stim-ulated the growth of the European beet industry, so the price umbrella covering sugar producers in the West began to encourage competition from cheaper alternatives. Once industrial processes allowed for sub-stitutions to sucrose from other monosaccharides, the relative costs of crops determined which would be used as raw materials. In the US, Japan and South Korea, for example, it was the surpluses bound up in the grain regime, along with technological economies of scale, which enabled the alternative liquid sweetener High Fructose Corn Syrup (HFCS) to become competitive. Crucially, this was enabled only by the existence and extension of the durable food system as liquid sugar could be used in large quantities simply impractical in home cooking. Further, and like the emergence of beet before it, these substitute pro-ducts were nourished by the formation of new industrial coalitions, this time the political alliance between corn refiners (namely, Archer Daniels Midland, Cargill, and, after 1988, Tate & Lyle) and sugar pro-ducers. As HFCS production leapt from zero in 1970 to 5.0mt by 1985, this alliance increasingly pushed for imports to be reduced to expand the domestic market in sweeteners. The Reagan administration duly obliged, cutting imports of sugar from 2.7mt in 1985 to 1.0mt in 1987.

The effect on the Caribbean Basin was ruinous as exports fell dramatically, causing a loss of 350,000 jobs and a crash in foreign exchange earnings.

In addition to the international structures of trade regulation identified, national inequalities in wage earnings were also a fundamental structure of the food crisis. Indeed, this was what made it a crisis: the fact that many of the poorest and hungriest people suddenly could not afford the basic grains needed to keep themselves alive (Friedmann 1982: 284). Contrary to the economistic perspective discussed previously, in which the crisis in sugar was really seen as a crisis of order, we suggest here that the political management of sugar production also affected the ability of the poor to pay for food and, in this respect, also implicated the commodity into the crisis of hunger. As already discussed, the production of sugar was becoming increasingly capital-intensive and decreasingly labour-intensive. In Jamaica, the Manley government attempted to reverse this trend by first declining Tate & Lyle's demands for mechanisation of the sugar harvest, then by buying the company out and reforming the industry so as to absorb rather than shed peasant labour. Between 1973 and 1980, roughly 36,000 small farmers (many formerly landless) gained access to 70,000 acres of land through extendible leases, and the state-held sugar estates were turned into worker cooperatives. But the cooperative scheme had inherited an industry in decline. Despite the guaranteed quota under Lomé, given insufficient investment, poor worker education, and dimming prices on the world market, the sovereignty of Jamaica's development planning began to yield to international financial institutions. The World Bank Rehabilitation Project in 1978 was the final turning point as loans were used in an attempt to improve the performance of the three largest estates through vast restructuring, whence, following their short-lived departure from the industry, Tate & Lyle reappeared as key participants in the management and partial ownership of the sugar economy (Weis 2004: 465).

Under the same broad process of structural adjustment, trade barriers across the agricultural sector were lifted as Jamaica found itself resubmitted to the old colonial logic of food trade: export sugar and import staples. In this way, sugar was implicated into the hunger crisis as land in countries across the globe was devoted to monocropping for export, the ranks of the rural surplus labour force were swelled, and traditional forms of agricultural knowledge were lost as more of the world's population was turned away from direct access to food and incorporated instead into capitalised food markets (Madeley 2002: 28–29). It is also worth noting here the subtle change that the concept of food security underwent. While the imperative remained, the means of obtaining food security shifted from directly controlling the production of dietary necessities to maximising the foreign exchange necessary to buy food. Thus the issue of providing food for the poor became construed as one of adequate supply rather than affordable access or guaranteed provision. At a national policy level, this meant finding one's place in the global economy and using export-led growth to secure the necessary foreign exchange to import essential foodstuffs. This was made possible by the acute need for finance in developing countries in the wake of the OPEC oil crisis, which overlapped with and contributed to the food crisis, and which the IMF and the World Bank satisfied with an intensified programme of loans. These came with conditionalities, so, in Peru and Guyana, for example, loans for sugar projects were made available for industry privatisation, while in Indonesia, they were supplied for President Suharto's migration programme to move people from Java to the outer islands and effectively exploit the potential of 'empty' lands through sugar plantations and mining (Toussaint and Millet 2005).

Maintaining our commitment to identify agency and contingency, though, it was evident that some developing countries were able to alleviate this bind through trade strategies that circumvented the world market. For instance, in response to high energy prices and under the rubric of national development, Brazil began its ethanol programme Proálcool to acquire alcohol-based fuel for cars from sugar cane. To do so, Brazil had to change the domestic demand function for sugar by institutionalising a substitute market in petrol and did so by keeping cane prices *below* the world market price and making huge funds available for infrastructural development. In 1978 Brazilian agriculture as a whole benefited from roughly $18bn in credit and loans, the bulk of which came from the state itself. Indeed, it has been claimed that, at the time, the state-owned Banco do Brasil was the largest agricultural lender in the capitalist world (Burbach and Flynn 1980: 97). The country also sought a way out the oil crisis through its 'counter-trade' with Nigeria, which involved a direct exchange of Nigerian oil for Brazilian sugar worth some $4bn (Strange 1988: 185). By swapping commodities rather than selling them onto the world markets, states that were able to offer each other a large and stable enough domestic market were able to offset the volatility of world markets and escape the expenditure of scarce foreign exchange. By far the biggest example of this activity, though, was the Cuban trade under the Soviet COMECON agreement, whereby the USSR set a price for purchases of Cuban raw sugar linked to the prices of Soviet-Cuban exports, including most importantly oil. According to Jorge Pérez-López (1991: 170) though precise measurement is difficult, in 1974 when the price of sugar first spiked, Cuba was estimated to have lost $463m under the arrangement, but, for every year since, Soviet transfers constituted a massive subsidy to the Castro government, somewhere in the region of $18bn between 1973 and 1984.

We have argued here that the contradictions of increased sweetener production in an environment of tight protection that were previously submerged within the national sugar regime were finally exposed during the period of the food crisis, which accelerated and made evident the unsustainable practice of increasing domestic production at ever more volatile and lower world prices. Many of the institutions that had supported this fragile balance such as inter-industry coalitions and national trade regulation evolved in keeping with the new era of market uncertainty while others, among them the International Sugar Agreements and the US preferential market, were pushed to the margins. In sum, the myriad trade regulations covering sugar no longer delivered stability, and the stage was set for a new regime to emerge.

An embryonic global regime in sugar

The two most important changes in international sugar trade during the 1980s and 1990s were the increased amount of sugar entering world market trade, which ended the predominance of the hub and spoke system of preferential trade, and the final inclusion of agriculture under the auspices of the World Trade Organisation, which internationalised the realm of decision-making over sugar policy to a degree never before witnessed. Each of these suggested the demise of the national dimension of production and trade and the emergence of a global regulatory order, that is to say, a regime that fostered international convergence in the ways of making and exchanging sugar (privatisation, deregulation, liberalisation in sugar and sugar-containing products, etc.). The economistic prescription of embracing market forces, if not its analysis, would thus appear to be somewhat vindicated. By exploring in this final section how these changes came about and what they actually entailed, we show how, on the contrary, the embryonic global regime in sugar did not represent a truly liberal market order but rather mutated and prolonged the national regime into the late 1990s.

Following our earlier assessment of export growth in the EU and substitutionism in the US and Japan, three of the historic major import markets, how was it that more trade suddenly started passing through the world market? The answer can be found in the increasing consumption of sugar in developing countries. Driven by population and per capita income growth – in many cases linked to oil wealth – countries such as Algeria, China, Egypt, Indonesia, Iran, Iraq, Malaysia, Mexico, Nigeria and the United Arab Emirates began to import sugar in increasing volumes.[3] In 1974, at the moment of the first price spike in sugar, developing countries accounted for just one quarter of all world imports. Within a decade this had doubled and within two, by 1994, they accounted for 69 per cent of total imports (Hannah and Spence 1997: 108). Moreover, without the legacies of colonial trade these countries looked primarily to the world market for supply, rather than striking preferential agreements, and, in doing so, increased both the absolute and relative size of the free market. This marginalisation of preferential trade was further aided by the dissolution of the Soviet Union in the early 1990s and the breakup of the COMECON trade pact with Cuba. By 1995, the share of the world market in total trade had risen to 70 per cent, up from 41 per cent in 1955 (Hannah and Spence 1997: 95). Entering the growing world market on the exporter side, meanwhile, were Thailand and, following deregulation of their domestic sugar programmes from the late 1980s, Australia and Brazil, which together filled the export market left by Cuba, as detailed in Table 4.3.

Table 4.3   International Net Sugar Trade, 1985–1994

Largest Exporters, MT			Largest Importers, MT		
1985	1990	1994	1985	1990	1994
Cuba	Cuba	Australia	USSR	USSR	India
7.21	7.17	4.52	4.30	3.94	2.63
EC	EC	Brazil	Japan	USA	Russia
2.98	3.63	3.60	1.98	2.04	1.96
Australia	Australia	EU	China	Japan	Japan
2.65	3.06	3.26	1.96	1.75	1.70
Brazil	Thailand	Cuba	USA	Mexico	China
2.59	2.50	3.19	1.91	1.55	1.24
Thailand	Brazil	Thailand	India	Canada	USA
1.78	1.64	2.72	1.74	0.92	1.13

Source: A. C. Hannah and Donald Spence (1997) *The International Sugar Trade* (Cambridge: Woodhead Publishing), pp. 93–94.

Although the 'thickening' of the world market was not due to liberal-isation as many commentators had wanted, but to the end of oligopsony, many welcomed the structural shift in the composition of world supply and demand nonetheless. G.B. Hagelberg and Tony Hannah (1994), for instance, favoured the increasing volume of imports by low income countries as they had more price-elastic demand functions, meaning they would buy relatively less as prices rose and relatively more as prices fell, keeping prices within a narrower band (though they also expressed dis-appointment that the break-up of the Soviet Union had led to the entry of new trading agencies to the detriment of market transparency). For their part, Donald Larson and Brent Borrell (2001: 10–11) praised the deregulation in Brazil and Australia and the ending of Soviet subsidies to Cuba as policies that made exporters more responsive to price, con-tributed to declining price volatility, and even made more apparent the costs of protection in the US, EC and Japan. The effect of this sustained pressure in free market prices would be that many of the less efficient exporters would be weeded out, which, for Simon Harris (1987) meant that the traditional exporters would have to improve the competitiveness of their industries through mechanisation or else have their governments take on the unions to force wages down. The implicit sentiment was that this was all to the good: the discipline of the market was the best way to undermine the political forces that held in place protectionist barriers and ultimately led to disorder (Borrell and Pearce 1999: 10).

Submitting sugar (but not support) to global regulation

Alongside this sea change in market structure was the comprehensive incorporation of sugar, and agriculture generally, into the multilateral trade negotiation framework. The Uruguay Round of the GATT (1986–1994) marked a watershed in trade governance when, as Sylvia Ostry (2002) put it, a 'Grand Bargain' was struck between the developed and the developing countries, implicitly exchanging the opening of OECD mar-kets in agricultural and labour intensive manufactured goods for the inclusion into the trading system of the 'new issues', such as services, intellectual property rights and investment. Finally, and almost as a last minute piece of the deal, to succeed the GATT a new organisation was also agreed to, the World Trade Organisation, within which there was also established a stronger and more judicious mechanism for settling conflict, the Dispute Settlement Body (DSB). The DSB was seen as 'the jewel in the crown' of the new rules-based trading system and came to play a major role in the restructuring of the international sugar trade when it later upheld a complaint filed by Australia, Brazil and Thailand against the EU's export subsidies; a far cry from 1978 when the same case was upheld by the GATT Dispute Body only to be dismissed by the EC without effect. The hope for the sugar industry, then, was that multilateral decision-making would institutionalise the deepening and broadening of market forces in the domestic economies of producers; a process that had already been initiated by the decline of preferential trade support and unilateral deregulation (Pearson 1993).

The Cairns Group, a coalition of exporters that came together to push for free trade in primary commodities, had promoted the inclusion of agriculture in the world trading system vigorously. The group comprised, among others, Australia, Brazil and Thailand, each of which, as highly efficient cane producers, stood to gain from any liberalisation of the sugar trade and thus became vocal advocates of this strategy. The emergence of these countries as bastions of free trade in sugar at this particular juncture is especially noteworthy. Taking the example of Australia (though any of the three could be used), the Colonial Sugar Refining Company had long been Australia's exclusive export marketer for the country's sugar cane crop, which was carried out under contract to the Queensland government with the distinctly illiberal aid of subsidies and insulation from domestic and foreign competition. Despite reforms that since the 1980s diluted these government-industry links, it is clear that Australia owed its position more to 'created advantage' than comparative advantage (cf. Krugman 1996). In this respect, the appeal to free trade and efficiency by such countries after their own structural adjustment through protectionism could be seen as a somewhat hypocritical and ahistorical argument (Baru 1987: 64).

It was not just low-cost exporters, though, that had an interest in agricultural liberalisation independent of any concessions that might be offered in exchange. Motivated by fiscal concerns attached to the seemingly unsustainable agricultural subsidy war, officials of the major industrial nations gathered at the Tokyo economic summit of May 1986 had explicitly recognised the problem of allowing vested interests to capture national policy:

> We note with concern that a situation of global structural surplus now exists for some important agricultural products, arising partly from technological improvements, partly from changes in the world market situation, and partly from long-standing policies of domestic subsidy and protection of agriculture in all our countries. This harms the economies of certain developing countries and is likely to aggravate the risk of wider protectionist pressures. This is a problem in which we all

share and can be dealt with only in cooperation with each other (Hathaway 1987: 18).

The pressures of the global structural surplus were no less apparent in sugar. In the EC for example, expenditures by the European Agricultural Guidance and Guarantee Fund (the financing tool of the CAP) on sugar had rocketed since the beginning of the decade. Prior to the major production push in 1980 expenditure averaged ECU 365m per year and by 1986 had grown five times over, to ECU 1,926m (Hathaway 1987: 76–77). After years of wrangling over the exact balance of concessions to be made, as neither wanted to feel that they were 'unilaterally disarming' in the face of the other, the US and EC finally managed to strike a bilateral deal. This 'Blair House Accord', settled in 1992, was then taken to the negotiating table to multilateralise among member states. In effect, the US and EC agreed to deal with the farming sector as a whole, thus ending the individual commodity regulation characteristic of the post-war era, and to explicitly tackle the three main trading barriers of export subsidies, import access and domestic support, whilst making important exceptions for US deficiency payments and EC transition payments. Under the resultant Agreement on Agriculture, 'decoupling' and 'tariffication' became the watchwords used to dismantle the policies that once worked in tandem to regulate agricultural trade. But, despite the institutional opportunity and the economic logic evident in reform, a tightly regulated and level-playing field in sugar was not forthcoming. Whilst the Agreement committed the US to give up Section 22 (which it had used to place arbitrary fees/quotas on sugar-containing products in the early 1980s) and the EC to cut export subsidies, as well as binding a minimum market access and a tariff reduction formula, the text allowed for significant continuation. It exempted farming deficiency and income payments from the Aggregate Measure of Support calculations, allowed Special Safeguard Measures to be introduced in relation to hard hit commodities, and enabled tariffs to be bound at high and prohibitive levels. The waiting game for multilateral liberalisation in sugar had begun.

Post-hoc analyses of the Uruguay Round have since suggested that it was especially difficult to liberalise long-protected agricultural industries such as sugar because of the support that would have be transferred to producers to alleviate the electoral pressures of protecting rural jobs (Hathaway and Ingco 1995). Again, this is an important but not an exhaustive political structure influencing outcomes. One institution overlooked in this account was the set of policies that tied together the various business interests implicated in the sugar industry and gave potentially antagonistic actors a stake in perpetuating the *status quo*. First, the incentive for cane refineries in the US and Japan to lobby for cheap imports instead of expensive domestic raw sugar was weakened by the system of support whereby refiners receive the higher government price, then pass a percentage onto growers, thus guaranteeing them a slice of the protectionist cake. Second, to enable cane refiners to fulfil their excess capacity, in the 1980s popular re-export programmes were introduced in the US and EC under which they were either given aid or made exempt from high tariff payment on raw cane imports, as long as the sugar processed was not sold domestically but sent back onto the world market. Finally, these programmes were also extended to the sugar-using industries, which had taken to importing semi-finished sugar-containing products in larger amounts to avoid the high domestic price of sugar. The re-export programme on finished goods allowed higher tariffs to be applied on semi-finished 'blends', thereby maintaining domestic protection for farmers, and allowed industrial food and drink manufacturers to compete in international markets.

These strategic coalitions and their policy institutions externalised the political conflict over trade from a conflict between economic sectors to one between countries, both dampening the willingness of heavyweight corporate interests to lobby against the protection of sugar production, a phenomenon which had so divided British policy in the 19th century, and perverting the logic of market competitiveness to which economists had appealed. The result? The global market in sugar, as envisaged by its neo-liberal protagonists, had been almost entirely averted.

Conclusion

Inheriting both domestic and international policy institutions from the pre-war era, the post-war management of sugar trade sustained the broad system of regulation characterised as the national regime. The commodity was able to fit quite comfortably into the provisos of the Development Project, jarred only by the Cold War leap of Cuban export from the US to the USSR, and the expansion of national production under the rubric of food security continued apace. With few exceptions, by the 1980s virtually all countries had established the means to cover a greater part of their sweetener requirements: in Bolivia, Chile, Ethiopia, Greece, Honduras, Malawi, Morocco, Pakistan, Swaziland, and Zimbabwe among others, this meant joining the ranks of the modern factory producers; in the US, Japan and South Korea, meanwhile, it involved the development of HFCS. But the contradictions of the regime could not be buried for long and reared most violently during the period of the food crisis, ultimately resulting in the disbandment of the ISA, the decline of US preferential access, and structural adjustment in trade deficit countries.

Across the globe, state participation in agriculture was rolled back in two stages. Development programmes were reconfigured in the 1980s and then flexibility to intervene in markets was restricted in the 1990s. Thus it was that the 'New Development Project' took shape: the conviction that liberalisation ensured cheaper and more stable food supplies by either reviving domestic agriculture through new export opportunities if a country held comparative advantage or 'releasing' (making redundant) excess capital and labour to more competitive economic sectors if it did not. For most countries, this meant that primary production passed from being a relative priority in national development – underpinned by a belief that the state had an important role to play and that the decline of agricultural employment could and should be reversed – to a place more or less at the margins (Weis 2004: 466). The organisation that emerged to cement this transition was the WTO, and the inclusion of sugar under its auspices signalled the dawning of a new era in the production and exchange of the commodity. But the global regime envisaged was not the one that materialised. The Agreement on Agriculture left a complex scenario in sugar. While the objective of liberalisation was entrenched various provisions were made for specific types of protectionism, meaning vestiges of the national regime, and within this legacies of the colonial regime, could still be seen. While the wheels of reform were set in motion, it would remain a contingent and political matter as to whether the sugar regime would ever arrive at its intended destination of upholding global economic efficiency.

5
Restructuring in the EU-ACP: Out of the Strong There Came Forth Sweetness

To recap, our theoretical argument up to this point has been that the worldwide production and trade of sugar could be hueristically understood as taking part within a national regime: a stylised constellation of rules and norms that fostered the tight management of sugar prices by the state but with the exact formation of this management differing between individual nations. The close of the Uruguay Round in 1994 had done little to dislodge this order as multilateral liberalisation of the international sugar trade was fudged. More precisely, though the rules agreed upon within the WTO ringfenced existing levels of protection and brought agriculture firmly within the organisation's remit, the tariff reduction schedules for sugar were ineffective, meaning there was little pressure to reform domestic policy. In the next four chapters, we examine the post-Uruguay Round era in greater detail and ask whether the terms of competition and strategies of accumulation in the industry have continued unchanged. In each case, the answer is negative, prompting us to enquire about the exact nature of the change, the reasons for this, and its distributive and developmental consequences.

Beginning with the case of the EU-ACP, we find that along with the Uruguay Round, sugar policy in the EU had also escaped liberalisation in the MacSharry reforms made to the Common Agricultural Policy in 1992 and the Fischler reforms in 2003. This may suggest that the regime erected in the post-war era had become well and truly entrenched yet, in 2005, the EU brought about the most substantial reform to CMO Sugar (the Common Market Organisation of Sugar) since the UK acceded in 1973, and two years after that, unilaterally denounced the ACP Sugar Protocol, bringing to an end 34 years of international commodity support. This chapter explores this striking transformation by first charting the changing structures of EU sugar production prior to reform, specifically the concentration and diversification of the leading sugar beet processors. Against this backdrop the next section explains, contrary to the assertions of many commentators that change 'simply had to happen', how an imperative for reform was actively constructed by the EU Trade Commission out of its adoption of the 'Everything But Arms' (EBA) agreement and judicial defeat at the WTO. The third section then details how this open-ended imperative split the various stakeholders in the regime with the final reform package favouring those European processors who were its prime beneficiaries previously, allowing them to both withstand international competition and facilitate renewed patterns of capital accumulation in its wake. Finally, the fourth section discusses the effects of reform on the traditional suppliers in the ACP countries and the contemporary suppliers offered new market access opportunities. In both cases, the argument is presented that the task of adjustment differs markedly in these countries from those in the EU but that the singular effects of CMO reform have been overstated in what will be an ongoing transition.

CMO sugar and the dynamics of concentration and diversification

To understand why sugar regulation in the EU had at first seemed so intransigent, it is necessary to delve into the byzantine CMO Sugar system. Forged through the Stresa Conference on the CAP in 1958, CMO Sugar had traditionally rested on three pillars: guaranteed prices, export subsidies, and import restrictions. Guaranteed prices were offered to processors for all sugar produced in-quota, that is, inside the allotted quotas set by the European Commission and distributed by national governments. Given that the sum of quota sugar and the guaranteed Sugar Protocol import from the ACP routinely exceeded domestic consumption, a structural surplus was effectively built into CMO Sugar. This surplus had to be exported, but as the world price of sugar is typically below European production cost, it could only be sold with an export subsidy. This came from a combination of levies paid by processors, which were effectively passed on to consumers in the form of higher prices, and finance taken from the EU's Development Budget equivalent to the 1.3mt ACP import, which was justified as a form of development aid. Finally, to prevent cheap foreign sugar competing with the allotted supply at home, import restrictions consisting of a flat rate tariff (€419 per tonne of refined sugar) and an additional variable tariff (€115 per tonne in 2003) were applied, creating a watertight seal on the European market (European

Commission 2004). This regulation was further complicated by the production of excess, out-of-quota sugar by EU companies, the so-called 'C-quota' sugar. For this sugar, no help was given and the commodity had to be sold below cost on the world market. As was made evident in the WTO court case ultimately brought against the EU, such sales were only possible because the profit margins that came with in-quota sugar were used to cross-subsidise C-sugar, thereby enabling it compete at low world prices.

In effect, then, CMO Sugar acted like a series of valves, carefully letting sugar flow out the EU, as subsidised in-quota or effectively subsidised C-quota, but not letting any excess flow in. Thus it successfully averted the stockpiling of sugar as happened in the case of 'butter mountains' and 'wine lakes' and thereby mitigated an acute political pressure point felt in other areas of agriculture. Moreover, the complicated and diffuse ways in which CMO Sugar was financed – through producer levies, development assistance and implicit higher consumer prices rather than through the usual CAP budget – resulted in the perception that the regime was self-financed and thus sustainable. This notion of sustainability was further enhanced by the political bargains made to cheapen inter-industry trade. As argued at the end of Chapter 4, potential antagonists to the high price of beet sugar were effectively paid off and given a stake in maintaining the *status quo*. To put some names and numbers on this, between 2000 and 2004, the annual EU expenditure on sugar ranged between €1,400m and €2,100m (European Commission 2004). Chemical refunds, a compensatory tool for firms using expensive European sugar in non-food products, were received by Tate & Lyle's Citric Division among others, while recipients of export refunds for processed foods included companies such as Nestlé. Tate & Lyle also received the lion's share of the refining aid, which was granted to cover additional costs related to the extra stage of cane processing (Rural Payments Agency 2004). The majority of expenditure, however, was for export subsidies, the major beneficiaries being Südzucker, Tereos (formerly Eridania Béghin-Say), British Sugar, Danisco, and, again, Tate & Lyle. Figure 5.1 details the exact division of support for 2004.

Within this regime, those companies originally granted quota by their national governments were further aided by the regulatory structure of CMO Sugar, which inflated and protected their individual markets. Through the system of quota allocation, CMO Sugar facilitated the emergence of 'national champions' in sugar as in the majority of member states quota production was held by just a handful of beet processors and tight regulations meant that this could not easily be transferred to potential

Figure 5.1   Explicit Costs of CMO Sugar, 2004 (€ millions)

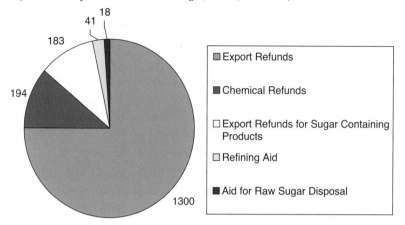

Source: European Commission (2004) 'EU Sugar Sector: Facts and Figures', Press Release, MEMO/04/177, Brussels, 14 July 2004.

competitors.[1] Moreover, as quota remained in the hands of the few, processors acted as both monopsonists (i.e. the only one possible buyer for farmers' beet) and monopolists (i.e. the one possible seller in the national/ sub-national market). This bore two consequences in terms of rent capture. First, processors were able to wrench a disproportionate share of the intervention price from growers, as, although they had to pay a minimum price for beet as set within the CMO, there was still the refining mark-up to be negotiated. Second, they were able to charge inflated prices by virtue of what the Swedish Competition Authority (2002) called 'tacit collusion'; an informal and legal arrangement whereby companies declined to compete with each other outside their national/ regional market and instead charged between 10 and 20 per cent above the already generous intervention price. Thus CMO Sugar facilitated neither a Single European Market, nor an international market, but was handmaiden to the domination of effectively sealed internal markets by a select number of processors.

Sugar beet was one of the most profitable crops to grow in the EU and sugar beet processors were arguably the prime beneficiaries. They were, in economic terms, the recipients of 'super-normal' profit; that is, profit that should be, but is not, eroded in the long run. By way of example, between 1994 and 2002 British Sugar's profit margins exceeded 20 per cent in every year bar one (Oxfam 2002a: 16). The logic of business management, however, dictated that this was not enough as profit streams had to be continually renewed and improved upon. For sugar processors, the options were limited as demand for sugar was flat – a result of income inelasticities and the shift toward reduced-sugar diets in Europe – and margins on inputs bought (beet/raw cane) and output sold (refined sugar) had been pushed to the limits. The remaining options were thus concentration and diversification.

Concentration allowed the aggrandisement of super-normal profit streams from different regions as processors bought one another out and then decommissioned the smallest among their number. The resulting changes in production locale were the only times that quota was transferred in practice. Between 1992 and 2002 30 per cent of sugar factories closed down, with the majority of the closures involving the smaller and/or independent plants. Moreover, given that many of the survivors were in the hands of the same parent company, it was estimated that just 30 companies filled the EU production quota, with a mere five – Südzucker, Nordzucker, British Sugar, Danisco and what would become Tereos – controlling the majority. This concentration of production led to reduced employment as technical advance and economies of scale raised the factor productivity of labour, meaning that less people needed to be employed to produce the same amount of sugar. Between 1992 and 2002 almost 20,000 jobs were shed in the processing industry, leaving just 38,500 people in work by the end of the period. This also affected the farming of sugar beet as those (typically smaller) holdings surrounding the decommissioned factories stopped growing the crop, while those remaining holdings increased in size. The biggest of these holdings could be found in France and the UK which had an average size of 100 hectares, compared to an average European sugar holding of 69 hectares, and an average agricultural holding of just 18 hectares (European Union 2003: 48–68).

Diversification, meanwhile, took place into both unrelated economic sectors via a parent company, or within the immediate economic sector into activities such as non-food sugars, distribution/trading or artificial sweeteners. In the UK, these trends could be witnessed in the activities of Associated British Foods, the parent company of British Sugar, which milked its cash cow for investments in property, and in Tate & Lyle, which acquired citric acid businesses and established trading houses and sweetener subsidiaries producing HFCS (this subsidiary operated in the US market as HFCS production was sharply constrained in the EU under CMO Sugar regulation). It is notable too, that these trends in farming and processing had a marked geographical distribution: those enterprises that remained in business tended to be located in some of the richest regions in the EU – the Paris Basin in France, East Anglia in the UK, and North

Rhine-Westphalia and Lower Saxony in Germany – thus exacerbating existing income inequalities across Europe.

Constructing the imperatives for reform

Guaranteeing high prices to European sugar beet farmers had thus resulted in a political economy 'house of cards' as successive stakeholder interests were finely balanced together and a regulatory regime slowly erected. What happened, then, to send this house tumbling? As a start, a number of critiques began to gather and together created a more hostile discursive climate in which the regime had to stand. The reports of the EU Court of Auditors (2000) and the Swedish Competition Authority (2002) highlighted the implicit costs, over-production and lack of competition within the regime; government departments challenged the notion that sugar should be treated as a unique industry (DEFRA 2006); and NGOs criticised the anti-development consequences of EU dumping (Oxfam 2002a, 2004). But the policies that made the need for change inevitable, by effectively pulling the rug out from under the regime, were the 2001 EBA agreement that prised open EU import restrictions, and the WTO dispute case that heralded an end to export subsidies. Without these, it is arguable that the impending CMO Sugar reform in 2006 could have dealt with its erstwhile challenges in a far more conservative manner.

The EBA began life as an idea circulating in the WTO around the 1996 Singapore Ministerial and proposed to give the 48 least developed countries (LDCs) duty-free and quota-free access to the EU market for all products except arms and munitions. The idea was picked up by Pascal Lamy, EU Trade Commissioner at the time, and via his intimate knowledge of the bureaucratic machinery of the EU was passed by the Council of Ministers just five months later. While the EBA did not cover any countries that could have flooded the EU market immediately, it constituted the thin end of a large and unsettling wedge for European producers. This much was recognised when sugar was made one of only three commodities denied immediate access under the agreement and instead backloaded until 2009, which along with a slight reduction in preferential imports (discussed later) was the only succour European producers were able to achieve once the wheels of the EBA had been set in motion.[2] The WTO case, meanwhile, involved Australia, Brazil and Thailand, all low-cost sugar producers with large export potential, taking aim at the EU's out-of-quota exports. The dispute did not challenge the EU's right to import ACP sugar at preferential prices but rather its use of development aid and effective cross-subsidisation, which was alleged to violate the Uruguay Round commitment of the EU to limit subsidised exports to 1.3mt. Despite European protestations, the WTO ruled in favour of the complainants and the EU was forced to abide by its initial commitment. The upshot was that around 4.0mt of EU sugar, which had previously found its way on to the world market, would have to be 'disposed' in another way.

At first glance, this victory appears to vindicate the strength of the WTO to universalise and enforce the rules of the multilateral trading system, providing a marked difference to the GATT and a compelling argument that globalisation has made even the most powerful states submit to the rulings of supranational bodies. Such an analysis here, though, would underplay the independent interests that the EU, specifically the European Commission, had in reducing domestic support on sugar anyway. What is suggested in the remainder of this section is that the EU acted in such a way as to use the WTO judgement to expedite reform to the sugar sector, which it sought to manoeuvre into a position consonant with its broader goals of WTO-compatible trade policy. This was not reform *by* the WTO but reform *for* the WTO.

First, it is apparent that the initiation of the EBA agreement by the EU was not just a long overdue pro-development policy, or, more cynically, an exercise in trade diplomacy, but was also, as one London sugar trader (2007) put it, 'an exocet missile designed to hit the sugar regime'. The point of note here is that most LDC exports received duty-free, quota-free access to the EU anyway under its Generalised System of Preferences (GSP), leaving the benefits of the EBA concentrated on just a few key products, one of which was sugar. Pascal Lamy (2001), EU Trade Commissioner at the time, was clear on the efficacy of this market opening:

> [Under the EBA] we decided to liberalise not only industrial products – including textiles and clothing – but also agricultural imports, and importantly, those that had hitherto been the most sensitive products... As you can imagine, the adoption of this initiative was not an easy task for us. *But we were determined to tackle entrenched domestic lobbies*, and as a result, I think the debate about trade and development in Europe has made a significant step forward. [Italics added]

Second, the waning commitment of the Commission to uphold the established practices of its sugar regime was evident in its WTO defence and subsequent response. Although the EU did present a defence in the WTO – not to have done so would have been political suicide – it was more out of a duty to challenge than a desire to win. One source even went as far as to claim that the EU did not fight its corner in the WTO particularly strongly as it was entirely equivocal about the outcome, noting that upon hearing the final verdict 'certain sections of the Commission weren't too unhappy about the result' (Australian WTO lawyer, interview 2008). It can be presumed that this referred in particular to the Trade Commission.

Third, the instrumental usage of the WTO judgement by the EU Commission can be seen in the restructuring of EU-ACP relations toward Economic Partnership Agreements (EPAs) and the ultimate denunciation of the Sugar Protocol. Although often conflated by the fact they were negotiated around the same time, the change in the sugar regime and the introduction of EPAs were actually far more integrated. Recall that the complaint over export subsidies was to be settled by reform to CMO Sugar; there was specifically no attack made at the WTO on the Sugar Protocol itself, or the right of the EU to import guaranteed amounts at above world price. The preferential treatment of the traditional exporters in sugar, and of the ACP in international trade more generally, was a separate issue regarding non-reciprocity, which was simultaneously under negotiation as the WTO waiver given to the 2000 Cotonou Agreement expired in 2007.[3] Yet the EU pushed the negative result of the WTO sugar case, along with that of the erstwhile bananas case, to suggest the incompatibility of non-reciprocal and discriminatory preferential treatment in the current trading order (Mandelson *et al.* 2007). This was undoubtedly made easier by the fact that within the European Commission, responsibility for ACP trade had passed from the Directorate General Development to Directorate General Trade, with the latter arguably more attuned to the need to harmonise EU trade regulation and less encumbered by the bureaucratic ties which had grown between DG Development and the ACP.

The preferred solution of the EU to the expiration of Cotonou was to conclude EPAs with the ACP and rewrite the Sugar Protocol within this framework. This would entail replicating the duty-free quota-free offer of the EBA and ending the system of guaranteed prices by breaking the link to the EU price, and allowing it to float and carry the benefit of making the EU's sugar trade with non-LDC ACP countries WTO-compatible. While the Sugar Protocol beneficiaries acknowleged that exact continuation of the Protocol was unlikely, not least because it ran against the principle of non-discrimination which was to be at the heart of any EPA legislation, they did still believe it was possible to safeguard the existing benefits of guaranteed EU purchases at negotiated prices (Jeffrey 2007). However, as many ACP countries stalled on the wider EPA negotiations, reluctant to accept stringent 'behind the border' policy changes proposed by the EU and to give up their remaining preferences, of which sugar was one of the most important, the EU made its threat material. Just as the expiry date of the Cotonou waiver began to close in, the Sugar Protocol was abruptly ended and its recipients made to face an even greater loss in export earnings should they not submit to the EPA juggernaut.[4] The exasperated response of Henry Jeffrey, Caribbean regional spokesman on sugar, to the request by the EU for the Caribbean to join with them in denouncing the Protocol says it all: 'If ever there was an absurdity, this was it!' (Stabroek News 2007).

For all the negative press and political upheaval it caused, it is worth asking why the European Commission was so adamant on concluding WTO-compatible trade regulation in sugar. In short, the answer has to do with the extent to which CMO Sugar interfered with greater trading priorities. This 'interference' was revealed by the steadfast refusal of Peter Mandelson, successor to Lamy as EU Trade Commissioner, to entertain ACP hopes of a renewed waiver; the renewal dismissed not so much because of its illegality but because of the costs associated with it. The Cotonou waiver was requested at the WTO Doha summit in 2001 in what was portrayed as a situation of 'exceptional circumstances'. Nonetheless, the EU still had to make trade concessions towards Thailand, Indonesia and the Philippines over canned tuna and towards Latin America over bananas to ensure member states would grant exception to the EU's preferential import system. Given the difficulty of construing the end of 2007 as *another* exceptional case, it was expected that the EU would have had to pay dearly for a second waiver. Moreover, defending the type of preferences as enshrined in the Sugar Protocol would be costly not only in terms of immediate concessions, but also in jeopardising longer term relations with far more important trading partners (Orbie 2007). The EU has much to gain from a credible and stable international trade system as institutionalised in the WTO, and reforming sugar gave it both room to manouevre in the Doha Round agricultural talks and the leverage to make enhanced demands of its own (Swinbank 2005). Mariann Fischer Boel (2007), EU Commissioner for Agriculture and Rural Development from November 2004, later stressed this point volubly:

> The example of sugar underlines our tough commitment to reform... we are deadly serious about having a CAP which can face up to the discipline of the international market and expectations of the public.... [But] It is not acceptable that we simply brush market access for

services and industrial goods to one side...No one can seriously expect the EU to make valuable concessions in the farm sector and come away from the table with nothing at all to show for them.

Finally, there was also a domestic trade incentive in bringing about reform: it could potentially bring about cheaper sugar for food processors, part of the broader EU strategy for shifting the region's trade profile toward value-added products (Mandelson 2006). While the Commission – and many other economic studies besides – typically touted the benefits of cheaper sugar as a boon for consumers, the fact is that any price reduction would have been somewhat negligible for the individual shopper. In the UK around just £0.16 would be saved on a kilo bag of sugar, and much less on products where sugar makes up a smaller percentage of the final cost.[5] Hardly the stuff of consumer liberation! As was anticipated, the real beneficiaries would be the sugar-using industry, which would be able to capture the reduced sugar input costs on domestic sales and ultimately be better placed to target foreign markets once the full price reduction took full effect and the reliance on export credits had ended (Laming, interview 2007).

In sum, reforming sugar was about the broader significance of the industry. This point was not lost on Franz Fischler (2004), then the EU Commissioner for Agriculture and Rural Development, when he announced to an audience of sugar workers on the eve of reform that the impending changes were 'not about reducing prices to consumers', though this was symbolically important, and neither were they about protecting jobs, as 'the trend towards rationalisation and job reduction would continue even without reform'. Rather, reform was about 'how the market fundamentals work', meaning a situation needed to be reached where the sugar regime was consonant with the other commodities in the CAP, thereby enabling the EU to take a positive rather than defensive position in future WTO negotiations. In achieving this objective, it is evident that the EU deliberately put WTO rules at the centre of the debate, portraying them as fixed and immutable and not the political construct they really are (Hurt 2003: 174).

Internalising regime change: the politics and agency of reform

So the rug had been pulled out from under CMO Sugar and reform made a necessity. The point to be made now, though, is that the precise nature of this reform remained an open question and that, given the complex and multiple interests at stake, there was still much to play for. The European Commission (2003) opened the debate on reform by releasing a working paper detailing three alternate scenarios to meet the necessity of reducing its volume of production – reducing producer quotas, letting the internal price fall, and full liberalisation – with preference firmly expressed for the price fall option. This would help bring sugar in line with the rest of the CAP commodities and also enable the duty-free, quota-free offers to be made with reduced risk of creating a flood of imports. However, this option held grave consequences for the less competitive producers, not just in Europe but also among the Protocol signatories and EBA eligible suppliers who benefited from the higher price their cane received in the EU. Yet the efficient beet producers that were able to withstand a price fall, namely, those in Britain, France and Germany, were reluctant to agree to a quota cut that would have been imposed uniformly across member states and in July 2004, the price cut option was decided as the path of reform.

In response to this threat, an unlikely alliance arose between the ACP cane exporters and (inefficient) sections of the European beet industry, advocating a 'shallow' price fall option. To make this compatible with the EBA agreement, LDCs agreed to voluntarily restrict their exports to the EU over the first ten years of the agreement, and, for their part, producers in the high-cost southern member states agreed to accept restrictions on production (ACP Sugar Group 2005a). This too failed to gain support. Both the trade and agriculture departments of the European Commission maintained that it would be an affront to the spirit of the EBA and to the letter of the WTO if the EU now reneged on the essence of the agreement and introduced sustained quota limits on exports *despite the fact this was what the LDCs actually desired* (Fischer Boel 2005). And, for their part, having already sidelined the fixed quota option, the efficient beet producers were in fact pushing their respective agricultural ministries to promote a *deeper* price cut to the one proposed by the Commission, in order to carve off as much potential competition as possible. In doing so, cleavages were created within the lobbying groups that had once united behind the preservation of the regime in its national guise. Representing farmers, Ricardo Serra-Arias, Vice President of the Committee of Professional Agricultural Organisations in the EU, called for a rejection of the final proposal, which he felt 'lacks solidarity as it creates a major division between producers' (European Parliament 2005). Likewise, the internal division also paralysed the organisation representing processors, the Comité Européen des Fabricants de Sucre (2004), which fell silent over the price cut and instead focused on preventing as many imports as possible – a move that would benefit the association as a whole irrespective of individual corporate cost structures. In contrast, able to promote its narrower corporate interests, British Sugar described the key to success as setting a price that 'drives as much of the inefficient production out' but which still guaranteed their minimum supply of beet, and, more plainly, Südzucker simply announced it would 'welcome' the lower price reduction (Fletcher 2006; House of Commons 2006).

Thus in June 2005, the cut in the reference price was deepened and the proposal taken to the Council of Ministers for approval. The inefficient member states were finally bought off with compensation payments thrown into the reform as it passed in November 2005; €2 billion found at the last minute to ease its passage. The CMO Sugar that resulted entailed a 36 per cent price cut to be phased in by 2009, partially offset by a direct payment which would compensate beet growers for 64 per cent of this cut for the first few years, and a restructuring fund which would encourage processors to leave the industry by paying them for production forfeited. To compensate refiners, a transitional package worth €150 million was released, the bulk of which would go to Tate & Lyle. In total, over €7 billion was made available to cushion the price fall adjustment and encourage producers to relinquish quota quickly and quietly to save the difficult political task of enforcing compulsory cuts. The ACP ultimately had to satisfy themselves with €1.33 billion in restructuring aid between 2007 and 2015, to offset estimated export earnings losses of €2.5 billion over the same period (ACP Sugar Group 2005b).

Renewing accumulation: concentration and diversification in the post-reform era

The argument presented so far is that the interests shaping reform cannot be understood apart form the historical terms of competition, and strategies of accumulation therein, which characterised the EU sugar industry. Moving this forward, the remainder of the section will show how these strategies not only conditioned reform when it came about but have also been renewed in its wake. Most obviously, the system of quota production has remained intact, albeit at lower prices, and it was this, not export subsidies, which was the source of structural advantage of European *vis-à-vis* foreign firms. The final reference price of €404 per tonne still compared favourably to an average world price of €130 per tonne and as such, those surviving firms are still guaranteed a protected profit stream as well as the opportunity to continue to engage in tacit collusion (Committee of Industrial Sugar Users 2005).[6]

In addition, the trend to concentration within the EU has continued to accelerate. As sugar production was ended or scaled back in countries such as Greece, Finland, Ireland, Italy, Latvia, Portugal and Slovenia, all softened by the restructuring package of course, between 2005 and 2008 the number of growers fell from 250,000 to 175,000 and the number of factories fell from 188 to 108 (van Campen 2008). This at the same time as the leading sugar producers continued to grow in capacity, aided at first by national governments in both Germany and France, which took up the offer of buying limited additional quota in the wake of reform, and since entrenched by the numerous mergers and acquisitions in the industry. France's biggest quota holder Tereos continued its vertical integration by merging with the beet growers union, Sucreries et Distilleries des Hauts de France, placing over 14,000 beet growers on its books, and, in 2008, ABF (British Sugar's parent company) bought Spain's biggest supplier Ebro Puleva for €385 million while Nordzucker acquired the sugar division of Danisco, bolstering its share of the EU market from 9 per cent to 16 per cent (F. O. Lichts 2008b: 863).

What *has* changed in the post-reform era, though, is the spatial extensity of this concentration. The introduction of the EBA, the widening of the EU to east Europe, and the WTO-enforced EU export withdrawal have all created greater incentives for foreign direct investment. To the extent that new opportunities in world trade are emerging, it is not just companies in Brazil, Thailand and Australia that stand to benefit, but many in the EU industry too – the supposed losers of the WTO dispute. The most notable in this regard has been British Sugar, which bought a controlling share in the dominant southern African producer, Illovo, for £317 million, since channelling a further £100 million through its subsidiary in 2007 to build a sugar mill and ethanol plant in Mali (Warwick-Ching 2007). Alongside its recent intention to 'harness the tariff free trading arrangements afforded to the LDCs' and begin refining cane sugar for the first time in the EU, British Sugar has also been closing its less productive factories, such as those in Yorkshire and Shropshire in Britain, while buying in Poland and even China to serve the attractive domestic markets there (Adamson 2007). Similarly, Tereos has been targeting foreign suppliers, investing in Mozambique and also in Brazil, where it plans to be processing 13mt of cane by 2012, while Tate & Lyle has acquired a 10 per cent stake in Lao Sugar and plans to refine the cane shipped to the UK (Tereos 2006; Agritrade News 2007). The effect of this concentration and multinationalisation of production is apparent in Figure 5.2; European corporations remain heavyweights of global sugar production.

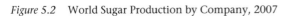

Figure 5.2 World Sugar Production by Company, 2007

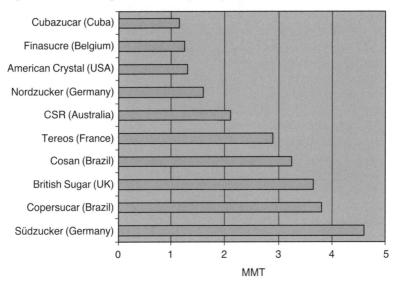

Source: F. O. Lichts (2008a) *International Sugar and Sweetener Report*, 140: 15, p. 471.

Strategies of diversification have also been maintained by Europe's leading sugar processors, adapted to the changed terms of competition created for the industry. In particular, two high-growth sectors have been identified: niche sweeteners and biofuels. The former has built on the successes of companies in branching out into chemical engineering and targets the health-conscious and 'wellness' markets. For example, Südzucker has developed the low glycemic sweetener Palatinose and Tate & Lyle has developed the artificial sweetener Splenda, an investment that has also seen the company embark on its first aggressive patent protection campaign to keep imitators out the American market. Market investors have already revealed the importance attached to these new planes of accumulation: when Tate & Lyle revealed the likely impact of EU reform, its share price was down only 1.7 per cent by end of day trading; when it revealed it had been 'over-optimistic' in consumer take up of Splenda, shares plummeted 15 per cent (Warwick-Ching and Shelley 2007).

The latter strategy of producing biofuel, meanwhile, maps on to the previous investments by processors in industrial crop transformation, and, like beet processing before it, has been aided by government support, the regulatory structure set down by the EU, and tariff protection, in this case on Brazilian ethanol.[7] The key target in the EU has been for 10 per cent of transport fuel to be biofuel by 2020 and to help meet this goal aid payments of €45 per hectare have been provided for crops grown for energy purposes, with national governments following in kind with tax breaks and production licenses (incidentally, all horizontal policies which elude WTO discipline). In response to these initiatives, British Sugar, Nordzucker, Südzucker and Tereos, and other companies either wholly or part-owned by these such as Agrana in Austria and Saint Louis Sucre, all announced multimillion Euro investments in ethanol plants, some using sugar beet, but most using wheat. As a result, ethanol production in the EU in 2007 had already reached 1.77 billion litres, with France and Germany the biggest national producers, and Tereos the biggest corporate producer (European Bioethanol Fuel Association 2008). Moreover, it was expected that the amount of sugar beet land dedicated to ethanol would double between 2008 and 2015, from 137,000 hectares to 260,000 hectares (F. O. Lichts 2009a: 24). Responding to the creation of this parallel regime in biofuel, one senior Commission official was quick to warn that 'what this is doing is creating a CAP 2, another system of subsidies', which will be hard to scrap when more advanced, second-generation fuels become viable (Mackintosh 2006). What has been illustrated here is that this issue of environmental efficiency is inextricably linked to the issue of ownership, as the survivors of the sugar regime capitalise on the growth of the 'green collar economy' and seek to establish productive control of the ethanol industry. Indeed, one policy opportunity that has already been closed down because of this has been the accelerated liberalisation of ethanol tariffs in the WTO, with Germany and France even pushing for the EU to designate the fuel as a sensitive product and thereby restrict any additional market access created out of the beleaguered Doha Round.

In sum, a *prima facie* analysis of CMO Sugar reform suggests that the EU and its sugar producers were 'losers' at the WTO while a more nuanced analysis may show how the axe fell down between efficient and inefficient countries. The focus here has been shifted from countries to companies, and not so much winners and losers but on changing opportunities for capital accumulation. From this vantage point we can see that, although all processors have lost revenue margins due to the lower price of sugar, those sizeable companies able to exploit the new trade opportunities and agro-industrial links that sugar affords have offset this loss and opened up new frontiers for future growth. As the chapter sub-title alluded to, quoting a biblical reference that still adorns tins of Tate & Lyle's golden syrup, it appears that in the case of sugar reform 'Out of the Strong There Came Forth Sweetness'.[8]

Alternative trajectories of accumulation: the troubles of raising cane

As many studies have pointed out, the effect of the Everything But Arms agreement and CMO Sugar reform is being felt unevenly across the developing and least developed countries that have access to the EU market (Gibb 2004; Milner *et al.* 2004; Chaplin and Matthews 2006). The most notable losers in this respect have been the traditional ACP exporters to the EU, which, as mentioned before, are expected to face a static shortfall of around €250 million per year. As Figure 5.3 reveals, the brunt of this will be borne by the biggest quota holders: Mauritius, Fiji, Guyana, Jamaica and Swaziland. In addition, the loss of Special Preference Sugar, which was terminated during the passage of the EBA in order to assuage the European beet industry, added another

Figure 5.3 Protocol and Special Preferential Quota Holders (DCs on left; LDCs on right)

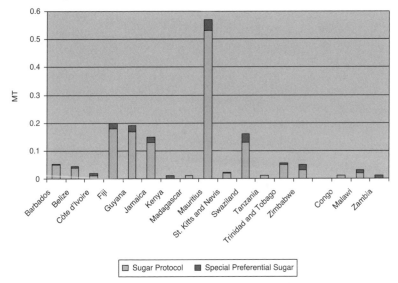

Source: Chris Milner, Wyn Morgan and Evious Zgovu (2004) 'Would All ACP Sugar Protocol Exporters Lose from Sugar Liberalisation?', *The European Journal of Development Research*, 16: 4, p. 793.

€40 million to this sum, a trade-off which Oxfam (2002a: 32) described as 'robbing the poor to give to the very poor'.

During the CMO reform process, while the ACP accepted that some reform was necessary – the EU could hardly pay these countries more for their imports than it did its own farmers – they also argued that their special circumstances had be taken into consideration. Accordingly, they pushed first for the 'shallow price fall' option to be adopted, and, once that had been skittled, argued for longer implementation periods and greater and more timely aid payments to help in the transition (ACP Sugar Group 2005b). At root, the circumstances to which the ACP referred grew out the alternate role that sugar played in their countries. First, sugar acted as an important source of foreign exchange, contributing 5.4 per cent of total foreign exchange across quota holders as a whole and over 20 per cent in Fiji and Guyana in particular (Insanally 2005). Second, compared to countries in the EU, traditional sugar exporters in the ACP typically have a narrower agricultural base, leaving the sugar industry as the major primary sector employer, if not the major employer for the whole country, especially given the industrial linkages it creates in haulage, packaging and supplies. For example, at the time of reform, sugar was estimated to support 101,000 jobs in Fiji, 93,000 in Swaziland, and 62,000 in Tanzania (Insanally 2005). Added to its sheer numerical importance was the *type* of employment that sugar was said to offer. Estate and factory workers are often provided with access to health clinics, housing facilities and social clubs; vital resources in countries with gaping safety nets, particularly in rural areas in which the restructuring effects will be concentrated. Finally, the crop itself was claimed to play a different role as cane had an aesthetic value which brought knock-on benefits in attracting tourism and also prevented soil erosion on the wind-swept islands (General Secretariat of the ACP 2005). In short, the ACP producers implicitly argued that when they 'lose' from reform the consequences were far more detrimental than when producers in the EU 'lose'.

For the ACP, then, maintaining production on the plantation was seen as necessary to prevent widespread economic upheaval and social collapse. Thus the crucial effect of the price cut in the EU market was not the financial 'terms of trade' loss *per se* but rather the extent to which their respective sugar industries were dependent on this preferential mark-up to sustain production and employment. In Trinidad and St Kitts and Nevis, for instance, the preference margin was so vital that the sugar industry has since been entirely decommissioned. For most ACP countries, however, adjustment to EU reform has been a question of scaling back to a point at which the industry becomes 'viable', i.e. able to sell above cost at home or abroad. As in the EU, this point of competitiveness was dependent on the dynamics at work prior to reform and, again like the EU, certain strategies of accumulation can be seen to have entrenched themselves. As Ian Drummond and Terry Marsden (1999) wrote, in the years leading up to reform and across the Caribbean as a whole, land under cane was declining, yields were poor, the sucrose-content of cane was below par and milling efficiency second-rate. Within Barbados (the authors' case study) industry stakeholders typically gave technical reasons for these falling standards: soil erosion, inadequate plant science, expensive credit, geographical limits to mechanisation, and poor labour relations among them. The authors contended, however, that while these certainly existed as pressing day to day difficulties, they were in fact symptomatic of a deeper crisis in sustainability rooted in the island's social structures and the external context of the Barbadian sugar industry. What had transpired was not simply that an increasingly unprofitable industry had been unable to attract the necessary investment, but that large elements of the planter community had systematically and objectively transferred capital out of sugar and into sectors such as tourism (Drummond and Marsden 1999: 130–139).

This represented something different from the rational relocation of industrial capital, as properly managed, sugar could arguably have remained profitable, or, at the very least, retired land could have been used to diversify food production and reduce dependency on expensive food imports. Rather, the capital transfer was an exercise in short-termism as the industry was, and continues to be, exhaustively mined for any remaining value. For one, ratooning – harvesting young shoots instead of waiting for them to mature – has been commonplace, a process which is agriculturally irrational for anyone wanting to remain in farming. And for another, landowners have been quite content to see their land go idle, easing the passage of residential planning permission and reducing domestic competition to the food importing sector; a sector itself pervaded by individuals involved in the island's sugar industry. In light of this, the Barbadian government has been encouraged by these same elites, and also by labour representatives, to subsidise where it can in order to avert the crisis of sustainability which had enveloped the industry.

This ongoing dynamic of divestment and extensive government support in Barbados has been replicated across a number of traditional sugar exporters. In Fiji, for example, the state has long bankrolled the nationalised and insolvent Fiji Sugar Corporation and has recently had to tempt landowners into taking up sugar with F$10,000 subsidies as they decline to renew the leases of their tenants and are reluctant to develop the industry themselves (Chand 2005). And, in Jamaica, divestment has been encouraged by the international financial institutions that guided the country into writing off national debt and preparing the sugar industry for privatisation, whilst simultaneously engaging in trade liberalisation to create investment opportunities in tourism and garment assembly for the 'captains of the Jamaican economy' (Weis 2004). Arguably only Malawi, Mauritius, Swaziland and Zimbabwe developed first-rate industries under the period of the Sugar Protocol, though, in Mauritius at least, this in part depended on the mechanisation of production and the employment of low-wage female workers to reduce the wage bill and improve profitability (International Labour Organisation 1994: 38–55).

A further importance of these processes is the extent to which they have compromised the objectives contained in the 'Sugar Adaptation Strategies' of the affected countries, the national plans upon which receipt of EU aid payments were made contingent. Within these plans the protocol recipients had to show how they would use the money to 'enhance competitiveness where this is sustainable, promote diversification of sugar-growing areas, and address broader adaptation needs' (European Commission 2005). In this respect, the first problem is the restrictions placed on effective pluralistic planning, given the economic impotence of the state and the short-termism of sugar elites, which is a direct concern for the more sustainable industry alternatives being mooted, such as ethanol and cogeneration energy projects that require concerted elite investment to lay down the necessary infrastructure. Second, the degraded and concentrated ownership of land and the deskilled and unmotivated labour that resides upon it have hindered the uptake of small-scale farming and the associated agrarian routes out of plantation dependence, leaving urban migration as the be-all-and-end-all of 'diversification' (Weis 2007b). Third, value-adding opportunities in the ACP are circumscribed by limited processing technology domestically and intense competition internationally. For example, the organic sugar market, which some countries earmarked for exploitation, is already reaching saturation point due to the entry of Brazil (Jolly, interview 2007). Thus the ACP are left prone to what Raphael Kaplinsky (2005) called the 'fallacy of composition', whereby a beneficial upgrading strategy for one country is not beneficial if all follow it as the rents associated with a particular market are unable to sustain ever more numbers of suppliers.

Finally, adding to these adjustment problems inherited from the past is the future uncertainty over continued preferential access to the EU market (albeit an access that is now less valuable). Where domestic European producers were given ample reassurances over the legislation of the reform programme, producers in the ACP were asked to restructure whilst crucial changes to the EU-ACP trade arrangements were still being negotiated, specifically the rewriting of the Sugar Protocol into the EPAs. Furthermore, even with the final adoption, there is still a safeguard on ACP sugar whereby up until 2015 an *automatic* cut will be applied if imports exceed certain amounts, after which a standard WTO-administered cut can be applied if it can be proved that 'serious injury' is being done to domestic producers.[9] Such regulatory uncertainty is likely to stunt the transformation of agro-industrial structures and lead to situations where adjustment becomes remiss and stagnation and depression entrench themselves further.

The indeterminate translation of export opportunity into export-led development

Not all poor countries are expected to face such trauma under the new European sugar regime. Recall that all LDCs gained full market access under the EBA, albeit temporarily forestalled by the backloading of EU liberalisation, and have accordingly been framed as 'winners' in the new trade arrangements. Although exact cost of production figures are closely guarded, it is widely held that among the most efficient sugar-producing countries covered by the EBA are Ethiopia and Sudan in east Africa and Malawi, Mozambique, and Zambia in southern Africa – the latter three countries in which Illovo holds 100 per cent, 28 per cent, and 91 per cent of production capacity, respectively. As such, it is assumed that these are best placed to take advantage of the changes in the EU sugar regime and will benefit accordingly (while some such as Malawi and Tanzania were previously beneficiaries of Protocol access, the amounts they were offered were so small that, on the whole, they can be expected to be better off under the new system).

This scenario lends credence to a common theoretical reading on the utility of preferences to help deliver development. As argued by Arvind Panagariya (2002b) among others, non-reciprocal preferences as offered in the Sugar Protocol are said to be based ultimately on political commitments which may wax and wane, precipitating over- or under-cautiousness in investment. More market-friendly arrangements, on the other hand, based on duty-free quota-free access as in the EBA and EPAs, were believed to represent a step forward in cleaning up the 'spaghetti-bowl' of preferences and help facilitate appropriate export capacity. What has become apparent in the initial years of the EBA, however, is that such faith in the market is misplaced, as predicted economic outcomes have not mapped neatly on to economic opportunities. This faith is misplaced for two reasons. First, thinking back to the theoretical framework set out in Chapter 2, the argument made above that politics distorts investment decisions overlooks our conviction about the inseparable nature of the state-market condominium and conclusion that 'the market' can neither be divorced from, nor emptied of, politics. Thus, in the case of sugar, the variable exchange rate differentials (manipulable through monetary policy, though not of course for reasons necessarily linked to sugar policy), the prospect of lower domestic tariffs resulting from the regional economic integration spurred by the EPAs, the ending of the fixed price system after 2012, and the possibility of quantitative restrictions in the EU have all created uncertainty over the price incentives that EBA countries are likely to face.[10]

The second reason why the smooth adjustment to a more market-orientated system of supply has been hindered is that, by its very nature, this system of provision depends on uncertainty to create competition. In the case of sugar, competition among the EBA countries themselves, but later the EPA eligible countries too, has meant that there is an uncertainty over the supply schedules an individual country will be facing. To mitigate these factors and translate market access into market share, LDCs have voluntarily agreed among themselves to share out the growing quota allowance to the EU to guarantee themselves a certain return on their investments (LDC Sugar Group 2007). In addition, some countries such as Mozambique have attempted to raise domestic prices by insulating themselves behind tariff walls, while others, such as Sudan, have targeted the markets of Gulf and north African countries alongside the EU in order to diversify their customer base (Reuters 2007a). Assuming these policies enable investment and low-cost production to take root, what needs to be questioned next is the type of development this will bring about. As such, this section concludes by offering some thoughts about the structural changes in land and labour management the pursuit of a sugar export market is likely to engender.

According to a report prepared for the UK Department for International Development (LMC International 2004: 62) unlike many traditional sugar exporters LDCs do not face significant land constraints and thus the expansion of cane production is not predicted to affect the availability of land for alternative crops and other economic activities. It is worth bearing in mind, however, that this land will need to be titled and irrigated; a privatisation of resources that will exclude other claimants and potentially create stubborn legacies of inequality. One only has to look at two more established African sugar producers, Zimbabwe and South Africa, to recognise the difficulties in eradicating these legacies if a changed political climate deems it necessary (cf. Cliffe 2000; Moyo 2000).

In respect of labour, sugar production certainly has a huge potential to increase paid employment in LDCs. Not only is the commodity labour intensive but also the supply-side problems that characterised traditional exporters are absent. Arguably, the shortages of dedicated labour experienced in the ACP were not caused by a lack of people looking for work but by the association of sugar with backwardness, hardship and poverty, and the looming comparison of modern urban or migrant jobs, which meant that people, especially the young, were simply reluctant to look for work on the plantation (Harrison 2001: 36). It also appears that the management of the expanding sugar companies in LDCs may be more benign than in traditional exporters. In southern Africa, the sugar estates run by multinational companies like Illovo have offered benefits more in line with Western expectations: training schemes, retirement packages, and health monitoring exist alongside the more commonplace estate provisions (London sugar trader, interview 2007). Compared to smallholder production, the vertically managed sugar farms provide higher wages and also insist on a stark gender division, with women and children excluded from hard labour in the fields (though also unlikely to ascend the hierarchies of management). Most importantly perhaps, the point to consider is that sugar production cannot be considered an unambiguous help or hindrance to development, given the many open ways it can be established. Nevertheless, it is worth reiterating the necessity of this potential being filled. In Ethiopia, an intended beneficiary of the EBA agreement, nearly half the entire agrarian population – 25 million people – are thought to be living below the national poverty line (International Fund for Agricultural Development 2007).

Conclusion

As set out in the 1958 Treaty of Rome, the CAP was designed to improve farm productivity, ensure fair standards of living for the agricultural community, stabilise markets, and ensure food security. Against all these criteria CMO Sugar must be acknowledged as a resounding success. But, as the tide of development theory and trade policy turned, the EU sugar regime became increasingly antagonistic to these shifts and was finally enmeshed within wider processes of international liberalisation. As it played out though, it was not the case that sugar reform constituted a free market coup by the elites of international organisations or by the sugar-using industry, but rather that the object of consolidating European sugar as a platform for capital accumulation helped delimit the parameters of debate when the window of opportunity was opened up. This consolidation was guided by the context of WTO compatibility and by the institutional legacies of CMO Sugar, which had privileged processors *vis-à-vis* farmers, and rich regions *vis-à-vis* poor, thus giving powerful vested interests the requisite material incentives in change. What resulted was not a global sugar regime in Europe *per se*, but a regime that, for the time being, became compatible with this wider, neo-liberal world order. Teasing out our account, the future of this regime, which is scheduled for inclusion in the next round of CAP reform in 2013, will likely be shaped by the ongoing dynamics of concentration, foreign direct investment and diversification into biofuels that have arisen within its parameters and which are significantly reshaping the sources of profit which sugar processors use to guide their influence of legislation.

Alongside these strategies of accumulation, the effects of the 2005 CMO Sugar reform on the EU's international trade relations have also featured both continuity and change, again illustrating the bounded evolution characteristic of regimes. Change has been evident in the source and value of imports into the EU while continuity has been apparent in the volume of imports permitted into the EU. While for the first time since the early 1970s the region became a net sugar importer again, this had more to do with declining exports than increased imports, which remained subject to automatic and potential cuts. Thus there has been a large element of trade diversion as the Sugar Protocol and Special Preferential Sugar quota holders have reduced supply while EBA suppliers have increased it. Perhaps the biggest change of all, however, has been the *de facto* end of the ACP group, which has been fragmented by the end of discriminatory preferences and reformed into regional groupings under the EPAs. In this sense, the regulatory dimension of the colonial regime first outlined in Chapter 3 has all but dissipated – nearly 400 years after it came into being – though it is clear that the markings of colonialism still run deep within the countries in question.

6
US Under Stress: Free Trade and Fracture in the National Regime?

The previous chapter outlined how the EU regime inherited from the national era was made consonant with the imperatives of the contemporary trade environment but with significant concessions that left its key protective measures intact if not inviolate. This chapter turns our attention across the Atlantic and moves to examine the evolution of the national regime in the US. Out of the three economies in North America, focus on the US is apposite here both because of its market importance (in 2006/07 the USA consumed 9.23mt of sugar, Mexico 4.98mt and Canada 1.43mt) and its political influence (ISO 2008: 15). As outlined in Chapter 4, the type of agricultural support adopted in the US was of crucial significance to the rules adopted within the trading system at large. This remains the case today. Through its position as the biggest agricultural exporter and its material and institutional power in the global trade architecture, the policy vision emanating from the US has had direct consequences for global agricultural trade. Within this vision, sugar has been a notable exception to the general thrust of aggressive market opening. During the Uruguay Round for instance, since the US had lowered its average trade distorting support under the 1990 Farm Bill and because tariffication and minimum market access provisions in sugar had already been set in place, there was no need for adjustment, and certainly no effort made to make this otherwise.

Despite evading multilateral change, there have been important shifts in the US sugar regime too. At the regional level of regulation, the free trade of sugar under the North American Free Trade Agreement (NAFTA) has finally taken effect, and at the domestic level of production the sugar industry has undergone significant restructuring. Following on from the previous chapter, we ask how traditionally protected markets have become subject to structural transformation and explore the relationship this has had to state policy and to issues such as equality. To do so, this chapter proceeds in three parts. The first section examines how the shift to rule-based trade in the US has fundamentally altered the previous system of supply-management in sugar and now placed the survival of current policy on a knife-edge. The second section argues that, despite the long-standing, though now precarious, protection afforded to them, sugar producers in the US have not 'grown fat' off the privilege. Mechanisation, chemicalisation, integration and more recently Genetically Modified (GM) crops have all been introduced to lower costs of production and maintain profit margins. Nevertheless, the efficiency drive is meeting limitations, forcing producers to look at ways of increasing demand as well as lowering supply costs. Finally, the third section shows how these trends of accumulation have fed back into the political debates shaping US trade policy. It suggests that the protection accorded to the US sugar industry has emerged from a confluence of factors, including the emotional appeal of family farming, coalitions between sugar producers and between the sugar and HFCS industries more broadly, and the evasion of antagonistic positions *vis-à-vis* other economic sectors. To the degree these became institutionalised, government support for sugar has seemed unassailable. However, as these institutions wear down, US sugar policy is likely to come under increasing pressure for change.

The US Sugar Program under constitutional trade relations

While it is correct to say that the US Sugar Program escaped reform during the Uruguay Round, it would be a mistake to conclude that its relationship to international trade has stayed the same. While the WTO succeeded in binding existing import commitments and disciplining trade policy, the concurrent conclusion of many Free Trade Agreements (FTAs) has steadily established more market access in sugar, threatening to erode the protective wall surrounding the US. The result is widespread fear among US sugar producers at the mere mention of new trade agreements and intense efforts to inoculate the Sugar Program against them.

In contrast to the 'three pillar' system in the EU, the US operates a 'two-legged' system of price support inherited from the 1934 Jones-Costigan Act, which is based on domestic marketing allotments and import controls. The level of price support is set through the loan rate, the amount that the US Department of Agriculture (USDA) temporarily lends to processors of cane and beet sugar. In the 2008 Farm Bill this rate was set to reach 18.75 cents per pound for raw sugar and 24.09 cents per pound for refined beet sugar. The processors pass a percentage of this loan to growers to pay for the crop, and, once the sugar is sold on the market, the USDA repaid. To make sure sugar does not flood the market and depress prices, the USDA operates domestic marketing allotments – a more flexible equivalent of the EU production quotas – alongside tariff rate quotas (TRQs) that apply a prohibitive duty on imports over a certain amount.[1] This is crucial for the operation of the Sugar Program given that the USDA loans are non-recourse, meaning that, by the time repayment comes, if processors have been unwilling to sell their sugar at the prevailing market price, the USDA is obliged to accept the commodity in lieu of cash. In other words, the government acts as a buyer of last resort.

As it is neither in the producer nor the public interest for the USDA to have to buy up unwanted sugar, the Sugar Program has a provision that it should be run at no net cost to the Federal government, i.e. forfeiture should be kept to an absolute minimum. It is therefore imperative that domestic production plus imports equals domestic consumption, as any over-supply would reduce the price of sugar below the loan rate and induce government purchase of sugar. Yet the efficacy of the two policy tools used to do this has been sharply circumscribed since the mid-1990s. First, imports cannot be unilaterally squeezed as they are now bound at a minimum level of 1.25mt under the WTO. This allocation is shared among the 40 traditional recipients of US sugar preferences through a TRQ, though just four – Dominican Republic (0.18mt), Brazil (0.18mt), Philippines (0.14mt) and Australia (0.10mt) – typically fill half the available access (Haley and Ali 2007: 29). In addition to this minimum import, a number of FTAs, in particular the North American FTA (NAFTA) and the Dominican Republic-Central American FTA (DR-CAFTA) have allowed for a growing amount of in-quota sugar to be imported into the US over time. Table 6.1 details the market access commitments which the US is obliged to fulfil, which, contrary to popular impressions of US sugar autarky, actually make it one of the biggest net importers in the world.

Second, the marketing allotments used to control domestic production volumes cannot be reduced to make room for more imports as US producers are guaranteed an 85 per cent share of total demand under the 2008 Farm Bill. It is only if US producers themselves produce too much sugar that measures can be taken for them to keep it off the market as stock. As a result, in the event of significant over-quota imports the hands of the USDA are tied and there is little it can do to manipulate supply and avoid forfeiture. The real imperative is to prevent this from happening in

Table 6.1   US Market Access Requirements in Sugar, 2008

Enacted	Agreement	Allowance	Comment
1994	WTO	1.25mt	Includes 0.11mt 'baseline' imports from DR-CAFTA
1994	NAFTA (Just Mexico as Canada is excluded from free trade in sugar)	Unlimited	In 2006/07 Mexico exported 0.55mt, net volume, to the US
2004	DR-CAFTA (Dominican Republic, Costa Rica, El Salvador, Guatemala, Honduras and Nicaragua)	0.11mt	Grows 0.003mt a year in perpetuity
2005	Peru FTA	0.01mt	Grows 0.0002mt a year in perpetuity
2006	Colombia FTA	0.05mt	Approved by Administration, awaiting Congressional vote
2006	Panama FTA	0.007mt	Approved by Administration, awaiting Congressional vote

Source: Jack Roney (2008) Director of Economic and Policy Analysis, American Sugar Alliance, Presentation to International Sugar Organisation, London, 19 November 2008.

the first place, a situation which has put the USDA and the US Trade Representative (USTR) 'shoulder to shoulder' with the domestic industry in opposing the loosening of import restrictions and setting future farm bills firmly against sugar trade liberalisation (Orden 2008).

From colonial to constitutional preferences

Focusing now on the trade dimension of US sugar policy, what has characterised the post-WTO era has been the profound shift from 'colonial' type preferences that were open to manipulation to 'constitutional' type preferences that are enshrined in law. Such manipulation was commonplace within the US sugar regime, as depicted in Chapter 4, when the import quota was tightened during the 1980s to alleviate downward pressure on sugar prices after competition emerged in the form of HFCS. The first signs of change came in 1994 when the US announced it would reallocate its TRQ for sugar-containing products away from Canada to fulfil its new commitments under the NAFTA. Canada reacted by threatening legal action against the US' own re-export programme, which facilitated the sale of US-manufactured refined sugar and sugar-containing products into its market and which Canada claimed was illegal under NAFTA laws prohibiting duty-drawbacks. Fearing arbitration, the US backed down and in 1997 agreed to reinstate Canada with an improved proportion of its TRQs for both refined sugar and sugar-containing products (Marsden 2002). While this retreat heralded the change in trade relations it would the decade-long dispute with Mexico under NAFTA that forced the point home: from now on trade wars would be fought in international judiciaries as well as the national legislature.

The source of the dispute with Mexico was present from the very inception of NAFTA. As momentum built toward this historic agreement, late deals had to be made to win support from its opponents, most notably a congressional bloc composed of ten Democrats and 13 Republicans from Florida who stood against its agricultural provisions. With their support, US sugar producers won the inclusion of a side-letter to the original agreement which stipulated that consumption and production of HFCS would be included in the evaluation of Mexico's status as net sugar producer. This was crucial as the original agreement allowed for greater exports of sugar from Mexico to the US as long as Mexico had a net surplus, i.e. it produced more than it consumed. It was assumed that this technical concession would preclude substantial Mexican sugar exports to the US throughout the 15-year phase-in period (Orden *et al.* 1999: 118). From the Mexican perspective, this concession not only threatened their exports but also their domestic market for sugar, as soft drinks manufacturers were expected to import increasing quantities of HFCS from the US once NAFTA came into force, something this traditionally powerful industry were unwilling to accept without a fight (Olson 2008).

So the stakes were high and this was reflected in the veracity of the battle that ensued over the NAFTA side-letter. The *status quo* favoured US producers; as long as the side-letter remained undisputed in law, the volume of Mexican sugar consumption would be inflated by counting HFCS. Thus Mexico made the first move, placing higher tariffs on HFCS from the US and later adding anti-dumping taxes as well. As the NAFTA legal system was not designed to deal with anti-dumping charges, the case was taken to the WTO on behalf of the corn refiners that manufacture HFCS, and, in 2000, the WTO Dispute Settlement Body judged that Mexico's anti-dumping duties were inconsistent with Article 10.2 and had to be rescinded. Sensing the power now held in the court room, Mexico responded by suggesting that it could take the US to NAFTA arbitration over failure to live up to the original tenets of the agreement – a slightly flawed plan given that the dispute stemmed from the very nature of what the NAFTA agreement actually was – and at which the US baulked. Revising its earlier strategy, Mexico instead took another swipe at the HFCS industry, taxing syrup-sweetened soft drinks rather than the product directly. As domestic taxes *did* fall under its rubric, at the behest of the US NAFTA was able to pass a ruling and requested Mexico to remove its duties. In a final twist, and showing it had learnt a thing or two from the way the US had made its own sugar quotas GATT-compatible, Mexico obliged, removing the duties and in their place erecting a TRQ for 0.14mt of HFCS (the precise amount of Mexican sugar allowed into the US at the time) with a prohibitive out-of-tariff quota of 210 per cent.

The main beneficiary of this long-winded dispute was the US sugar industry, but to the extent that it managed to perpetually hinder imports of HFCS, the Mexican sugar industry also prevailed. The US corn refining industry, meanwhile, was on the sharp end of this dispute and was understandably aggrieved that the result of safeguarding sugar in the US should be the seizure of its freedom to export to Mexico. In deference to the growing agitation of the corn refiners, and because the NAFTA was to move to duty-free quota-free trade in sugars and syrups by 2008 anyway (regardless of the validity of the side-letter), in July 2006 the respective sugar industries of Mexico and the US agreed to see out the following 18 months of the phase-in period without resorting to discriminatory action.

In sum, what the NAFTA dispute made evident was the growing constitutionalism of trade relations under the multilateral trading system, that is to say, the elevation of the rule of law above politics. Specifically in this case, we witnessed the elevation of rules against anti-dumping charges and discriminatory domestic taxes above the political argument as to whether such economic infringements were justified in the first place (namely, Mexico's claim that the US had unilaterally modified the NAFTA text). A palpable consequence of this constitutionalism has since been an emphasis on 'getting the rules right' at the outset of a trade agreement, as producer groups and trade negotiators alike have become increasingly aware of the difficulty of pushing through policy changes that contravene the stipulations of a given text. This in turn has led to heightened concern regarding the negotiating 'precedent' given that what tends to be included in one FTA is also included in the next; a particular worry for US sugar producers who sense that increased market access as offered in NAFTA – the trade dimension that needs to be most tightly defended – is being made a permanent feature of US trade policy.

This fear about the ratcheting of market access across successive FTAs has been conditioned by the broader trajectory of US trade policy, which since the early 2000s has tended to prioritise bilateral negotiations. According to Nicola Phillips (2004) this bilateralism has emerged as a political response by the US government to the difficulties encountered in realising its particular vision of the Free Trade Area of the Americas, and, we might also add, its vision of the Doha Round at the WTO. This vision is one in which the US seeks access to services markets for concessions on its goods markets, but, equally, excludes the wholesale liberalisation of domestic agriculture and modification of legislation on trade remedies. In each of the FTAs covering sugar, the US has followed this mandate and insisted on limiting disruption to its domestic supply management. In the NAFTA there was the side-letter; in the DR-CAFTA there was a clause under which the US can refuse its obligation to import sugar and pay the countries compensation instead (a first in US trade policy history); and in the remaining FTAs there were only tiny import allowances actually offered. For their part, signatories to these US-envisioned FTAs have been willing to ascent to these concessions as, somewhat paradoxically, increased market access has not been the real incentive of a free trade agreement. Rather, as scholars such as Kevin Gallagher (2008) and politicians such as El Salvador's President Elias Antonio Saca (2005) have suggested, the smaller and/or developing economies that have negotiated with the US have done so primarily seeking geo-political goodwill and to lock-in existing preferences in constitutional form.

Yet sugar producers in the US remain displeased so as long as any additional market access is created. They would much rather exclude sugar from bilateral FTAs in the first place than let exporters get any type of foot in the door. On only one occasion have sugar producers achieved this, in the bilateral agreement with Australia that passed in 2004.[2] After months of intense debate, and with the issue hanging in the balance right up until the end, the commodity was eventually pulled from the agreement. In the wake of this success, the sugar industry attempted its own piece of precedent setting, pointing out that a sugar-exclusive FTA was plausible and could 'serve as a template for all future negotiations' (Jurenas 2007: 14). A more sober reading would suggest that the sugar industry was the beneficiary of circumstance. In the US the presidential election was approaching and in the swing states the sugar vote was crucial, while Australia had sunk too much political capital into the agreement and secured enough access in other areas to want to play brinkmanship for what would, in all likelihood, have been a relatively small increase in its export allowance (Australian diplomat, interview 2008).

In conclusion, US sugar trade policy has always been intertwined with domestic policy, but where once the former took its cue firmly from the latter, under a world and regional trading system inclusive of agriculture and enjoining of constitutionalism, that relationship has begun to assume a more pronounced dialectic. No longer can the US forcibly squeeze imports to maintain the domestic price and, never having had export subsidies built into its Sugar Program as they were in the EU, neither can excess domestic supply be reduced through exports. As a result, excluding sugar from every trade agreement has become paramount for producers, which view import prevention as far superior to legislative cure.

Agro-industrial transformation: running to stay still

Increased imports are the most imminent but not the only threat to the US sugar industry. While the 'flooding' of the US market has been abated the regime has not been intractable to change. Just as in the EU external protection has gone hand-in-hand with internal transformation as major structural changes have occurred in the way sugar is farmed and processed. This change in production has not been levied by market forces, which as described earlier are kept at bay by the supply management of the Sugar Program, but by a simulacrum of market competition: declining real prices. Recall that the loan rate is the means by which the USDA sets the level of support for sugar producers and so, if this remains unchanged, so too does the price that farmers and processors ultimately receive for their product. Until the 2008 Farm Bill, this rate had remained unchanged for 23 years. The implicit agreement struck between the industry and government during this period was that improved productivity would counteract the inflation-adjusted input prices and thereby maintain revenue margins (American Sugar Association, interview 2008). So, in response to rising fuel, fertiliser, labour and machinery costs, sugar producers had to continually find ways to lower costs and increase their yields, crop sucrose content, and processing efficiency.

The foremost way in which this exercise has been conducted has been through concentration. The long-term trend has been for fewer farms and factories meeting America's sugar needs; a trend that has taken place across the beet and the cane sectors. In respect to farms, this been possible both because the average farm size has grown, thereby maintaining the area of sugar harvested, and because of agronomic productivity gains. To illustrate, between 1997 and 2002, the number of farms growing sugar beet fell by 2,100 and the number growing cane by 126, at the same time as the average sugar beet holding increased 32 per cent and the average cane holding increased 24 per cent.[3] Those farms closing were typically smaller and/or in states with a history of higher costs and so it was that those sugar producers in the West reduced acreage while the already large holdings in the Mid-West and East increased in size (Haley and Ali 2007: 54). There was also a marked political dimension to this, as not only did existing crop acreage concentrate but also *potential* crop acreage was suppressed. When sugar cane growers in Arizona attempted to enter the sugar market, for example, existing cane growers testified to the USDA that 'the allocation of allotments is a zero sum game' and recommended that marketing allotment only be granted if the applicant could prove in advance they were capable of succeeding; a business model that does seem to put the cart before the horse somewhat (Yancey 2003). So while sugar is still grown in many states, between 2000 and 2004 just four – Minnesota and North Dakota (beet) and Florida and Louisiana (cane) – accounted for two thirds of the entire national crop.

This concentration in land has its parallel at the factory level, as industry ownership has condensed through the closure of some factories and the integration of others. From 1985 to 2007 the number of beet factories and cane mills declined by half, to just 23 and 18, respectively (Roney 2008). Moreover, despite the creation of the US re-export programme, which was designed to ensure that cane refiners could operate at full capacity without disrupting domestic supply, ten refineries closed down between 1985 and 2007 as raw imports contracted and domestic processing costs could not be reduced far enough. Seeking to shore up the processing capacity of the cane sector and attracted by the bigger margins made possible from vertical ownership, the three major sugar cane companies in the industry – Flo-Sun and US Sugar Corporation (both Florida) and Louisiana Sugar Cane cooperative – have invested heavily in the sector.

For 'Big Sugar' especially, as the Florida producers are collectively known, this strategy of downstream acquisition has represented a significant break with the past as efficiency gains were formerly sought through lowering the wage bill and polluting the Everglades (Hollander 2004). Low wages were possible thanks to the agricultural Guest Worker Program that provided temporary visas for seasonal Caribbean migrants, and around 10,000 would arrive in Florida every year for the annual sugar harvest. In the early 1990s the class action lawsuit *Bygrave vs. Florida Sugar Cane Growers* exposed incidences of endemic under-payment within this system and a payout of $51 million was initially awarded to the cane cutters. Forestalled pending appeal, the US Sugar Corporation later settled for $5.1 million, fearful of the ongoing public relations damage caused by the case, but the owners of Flo-Sun, the Fanjul brothers, decided to ride out the storm and ultimately oversaw defeat of the charges in the subsequent trials. Perhaps the bigger defeat though was that the case had the ultimate effect of convincing the Florida cane growers of the need to end reliance on migrant labour. As the Fanjul's lawyer, Joseph Klock, warned his employers during the trial, 'Unless you want to move into Belle Glade, drive a pickup truck and supply cars and two-bedroom apartments to all the workers, get out of this business' (Brenner 2001). Foreseeing the increased employment costs attached to cane cutting, by 1997 the Florida producers had moved entirely to mechanised harvesting.

The acquisition of existing companies and investment in new facilities has prompted two important changes to the mode of accumulation within the sugar regime. First, there is evidence of 'proto-internationalisation' as companies prepare, if not commit to, regional free trade in sugar. Flo-Sun, together with the Florida Sugar Cane Growers cooperative, have bought the Redpath refinery in Canada and Ingenio refinery in Mexico, while the Louisiana Sugar Cane cooperative and Cargill have entered a joint partnership to build a new refinery on the Mexican border capable of supplying either market and sourcing from either too. Given that Flo-Sun already owns 250,000 acres of sugar cane land and a stake in the Central Romana mill in the Dominican Republic, should there be any significant changes in the sugar supply under NAFTA or DR-CAFTA, these companies will be best placed to adapt (though arguably they would prefer to forgo this eventuality and keep guaranteed prices intact). Second, the strategy of downstream acquisition has had the effect of integrating the industry horizontally as well as vertically. Flo-Sun and Florida Sugar Cane Growers also bought out Tate & Lyle's three US-based refineries in 2001 and California & Hawaii Sugar's refinery in 2005, giving them control of five of the nine refineries in the US and 32 per cent of domestic processing capacity (Williams Walsh 2008).

Perhaps most significantly, this tendency for concentration will extend even further under legislation passed in Florida in 2008 mandating a state to buy-out of the 181,000 acres of land owned by US Sugar Corporation for $1.34 billion. The deal would be one of the largest environmental land purchases in US history (equivalent to the size of Chicago city) and is designed to restore the flow of water from Lake Okeechobee to the north of US Sugar to the Everglades in the south. Under the deal US Sugar is to keep its integrated mill-refinery (claimed to be the world's biggest), citrus processing facilities and railroad network and also is allowed to lease back the land at a quarter of the market rate and keep farming for seven years, perhaps longer if the district delays breaking ground on restoration projects (F. O. Lichts 2009a: 4). It is therefore possible for US Sugar Corporation to stay in business by refining sugar from Florida's other cane growers or Mexico, or move into the production of alternative energy. Indeed, this has led Flo-Sun to challenge the deal with Gaston Cantens, Vice President of their subsidiary Florida Crystals, criticising it as an 'improper and ill-conceived use of public funds to subsidise… cloaked under the guise of environmental restoration' (Quinlan 2009). But this attack masked the benefits of the deal for Flo-Sun themselves. As the state also needs a 40,000-acre chunk of land owned by Flo-Sun to make the restoration viable and as the US Sugar Corporation could still choose to sell its assets, it is possible that the Fanjuls will use the buyout as an opportunity to expand their holdings in southern Florida, trading some of their land for the excess US Sugar land in a swap orchestrated by the state (Williams Walsh 2008).

In the sugar beet sector, meanwhile, the dominant producer is American Crystal, which farms 500,000 acres of beet in the Red River Valley of North Dakota and Minnesota. As opportunities for further vertical integration are limited in beet production as the mill-refinery distinction does not exist, growers owning this company have put their faith in agronomic transformation to deliver efficiency gains. In the early 2000s, sensing that industrial and consumer concern about genetic engineering had subsided, American Crystal and the biotechnology corporation Monsanto began to develop a herbicide resistant seed, which in 2008 became the world's first ever GM sugar beet planted (Pollack 2007). The benefit offered by the crop is that it reduces chemical and cultivation costs, as it requires application of just one powerful herbicide, Monsanto's 'Roundup'. Furthermore, as no DNA alteration is passed through to the actual sugar, no special labelling has to be put on the final product.

As happened in the Everglades, however, a number of pressure groups have called into question the environmental externalities that have resulted from intensifying sugar production. The Center for Food Safety (2008) has claimed that the wind-pollinated GM sugar beets will inevitably cross-pollinate with related crops being grown in close proximity, and, contrary to the industry's mantra that these plants reduce chemical use, has argued that herbicide use will actually *increase* as weeds adapt to the herbicide and force farmers to rely on ever more toxic applications. Seeking both legal and demand driven barriers to GM beets, in January 2008 a coalition of consumer and conservationist groups filed a lawsuit against USDA protesting the approval of GM beet, and in March 2008, the Interfaith Center on Corporate Responsibility called on consumers to write to companies such as Heinz, General Mills and Kraft to ask them to renounce the use of GM sugar (Birchall 2008). As Tony Weis (2007a: 77) has noted, such challenges remain possible precisely because of the conceptual dichotomy that all GM foods must straddle: on the one hand, demonstrating that the innovation is different enough to represent intellectual property, while on the other, asserting the substantive similarities between the new and the traditional plant.

The politics of demand: creating markets in food and fuel

So far focus has been laid on the attempts by the sugar industry to cheapen the supply of sugar in the face of a static loan rate. This was partly eased by the raised loan rate in the 2008 Farm Bill, but with inflation ever present and with the increased attractiveness of this higher price to Mexican exporters, the incentives remain to improve efficiency where possible. To lessen dependence on this one form of alleviation, the US sugar industry has also sought to reconfigure government guidelines on diet and encourage the take up of sugar as an ethanol feedstock. In other words, it has tried to change the nature of demand, and so, following the lead set in Chapter 3, we now attempt to endogenise contemporary patterns of sugar consumption within our analysis.

It will be recalled that the US is quite unique in that sugar vies with HFCS for the dominant share of the sweetener market. As part of the trend during the 2000s for lower-calorie diets, per capita consumption of HFCS fell and while sugar did begin to recover to its peaks in the 1990s, as illustrated in Figure 6.1 it was the uptake of artificial sweeteners that began to capture a greater proportion of total market share.

The alternative sweetener field is composed of sugar alcohols, such as sorbitol and xylitol, which have fewer calories than sugar and do not promote tooth decay, and artificial sweeteners, such as the 'Nutrasweet' aspartame, the 'Sweet 'n Low' saccharin and the 'Splenda' sucralose, which contain no calories at all. As sugar alcohols are not as sweet as sugar, and as artificial sweeteners lack bulk and often carry an unpleasant aftertaste, these alternatives are often combined with each other, or with traditional sweeteners, to create alternative product attributes. For

Figure 6.1 Sweetener Market Share in US, 1995–2007

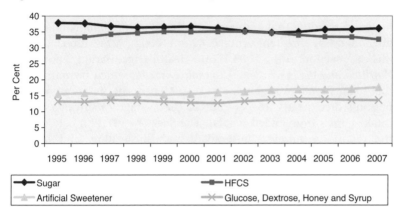

Source: Jack Roney (2008) Director of Economic and Policy Analysis, American Sugar Alliance, Presentation to International Sugar Organisation, London, 19 November 2008.

example, Wrigley's Extra chewing gum is sweetened by sorbitol, glycerol, mannitol, aspartame and acesulfame K, the Diet Coke Plus drink by aspartame and acesulfame, and the Kellogg's Nutri-Grain cereal bar by HFCS, corn syrup, sugar, glycerin, maltodextrol, honey, dextrose and sorbitol (author's own product check). In short, as more sweeteners become available, more product innovation is possible, and more market niches can be sought out. Crucially, US sugar producers have been excluded from this structural change as the alternative sweetener market has been captured by multinational agricultural processors and chemical engineers, among them Roquette, Danisco, and Tate & Lyle in Europe, Archer Daniels Midland, Cargill and McNeil in the US, and Mitsubishi International in Japan. Moreover, approval of new sweeteners by the US Food and Drug Administration (FDA), a necessary entry point should the sugar industry wish to enter this market, has been thwarted in the past, most notably in the refusal to grant approval to the stevia-based sweeteners (although this has since been accepted with PepsiCo and Coca-Cola launching new drinks containing this immediately).[4]

Responding to these challenges, the sugar industry – through its educational and scientific organ, the Sugar Association – has pursued a two-track strategy. First, it has tried to prevent erosion in the sweetener market as a whole, which fell from 151 pounds per capita intake in 1999 to 142 pounds per capita by 2005, by opposing government advised reductions in sugar/syrup consumption (Haley and Ali 2007:

32). This has involved representatives of both the sugar and sweetener-using industry seeking to neuter government dietary reports by insisting upon wording that emphasised 'choice' rather than 'compulsion' in moderating sweetener intake (Nestle 2002). More direct though was the reaction to the 2003 World Health Organisation report *Diet, Nutrition and the Prevention of Chronic Diseases,* which recommended that sugar should exceed no more than 10 per cent of the calories in a person's diet (nearly 16 per cent of the average American's calorie intake comes from added sugars). The Sugar Association condemned the report as 'unfair', 'misguided' and 'misleading' and lobbied Congress to withdraw its annual $406 million funding for the WHO unless promotion of the report was ceased (Dalmeny 2003). For their part, the Sugar Association (Digges, interview 2008) have maintained that the 10 per cent guideline did not reflect the views of the full scientific community, which remain 'undecided on the level at which sugar can safely form part of a person's calorie intake'. The fact that some of the organisations – such as the International Life Sciences Institute or the Centre for Consumer Freedom – that form this community are funded directly by companies that rely on sales of sweetened products no doubt helps stoke this indecision.

The second strategy has been to demarcate a larger space for sugar within the sweetener market by distinguishing it as a unique and superior sweetener. In 2004, for example, the Sugar Association sued McNeil, the distributors of Tate & Lyle's Splenda, for claiming that it falsely promoted Splenda as a natural product 'made from sugar, so it tastes like sugar' when it was in fact a chlorinated, artificial sweetener. McNeil hit back in 2005, accusing the Sugar Association of conducting a 'smear campaign' and creating a website – truthaboutsplenda.com – that contained allegedly false statements about the product. The contending lawsuits were settled in private in 2008 (F. O. Lichts 2008c: 903). More recently, the Sugar Association have attempted to get the FDA to redefine the label 'natural' to distinguish between sugar and HFCS. The argument put forward by the Sugar Association (2006: 5) has been that the 'natural' definition should refer to products containing nothing artificial, synthetic, or more than 'minimally processed'. Accordingly, HFCS is said to fall outside this category as its production requires changing the molecular structure in a naturally found product, whereas, when sugar is refined, this molecular structure is merely 'extracted'. Replying in kind, the Corn Refiners Association (2006) have countered that the 'minimally processed' definition cannot reasonably be applied to highly processed foods such as sweeteners, but, even if it were to be accepted, HFCS would still qualify as natural as it uses enzymes rather than chemicals to transform the starch into syrup. Interestingly, an argument not made by the corn refiners was that designating sugar as natural could result in a situation where products containing GM sugar beet could legitimately claim to be 'All Natural'. Arguably the reluctance to make this case is a reflection of the de-politicisation of GM-technology by the corn industry itself, which would stand to lose more than it gained if it were seen to give credence to the idea that GM is in some way unnatural.

Regardless of the final outcome, what both these debates over consumption reveal is that diet and labelling are not matters that can be resolved by scientific fact as what has to be judged are not the facts in themselves (which are invariably valid in their own context) but the social question of how these facts will be interpreted. Though lobbying groups repeatedly stress the value of individual choice, and in doing so try to empty politics from the act of consumption, their actions belie the reality that setting the parameters of choice, and thereby institutionalising demand, remains an intensely political matter.

The other demand shift that has affected the US sweetener regime has been the huge uptake of ethanol, which in contrast to the nutritional debate has been highly politicised throughout. Satisfying the goals of reducing energy dependence post-Iraq, undercutting the regional impact of Venezuela's oil diplomacy, and contributing to the rural economy at home by driving up corn prices and creating jobs, promoting ethanol has been seen by many in the US as an international and domestic win-win policy. As such, the US Congress has repeatedly sanctioned higher biofuel production, expanding the mandate for ethanol in the 2007 Energy Independence and Security Act to 36 billion gallons by 2022. The US government has been a lynchpin of this explosion in production, supporting the nascent industry with a tax credit of 51 cents per gallon to ethanol blenders, and, to ensure that this is used for US-grown feedstock, a tariff of 54 cents per gallon placed on semi-processed ethanol from abroad. As a result, in 2007 the US stood as the biggest biofuel producer in the world, illustrated in Figure 6.2.

As in the artificial sweeteners market, the market expansion in ethanol has also eluded US sugar producers. A major handbrake on farmers entering the industry has been the high cost of producing ethanol from US-grown sugar; according to Haley and Ali (2007: 39) one gallon can be produced from corn at around \$1.04, from sugar molasses at \$1.27, and from sugar beet and sugar cane at \$2.35 and \$2.40, respectively. Consequently, around 97 per cent of ethanol produced in the US comes from corn feedstock, giving the corn refiners,

Figure 6.2   World Biofuel Production, 2007

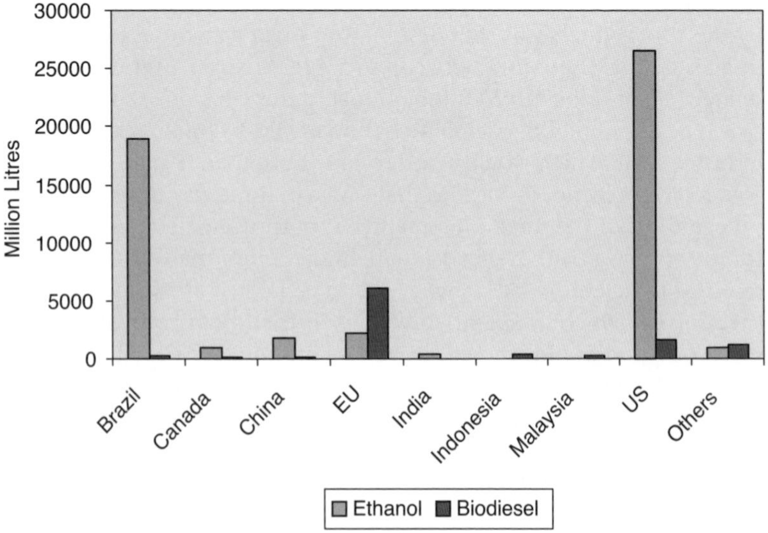

Source: Food and Agricultural Organisation (2008) *Biofuels: Prospects, Risks and Opportunities* (Rome: Food and Agricultural Organisation), p. 15.

and Archer Daniels Midland in particular, the upper hand in the ethanol processing also.

To gain some succour from this new plane of accumulation, the sugar industry successfully lobbied for a 'Feedstock Flexibility Program' to be amended to the 2008 Farm Bill. This obliged blenders to process any surplus sugar on the US market into ethanol, with the government making up the difference between the price at which sugar sells (around 26 cents per pound) and the price at which blenders can profitability turn it into ethanol (estimates vary between 18 cents to 5 cents per pound (American Sugar Alliance, interview 2008; Promar International 2008)). The benefit of this scheme is that it makes viable the US producers' demand that they maintain an 85 per cent share of the domestic sugar market. Now, if imports were to rise above 15 per cent, the Feedstock Flexibility Program would ensure that this would be diverted into ethanol production and prevent depression of the sugar price. Moreover, as the government payments would come out of energy spending, its supporters also argued that the Sugar Program would then be able to continue as a 'no net cost' agricultural programme. In essence, then, this programme has effectively replaced marketing allotments as the means by which in-quota imports and domestic production are to be controlled but with two important differences. First, the burden of reducing output in times of over-supply is shifted from US sugar producers to the US tax-payer. And second, the cost of the policy is now totally indeterminate as the taxpayer must pay for *all* surplus imports to be turned into ethanol; an aspect which led the White House Administration to label the programme an 'egregious new sugar subsidy' not least because Mexico can now export unlimited amounts under NAFTA (Bush 2008).

In addition, the sugar industry has also been seeking to capitalise on second-generation fuels and thereby overcome the cost inefficiencies of the sugar feedstock. 'First generation' biofuels are derived from starch/sugar crops to make ethanol and from oil crops to make biodiesel, while 'second generation' biofuels are derived from cellulose, hemi-cellulose and lignin – the woody parts of grasses, bushes, trees and plants such as sugar cane – which are broken down into ethanol. Alongside the Flexibility Program, the 2008 Farm Bill also featured generous $1.01 per gallon tax credits for ethanol made from cellulose and offered loan guar-antees for second generation farm and factory investment (Reuters 2008b). Arguably, Flo-Sun is best positioned to take advantage of these incentives, having already begun to develop cellulosic ethanol technology based on its experience in energy production from the sugar cane by-products and financial assistance from the Florida state 'Renewable Energy Technologies Program'.

In conclusion, two main points can be discerned about the structural transformation of the US sugar regime. First, despite the relative success of sugar producers in protecting themselves from import pen-etration under bilateral and multilateral trade agreements, structural transformation has still taken place. The very workings of the Sugar Program have exerted a slow squeeze in the form of declining real prices, leaving producers 'running to stay still'. This productivity tread-mill has split the sugar industry between those growers, processors and refiners that are able to extend and intensify production – essentially the big four of American Crystal, Flo-Sun, and the Sugar Cane Growers' cooperatives of Florida and Louisiana (and prior to the buy-out US Sugar) – and those smaller entities that have slid toward the precipice. Second, the type of transformation that has occurred cannot be under-stood apart from the dynamics in the corn industry, and, in particular, apart from the activities of its big refiners: ADM, Cargill, Tate & Lyle and Cerestar (part of the Tereos lineage from France). Benefiting twice over from protectionism – first for HFCS which received higher prices under price umbrella of the Sugar Program and second for ethanol – the corn refiners have since been able to increase efficiency and institutionalise political networks and consumer demand to the point where they are now able to exert a purer and less contestable pricing power over sugar producers.[5] This power asymmetry has limited the options open to sugar producers to embed new strategies of accumulation and has also had major consequences for trade policy, as the traditional alliances between sugar and HFCS producers have broken down and the political economy of sweetener production been fundamentally reshaped.

Explaining trade preferences: from timeless solution to institutional evolution

In 2008, then, the US sugar regime had arrived at a definitive set of crossroads as the initiation of free trade in sugar and HFCS in NAFTA and prospective conclusion of the WTO Doha Round and a number of FTAs all loomed simultaneously. This final section poses the crucial question of how the US government can be expected to manage its international and domestic political relations from this juncture, and to what extent these decisions are shaped by (and in turn reshape) the institutions and actors of the extant regime.

Much existing literature on the policy preferences of US state elites in respect of sugar has focused on the relationship between political donations and Congressional decision-making (Brooks *et al.* 1998; Chiang 2003; Gokcekus *et al.* 2004). This pluralist approach, which once again draws heavily on the collective action dilemma, posits that the sugar industry is *able* to raise money and votes as it possesses a strong coordinating lobby, i.e. the American Sugar Association, that presides over a group populous in a number of states, and is *willing* to mobilise these resources because it has more to lose from liberalisation than the dispersed and fragmented sugar users have to gain. In short, the sugar lobby can put a greater amount of votes and money on the Congressman's table.

Arguably the popularity of this approach can be put down to two factors: the amenability of the subject matter to the quantitative methodology that many political scientists choose to work with, and the notoriety of the sugar industry when it comes to financial donations. Though it accounts for just 1 to 2 per cent of American farm receipts, sugar is the largest single agricultural donor to political campaigns. In 2006, the sugar industry gave \$3.3 million to federal candidates and parties, compared to just \$2.0 million by the entire food manufacturing industry (Riley 2007). The perception that sugar can readily 'sweeten the legislature' is further encouraged by comments of Congressman like John Breaux, who once confessed in relation to sugar that, while his vote cannot be bought, 'it can be rented' (Chait 2005). Most notorious of all, however, is the Fanjul family, owners of Flo-Sun, who have contributed millions of dollars to election campaigns both directly and through Political Action Committees. Wisely splitting their political sensibilities, Alfonso Fanjul and his brother Pepe have also held top posts in the fund-raising operations of the Democrat and Republican parties respectively. Indeed, so important a donor is Alfonso Fanjul that in 1996 Bill Clinton interrupted a critical Oval Office meeting with Monica Lewinsky aimed at surreptitiously ending their affair to take a phone call from him (Starr 1998).

Yet, despite such notoriety, the extensive literature on campaign donations and policy outcomes has failed to generate conclusive evidence that the sugar industry is able to 'buy protection' (Alvarez 2005). At most it has been able to confirm a number of expected outcomes: that being in a sugar-growing state, being an 'insecure' freshman, and being a member of a key Congressional committee all increase the probability of a larger donation.[6] What these accounts fail to consider is that obtaining a 'pro-sugar' decision from Congress depends on more than the 'timeless solution' of delivering a certain amount of money and votes. Posing a different tack to these more parsimonious and quantitative approaches, this section explores the cultural dimension of sugar production, the relationships between the sweetener coalitions, and the impetus and structure applied by the regulation of the WTO in order to explain the (non) reform of US sugar policy. In other words, the institutions of the sweetener regime, and how they evolve through time, are brought to the foreground.

The cultural economy of sugar: the premium of solidarity

Staying with donations temporarily, in 2007 journalist Dan Morgan noted how sugar groups had been able to expand their influence far beyond the 15 states and few dozen congressional districts where sugar is grown, reaching Congressman such as Maurice Hinchey of New York and Michael Michaud of Maine. What was notable in this report was not so much the (relatively small) campaign donations received by these politicians but the reasons they gave for casting their votes in line with the lobbyists' demands. For Hinchey, support for the Sugar Program was a family farm issue, while, for Michaud, it was about disavowal of cheap labour imports undercutting American jobs. In this light, we begin to see campaign donations more as a catalyst than a cause of Congressional support. What is more important than the sum of money is the discursive appeal that accompanies it, an appeal which draws on the deeper political sentiments concerning the values and traditions of their industry, namely, the honest labours of the farmer.

This appeal is not totally without foundation; even in Florida, 'Big Sugar' has coexisted with 'Little Sugar' since the 1940s when ranchers and farmers in the area were encouraged to diversify by planting sugar cane (Hollander 2004). Yet to characterise the industry and its major producers as bastions of smallholder family production is laughable. How, then, has the industry been able to sublimate this glowering contradiction? With its trump card: industry coherence. By calling upon the minority, small-scale landowning farmers that remain in business to represent the human face of US sugar production and combining these with political donations from the larger entities, the industry has been able to project an image of itself as integral to American rural communities. This is bolstered by the political letter-writing campaigns promoted within the sugar-producing communities and the comparisons made between the high environmental and labour standards at home and the low standards encouraged abroad (American Sugar Association, interview 2008). The premium of solidarity was fully recognised by a spokesman of the Sugar Cane League (2008) who commented in an interview that 'our position is that everyone that's in business is to stay in business...Having a larger group helps make us stronger, more vibrant.' Moreover, by perpetuating the idea that the industry is without internal conflict, policy elites are more likely to view the Sugar Program as a successful, if highly complex, reflection of the various needs within the industry rather than a system which privileges dominant agri-capital. As the former Congressmen William Robert Poage testified, 'Aerodynamic engineers cannot tell you how the bumblebee flies, and I cannot tell you how the Sugar Program functions, but for 40 years it has worked quite well' (Hemsted 1991: 18).

Maintaining the perception that the sugar industry exists as a self-sufficient and culturally bucolic entity also helps explain why sugar producers are so keen to avoid forfeitures, as happened during a two year period of excess domestic production in 2000–01 when the USDA had to buy up $100 million of US sugar and effectively pay farmers not to plant. In spoiling the 'no net cost' claim of the industry and by suggesting that it may no longer be capable of managing itself, the danger is that the emotive culture of sugar gets replaced in the popular imagination by a starker economic balance sheet upon which the commodity appears as an irrefutable liability. What we suggest here, though, is that the greatest enemy to preserving the *status quo* in sugar may not be the risk of forfeitures, which in the long run have appeared only spasmodically, but rather the passage of time. Under the intensification of production and concentration of ownership highlighted previously, between 1997 and 2002 the 'productivity treadmill' reduced sugar factory employment from 16,500 to 14,600 and the number of farms from 8,136 to 5,980 (Haley and Ali 2007: 25).[7] The problem is that as the industry gives fewer people a stake in the perpetuation of the current regime, especially those people who provide the cultural qualities on which the industry has made its bed, it undercuts its own support base and economic identity. Diverting attention from any costs incurred by the Sugar Program may well be futile if the gaze of Congressmen and the American public has nothing to settle on bar a capital-intensive and de-populated industry.

Between conflict and cooperation: the shifting sands of sweetener coalitions

Turning now from the relationships between sugar producers to those between sugar producers and other actors complicit in the US regime, we consider first the role of the sugar-using companies on sugar policy. The central charge laid by their industry association, the Sweetener Users Association (SUA), has been that the high prices guaranteed to domestic producers has had the effect of encouraging those companies manufacturing sugar-containing products (SCPs) in the US to relocate abroad. This immediately presents us with something of a policy puzzle, given that the SUA comprise many rich and well-connected food and beverage manufacturers and so one would expect them to be able to suppress US sugar prices in line with the world market price, the cultural economy of sugar notwithstanding.

On the face it, the charge by the SUA of forced cost reduction and relocation of a proportion of its members certainly seems valid. Between 1997 and 2002 employment in the SCP industries in the US decreased by more than 10,000 jobs, without even accounting for the new jobs created abroad in the first place (International Trade Administration 2004: 2). Most of the relocations have taken place within the NAFTA area, with confectionery companies such as Brach and Sunrise moving to Mexico, and chocolate companies such as Hershey's to Canada. Manufacturers are able to access cheaper sugar in these countries as Canada's sugar prices stick close to the world price and Mexico operates a 'Maquila Re-Export Program' in which sugar can be imported from the world market as long as it is exported in a processed product within six months (Mexico's own sugar prices are not that much lower than in the US, and in certain years are actually higher).[8] As North American trade in SCPs rose during the course of the NAFTA phase-in, the trade deficit of the US in SCPs grew larger. By 2005 it was over 17 times higher than in 1995, as imported products grew from 10.7 per cent of demand to 33.9 per cent and exports moved in the opposite direction (Haley and Ali 2007: 49).

Yet simply highlighting an adverse trade balance in SCPs is not enough to indict US sugar policy with a causal role in food processing job losses. Food manufacturers that moved to Canada and Mexico have benefited from lower costs not just in sugar but also in tax and labour expenses (Grocery Manufacturers Association, interview 2008). These additional savings are likely to be far more instrumental in encouraging relocation. Taxes paid by firms in the sugar-using industry are around a quarter to two thirds the level in the US, while wages and health care insurance can fall even further, especially in Mexico (Peter Buzzanell & Associates 2003). To put these in context, while sugar may contribute a significant percentage of raw material costs – 30 per cent in case of breakfast cereals and confectionery (International Trade Administration 2004: 6) – raw materials do not actually contribute a large percentage of final cost. Moreover, the final cost faced by manufacturers is far below the price they charge retailers, as they are able to extract significant rents through branding, and, depending on the outcome of a Competition Bureau enquiry, possibly price fixing as well (Associated Press 2007). To illustrate this gulf between costs and revenue in the food processing industry, in 2007 the profit margin across the chocolate, confectionery and gum sector was 35 per cent (National Confectioners Association 2008). Based on this assessment, we suggest that the lack of success for the sugar-using industry to lower the cost of US sugar may in part be down to antipathy among its most powerful members. Given the opportunities to restructure under NAFTA, and because the SCP re-export programme assuages the high cost of sugar for exporters, US sugar policy is only a major problem for domestic-bound, domestic-orientated manufacturers; precisely those companies with the least resources to lobby for change.

While the potential conflict between the sugar producers and sugar users has been muted, the coalitions between sugar producers and other agricultural producers have been both more volatile and more influential in shaping sugar policy. Specifically, it has been the withering of historical inter-commodity solidarity with the peanut, tobacco and corn refining groups that has done most to challenge the fortunes of sugar producers. The peanut and tobacco alliance was based on the fact that all commodities were subject to price support programmes and disappeared when these two became subject to a government buy-out that lobotomised their respective support policies. The alliance with corn refiners, meanwhile, was based on shared markets and has disappeared as these have separated. In the sweetener market, for example, during the 1980s HFCS and sugar were largely price compatible, meaning corn refiners would feel any erosion in sugar support and thus gave them a clear interest in backing the Sugar Program, which they did through their membership of the Sugar Alliance.

Since 1993, however, the price of HFCS has diverged from sugar due to technical advances in production and greater economies of scale at the same time as the possibilities for substitution have become more limited as the taste for syrup sweetened drinks has solidified and a greater range of HFCS products has created more specialised sweetener markets. As a result, even if the price of domestic sugar fell, it is arguable that the impact on the price of HFCS would be limited; the biggest factor in final cost being the price of corn now supported under the ethanol programme. Coupled with opportunities to export abroad, corn refiners have thus been willing to step out from under the protectionist sugar umbrella and embrace extensive trade liberalisation. As part of this policy shift, in the early 2000s they renounced membership of the Sugar Alliance, and, in a position totally at odds with the American Sugar Alliance, have also supported the use of Trade Promotion Authority, which gives the President the ability to negotiate agreements that Congress can accept or reject but not amend or filibuster (Corn Refiners Association, interview 2008).

The impacts of this coalition breakdown have been most visible in US trade policy. In the run-up to the DR-CAFTA agreement, the US sugar industry began lobbying other agricultural trade associations to oppose the deal, distributing a study that predicted that the agreement would lower not only sugar prices but also prices for grain-based products, such as fructose and ethanol (Alden and Buckley 2004). Fearing a repeat of the NAFTA debacle in which HFCS exports were negatively affected, the agricultural exporters did not bite, dismissing the pleas of the sugar industry and banding together behind the Administration's existing deal, which included sugar. Despite this defeat, the US sugar industry pushed again for a similar trick on the NAFTA, determined to stem imports from Mexico after 2008. Deciding now to work with their erstwhile opponents across the border, the US and Mexican sugar producers proposed that a kind of international cartel be established whereby both sets of producers would limit sweetener exports in a bid to maintain sugar prices. This proposal caused outrage not only among the corn refiners, who would be required to 'manage' exports of HFCS to Mexico, but also among the wider US agriculture sector that feared an unravelling of NAFTA if other commodities were also submitted to controls. Charles Conner, Acting Secretary of Agriculture, got to the nub of the proposal's problem: 'This is way bigger than sugar' (Morgan 2008). In trying to reshape the NAFTA in its own import sensitive image, the sugar industry had 'over-reached itself' and had its fingers burned accordingly (Corn Refiners Association 2008). Only where the US Sugar Program has actively impeded the trade agenda of other agricultural sectors has its support in government been compromised.

Sugar under the WTO: an exercise in evasion

In the final sub-section, this idea of sugar 'impeding' the trade agenda of other sectors will be explored more fully. As a heavily protected and lucrative market for many sugar exporters, the general exclusion and/or minimal concessions offered by the US government in international trade agreements impedes the agenda of many of its export-orientated sectors. The previous sections have offered two reasons why this has been overlooked, namely, the Congressional support for sugar drawn from the cultural economy of sugar production and the antipathy of industrial sugar users based on the relief offered by NAFTA and the re-export programmes. But these cannot be considered insurmountable barriers, not least because of the institutional transformation engendered by the WTO and the leverage this has offered to many export-orientated industries. As Nitsan Chorev (2007) has noted in the realm of trade policy, the internationalisation of the state as conceived by Cox has meant that many domestic actors with protectionist agendas have found that the political organs upon which they have traditionally depended for support are now subordinated to internationally linked domestic agencies. For example, while the US steel industry has retained its influence over Congress and the Department of Commerce, it is now the USTR that actually has more power over trade negotiations and, in any case, Congressional and Administration decisions that are made have generally been compatible with international obligations and therefore biased in favour of free-trade principles anyway (Chorev 2007: 663). The relevance of this for our case is that the importance we granted to inter-commodity coalitions would be of minor importance if the agricultural sector itself held little sway over trade policy.

In theory, agriculture should indeed be of minor importance. The USTR is responsible for pulling together the US position for trade negotiations and ostensibly is able to remove itself from vested bureaucratic interest and sectional political demands upon which the agricultural sector typically depends for influence. In practice, however, matters of agricultural trade policy are still largely autonomous (US International Trade Commission civil servant, interview 2008). The USDA has a number of key advisors working at the USTR and nor has the sector lost the ear of the Administration, which has established an Agricultural Policy Advisory Committee for Trade and sets of Technical Committees for Trade – one of which is dedicated solely to sweeteners – to act as vehicles for the private sector to communicate its views directly to government (USDA 2007). Moreover, the key agricultural committees in Congress have jealously guarded their position as initiators of legislation, resisting the internationalisation process of which Chorev writes. In short, to the extent that a given commodity can avoid becoming incompatible with other sectors of agriculture, there is little pressure that internationally linked agencies can bring to bear on its programme, cotton perhaps being the best example (Lee 2007).

In addition to the control maintained by the USDA, supporters of the Sugar Program have also benefited from the attempts of the US to preserve the autonomy of its agricultural policy more generally in the WTO. Whilst certainly not avowing free trade theory, the US has been manoeuvring to replace 'market disrupting' forms of intervention with those more compatible with liberal principles. This has involved reworking its counter-cyclical payments so they can be moved out of the 'Amber Box', a WTO category of support measures that are scheduled for reduction and have annual ceilings placed on their usage, and into either the 'Green Box' category, which imposes no limits on spending, or the 'Blue Box' category, which equally poses no limitations but is supposed to encounter negotiated reductions in the future. In addition, the US has also sought to keep those policies that do present legal problems, i.e. the ethanol tariff, out of WTO purview. This two-track strategy has meant US negotiators have not had to choose which commodity should 'feel the pinch' of tightened WTO provisions, a choice which would likely be problematic for sugar producers. For instance, as a price support programme, sugar counts towards the domestic support calculation, contributing approximately $1.1 billion out of a total permissible $19 billion in the Amber Box, a disproportionate amount given its value to the US economy.[9] With the prospect that current WTO talks might ultimately require a reduction of 60 per cent or more in the US Amber Box, sugar would be in direct competition with the other US programmes in that box, chiefly the dairy programme and loan deficiency payments for major crops, for permissible allowance. Thanks to the manoeuvrings above, this choice has been avoided.

To conclude, this section has offered an analysis that emphasises the triumvirate of ideas, interests and organisations in shaping trade preferences. The challenge made to protectionist sugar policy by the sugar-using industry failed as it had no cultural economy on which to draw, insufficient desire to bring about change, and few efficacious links either to agricultural or trade-making institutions. Compare this to the corn refiners, which have been able to match the sugar lobby on all three fronts. Moreover, it has been stressed that wherever institutionalisation has taken place in a set of social practices – for instance, in the belief that the Sugar Program protects the family farm, the desire for consumers to have their soft drinks sweetened with syrup rather than sugar, or the influence of agricultural officials over trade policy – the pattern of preferences can be expected to continue. But, by recognising that institutions are simply ongoing and embedded practices, we also see that evolution is necessary as structural transformation continues, production prices change, and WTO provisions contract. All this goes to show that the sites of power that keep the Sugar Program in existence at the moment may not be present in the future, and that in accounting for policy outcomes, we should look to 'institutional evolution' rather than the 'timeless solution'.

Conclusion

Under the squeeze of declining real prices and constitutional import allowances, the US sugar industry has been put under increasing stress in defending its profit margins, relieved only temporarily by the loan rate increase in the 2008 Farm Bill. The initial attempts to alleviate this stress through increasing efficiency have now but all been exhausted. Within the natural environment and socio-legal framework of the US, all unit costs that can be minimised have been, and the introduction of GM crops arguably represents the last throw of the dice in these input cutting exercises. In terms of mitigating this pressure by increasing the value of sugar, as producers of a largely undifferentiated commodity, sugar farmers and processors have not had the option of insulating themselves from price competition through branding, innovation or market segmentation, and so have to put their faith instead in arduous political campaigns to maintain increasingly de-legitimised border tariffs. Yet despite the efforts of the US sugar industry to secure favourable supply-management through political patronage, and in doing so defer the end of the national regime and the emergence of a regional regime, a degree of competition for the domestic market has now been embedded.

Arguably, the main hope for the industry now is that older, national patterns of trade will persist due to the ethanol boom, which has raised the price of corn and HFCS and dissuaded Mexican soft drink bottlers from turning away from sugar, leaving fewer surpluses to enter the US.

Two broad directions thus seem plausible for the US sugar industry to take. One option is to continue to promote policy innovations such as the 'Natural' labeling regulation or the 'Feedstock Flexibility Program' that alleviate the pressure of declining real prices or import competition. Following this path of institutional bricolage would in fact represent a moment of longer continuity for the US sugar regime. As Anne Kreuger (1990: 210) noted nearly two decades ago, the regime has always been in a process of evolution as increasingly complex policy instruments have arisen to deal with competing interest groups and subvert the sorts of market responses perceived to be detrimental to its immediate perpetuation. Alternatively, if import control becomes untenable under NAFTA or if a dramatic trade concession is offered, then the window of reform will be levered open and the industry forced to renegotiate more sweeping change. In this instance, the industry can be expected to fracture along the fault-lines developed under structural transformation, with the 'big four' – and Flo-Sun in particular – best placed to shape the new regime and profit under it.

7
Antinomies in Asia: Political Conflicts in Protected Markets

The previous two chapters have focused upon the evolution of the regimes surrounding the North Atlantic, and in this way, trace a line from the colonial era depicted in Chapter 4 up to the present day. Complementing these historical trajectories in the West, this chapter will now foreground the countries in Asia and shift the focal point toward a markedly different set of states and regime dynamics. There is certainly an empirical obligation in choosing this particular region as a case study. In 2005, over 60mt of sugar was consumed in Asia, compared to 36mt in the Americas and 31mt in Europe, suggesting that the way sugar production is managed in Asia will have important consequences for the world market as a whole (Lichts 2008d). More than this, though, as outlined in the introduction, focusing on Asia is considered here a theoretical necessity, as both a counterpoint to Western- and colonial-oriented analyses and as an essential component of the international sugar industry regardless of its effects on world prices. As Frederick Söderbaum (2005: 239) has argued, such comparative methodology is essential in the construction of a more global IPE as it helps 'guard against ethnocentric bias and culture bound interpretation that can arise in too specialised or isolated an area study'. The construction of this comparison will take place as follows.

The first section opens with an account of the prevailing system of trade relations in Asia, which is defined as a starker version of the bilateral policy witnessed in the US that differentiates between export-oriented and import-sensitive sectors. Built on the premise of an 'embedded mercantilism', sugar has been placed firmly within the import-sensitive category, meaning that political pressures to reform the sector emanating from the trade environment have been relatively subdued. The second section then examines the processes of accumulation within these distinct national regimes, finding that, although international pressure may be weak, the dynamics of agrarian capitalism have still been volatile enough to cause substantial crises in the countryside. In this respect, the point is made that both the underlying tensions and the ultimate government responses to dysfunction in the sector have been mediated according to the state-society in question, and that protectionism has been no panacea for rural instability. Developing this argument, the final section looks at the 'nutrition transition' in Asia toward diets with higher sugar content and argues that, here too, pressures have been placed on states in the form of growing health risks and increasing opportunities to benefit from the processed food trade that cannot be avoided simply by abiding to an embedded mercantilist policy orientation. In conclusion, we suggest that there are certain antinomies, or mutually incompatible principles, within the current objectives guiding sugar policy in Asia and that as these become exposed they will generate increased demand for change, albeit in a manner reflecting the domestic politics of the state in question.

The regional project of embedded mercantilism

As in the EU and the US, the conclusion of the Uruguay Round meant little change for sugar regulation in Asia. In terms of import tariffs, those countries that took on specific reduction commitments chose relatively slender levels of liberalisation and, in the case of Japan, mitigated these with changes to other surcharges and levies (Australian Bureau of Agricultural and Resource Economics 1999: 50). Most developing countries in Asia instead chose to bind ceiling tariffs, an option which eschewed tariff reduction and in fact permitted countries to raise tariffs up to the newly bound level, a prerogative that both Indonesia and India have since taken advantage of (International Sugar Organisation 2000). In addition, scant reduction in domestic support was brought about, primarily because most countries in Asia could not afford it to begin with, and little compulsory market access was created, with the notable exception of China, which had to open up a TRQ upon WTO accession in 2001.

As was noted in the previous two chapters, the momentum for the (limited) liberalisation in the EU and US in the wake of the Uruguay Round was actually borne by free trade agreements, specifically, the EBA/EPAs and NAFTA/DR-CAFTA. Judging the broader successes of these agreements in Europe and the Americas, and stimulated by the simultaneous failure of the Asia-Pacific Economic Cooperation forum to garner a consensus approach to trade reform, Asian state elites have also turned to bilateral liberalisation as a route to economic growth. However, this is where sugar trade policy in Asia differs, as there has been a stronger commitment to keep this sensitive product out of the plethora of trade agreements that now tie the region together. Of the 25 such agreements featuring one or more Asian countries concluded between 2000 and mid-2008, sugar has been conspicuous by its absence in nearly all (World Trade Organisation 2008a).

In explaining this regional phenomenon John Ravenhill (2003) has identified the same utility in trade bilateralism for developed countries in Asia as Nicola Phillips did for the US, namely, that bilateral agreements offer political leverage over smaller economies and require less than full coverage to be legal under multilateral law. So in Japan, for example, sugar was one of the 1 per cent of total product lines excluded from liberalisation under its FTA with the Association of Southeast Nations (ASEAN). It was also excluded from the FTA with the Philippines signed in 2004, and with Thailand in 2007, despite the fact that significant benefits, such as lowered tariffs on automobiles in Thailand, had to be foregone as a result (Mulgan 2006). History has also played its part in the ringfencing of sugar from Japanese trade policy. In contrast to the EU and the US, which maintained supplies from colonial/traditional suppliers and thus embedded an import quota within its domestic supply management system, after the Chinese national party assumed control of Taiwan in 1946 and nationalised the assets of the sugar industry, Japan lost control of its sole sugar colony. Since then, Japan's prevailing import policy has placed domestic producers first, only seeking imports to fill shortfalls between domestic production and consumption.

Among the smaller Asian economies, liberalisation of sugar has been postponed, rather than completely excluded. The six original ASEAN signatories – Brunei Darussalam, Indonesia, Malaysia, Philippines, Singapore and Thailand – initially agreed to reduce tariff rates on a wide range of goods to no more than 5 per cent and to eliminate quantitative restrictions and non-trade barriers by 2002. This has since been extended to cover import duties on all goods by 2010. The four countries that joined later – Cambodia, Laos, Myanmar and Vietnam – are expected to reach this latter target too by 2015, suggesting that, for sugar, a partial free trade area in Asia is imminent (Secretariat of the ASEAN 2002: 4–6). However, having significant and relatively uncompetitive sugar industries, both Indonesia and the Philippines have moved to forestall the immediate reduction of sugar tariffs and, indeed, their ultimate abandonment by transferring the commodity on to the sensitive products list.[1] Finally, for the two giants of Asia – China and India – sugar has also been handled with kid gloves. In the China-ASEAN talks that led to a 'limited' FTA signed in 2005, sugar was placed on the 'highly sensitive' list, thereby requiring both sides to reduce their tariffs to just 50 per cent by 2015 (Asian Economic News 2004). And in the framework agreement signed in 2003 between India and the ASEAN, the 'Early Harvest Program' specified that members should eliminate mutual import tariffs on almost all agricultural goods by 2010 but had sugar listed as a commodity for which only 'feasible cooperation' was to be explored.

As sugar has been excluded and/or backloaded in successive FTAs, states have been shorn of the responsibility to reform their domestic policies in line with international trade obligations. Of course, trade agreements are by no means the only source of public, external pressure that can push states into reform. Many commentators have noted how the actions of the IMF to curtail state intervention in the 1990s, particularly in the wake of the East Asian financial crisis in 1997, have impacted on sugar policy. In Indonesia, for example, to cushion the price increase faced by consumers following currency devaluation, tariffs on raw sugar were temporarily reduced and import controls deregulated, ending the monopoly of the state trading enterprise BULOG in the process (Asian Economic News 2000). And, in the Philippines, Michael Billig (2003) has written how defeat of the 'Import Rationalisation' bill of 1994, which proposed an increase in the tariff on sugar from 75 per cent to 100 per cent, was prompted in part by the government's acquiescence to the liberalisation discourse of the IMF and other international agencies. Nevertheless, as Table 7.1 indicates, there has yet to be systematic withdrawal from the market management tools typically used by governments. These include: 1) those that maintain domestic prices, referring to the 'three pillars' of export subsidies, import restrictions and domestic supply management; and 2) those additional supports on inputs that lessen the financial burden on producers.

The consequence of these trade controls has been an absence of secular change in trading patterns, barring the stochastic imports made in response to domestic production shortages. As Figure 7.1 shows, over a period of ten years, the trend has been for a relatively stable relationship between production and trade, as opposed to the progressive inclines or declines one would expect to see if trade was growing in importance. It is especially noteworthy that the two biggest consuming nations – India at 20.1mt and China at 11.9mt – have a tendency to self-sufficiency,

Table 7.1   Government Supports in Selected Asian Countries

	Export Subsidies	Import Restrictions	Domestic Supply Management	Input Supports
China		1.95mt TRQ at 15% Out of quota tariff at 50%	State owned sector able to influence stock releases and prices	
India	Transport subsidy $15 per ton	60% tariff Countervailing duty of Rs850 per ton	Monthly quotas divided among mills	Land maintenance subsidies
Indonesia		23% on raw sugar, 20% on refined Import quotas determined by domestic demand	No, but an annual minimum price is established	Credit subsidies
Japan		0% on raw sugar, 7% on refined High effective tariff set via compulsory state import purchasing agency	No, but an annual minimum price is established	
Philippines		0.05mt TRQ at 50% Out of quota at 65%		
Thailand		0.01mt TRQ at 65% Out of quota tariff at 96%	Quota applied on volume that can be sold in domestic market	Debt rescheduling, credit for pre-financing cane crop and loans to growers

Source: LMC International (2006) *Review of Sugar Policies in Major Sugar Industries* (LMC International: Oxford). Note: China as of 2004; India as of 2003; Indonesia as of 2005; Japan as of 2003; Philippines as of 1999; Thailand as of 2003.

Figure 7.1   Trade as a Percentage of Production in Asia, 1997–2007

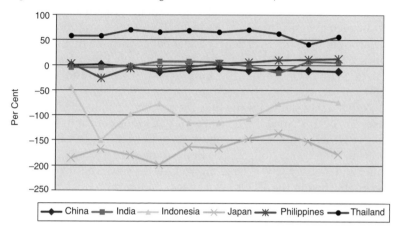

Source: F. O. Lichts (2008) *International Sugar and Sweetener Report, 1997/98–2006/07* (F. O. Lichts: Ratzeburg, Germany), p. 31.

given that any change in their ratio of trade to production would have a proportionately greater impact on supply and demand and act as a significant spur for regional trade as a whole (International Sugar Organisation 2008). Thus, the only real regional dimension to trade relations in Asia is the fact that Australia and Thailand supply the bulk of Japan, Korea and Indonesia's import, although, as noted before, this has less to do with liberalisation and the integration of markets than with post-hoc world market purchases. In other words, despite the myriad trade agreements concluded in the region since the Uruguay Round of the GATT, the theory of comparative advantage has failed to find expression in the international Asian sugar trade.

The failure to include sugar in the lattice of integration being built in Asia should not be surprising. Indeed, many scholars have argued that this burst of regionalism has come about only *because* of such exclusions. According to Kanishka Jayasuriya (2003) the regionalist project in Asia has been designed to reflect the 'embedded mercantilism' that is characteristic of its national political economies and, in doing so, has consolidated the set of trade-offs between the export-oriented and import-sensitive sectors. In practice, this has meant assembling policies that would compensate the non-export sectors of the economy; sectors that were critical to secure the political coalitions required for the pursuit of export-orientated industrialisation strategies. In the case of Japan, for instance, it is notable that, at the same time as the economy was undergoing rapid industrialisation in the 1950s and 1960s, the state was distributing the fruits of this economic growth among other sectors such as agriculture in order to ameliorate the conditions of relative economic decline and deliver social policy through distributional politics. Such interventionism has since continued into Japan's low growth period, entrenched by bureaucratic interests and pro-farm politicians across the party spectrum (Mulgan 2005: 50).

In other Asian states, meanwhile, the practice of embedded mercantilism has been shaped by the emergence of groups of capitalists with links to either ethnic Chinese networks or powerful political families and who then formed oligopolies in the domestic sector. In Thailand, Doner and Ramsey (2004) have shown how the sugar milling industry was established in the 1950s by overseas Chinese with links to powerful military patrons and commercial banks and then modernised during the 1970s with the institutional support of the state (although it later became an important export industry, it has never been open to imports and can thus be considered part of the import-sensitive sector). While in Malaysia, the entrepreneur Robert Kuok – now the richest man in Southeast Asia – first entered the sugar trade alongside the government in the 1960s, going on to act as the major distributor for sugar in Malaysia and Singapore before later entering into partnership with Liem Sioe Liong, a fellow Chinaman from Fuzhou with links to the Suharto family, to grow and refine sugar in Indonesia (Koon 1997). To reiterate, the argument being made is that sugar was never likely to be liberalised under the internationalist strategies predominant in Asia; indeed, its protection has been necessary to deliver, along with other import-sensitive industries, the political coalitions that have made such internationalism possible. For Ravenhill (2003: 308) this balance has enabled bilateral trade policy to offer 'a means by which the circle can be squared... a liberalisation without political pain'.

Intranational tensions: India, Thailand, China and the Philippines

In respect to sugar, this reading of the international political economy in Asia suggests that the various national regimes that were institutionalised in the context of the post-war development project have been largely inviolate from the recent policy changes associated with globalisation. Extrapolating from this, one could be tempted to conclude that the sugar industries in Asia are essentially stable and, as a consequence, tell us little, if anything, about the exercise of power and the shift toward a global sugar regime more generally. The rest of this chapter cautions against such a conclusion. Whilst embedded mercantilism has foreclosed regulatory change there still exist many sites of tension and change (Ravenhill's 'political pain') each of which has required concerted political action to sublimate or manage. In addition, a number of important global and non-regulatory shifts have occurred across Asia, most notably the unprecedented increase in sugar consumption. By looking a little closer at these currents we reveal how change can be located in arenas of the sugar industry often overlooked – i.e. those that exist below the surface of international regulatory agreements – and, as part of this, interrogate how power is implicated in the perpetuation of inequality and the creation of intra- and inter-industry conflict.

India

We begin our case-by-case approach to Asian sugar production in India, where the contradictions of the extant regime have arguably had their most shocking manifestation. India is the second biggest producer of sugar in the world after Brazil, fed by the big cane growing states of Maharashtra, Uttar Pradesh and Karnataka, respectively. Together this industry supports 50 million cane farmers and dependents, which, along with ancillary workers, constitute around 8 per cent of the entire rural population (Jain 2008). On paper, the regulatory system that exists in India is set up to ensure that this vast and labour-intensive cane sector is well protected. As described above, significant tariff protection and production quotas are used to ensure that a minimum cane price is set nationally. Moreover, there are legal obligations placed on millers to ensure that they cannot refuse to take cane from growers at these prices. Nevertheless, there is still immense hardship in the industry, culminating at its bleakest in the recent outbreak of farmer suicides. The question we set ourselves here, then, is why do tightly regulated markets still not work for the poor, and what is to be done about it?

The main reason given for hardship has been the lack of liquidity in the industry. The monthly release system is used to ensure that the supply of sugar by Indian mills is enough to command the minimum price but, given that the mills are obliged to take as much cane as is offered, has often left them holding large stocks of unsold sugar and unable to pay the full price to farmers. This is made worse, from the miller's perspective, by the fact that many states mandate higher minimum prices than the national government, in some cases up to 50 per cent more (International Sugar Organisation 2003: 8). As a result, a number of mills and cooperatives have obtained high court orders from state governments to sell sugar in excess of the monthly quota and also filed a case in the Supreme Court of India to be allowed to pay the lower national government price to its cane suppliers (LMC International 2006: 35). Concurrently, cane growers have continued to face delayed payments and to address their objections, the national government has been forced down a path of sporadic interventionism, releasing financial bail-outs in July 2003 and December 2007 to cover arrears in cane payments, the latter amount worth $600 million (Business Standard 2007).

Yet for all the soft loans thrown at the industry, the government has not been able to prevent the widespread ruin of cane growers as many continue to become mired in debt. According to Christian Aid (2005) this is common to many cash crop farmers in India and is due to a steep rise in the costs of inputs, particularly as government fertiliser subsidies have fallen away, and a lack of access to formal lines of credit as regional banks have pursued a more commercial mandate, raising interest rates and following a more aggressive recovery policy. These monetary constraints have been brought into sharper focus by the tendency for farmers to collectively over-estimate market prices, conditioned by the volatile domestic price and the temporary incentives to export such as the currency devaluation in the early 1990s. It is this cycle of over-investment and lagged over-supply that has given the Indian sugar market its odd status as a swing-trader, oscillating between a net exporter and a net importer, and which has forced sudden credit crises on millers and farmers. The consequences of this are tragic. Crippled by debt and unwilling to make their family destitute by selling their land, farmers have been killing themselves in huge numbers. India's federal agricultural minister recently conceded to parliament that more than 100,000 farmers have committed suicide between 1993 and 2003 – the majority of whom worked in the country's sugar and cotton industries – with debt identified as the most important factor (Weis 2007a: 110).

Both from a human and a business viewpoint this is clearly an untenable situation and regulatory reform could arguably do much to alleviate some of these contradictions. But what we caution against here is a knee-jerk response that would suggest that because protectionism has not worked, liberalisation must be the answer. By revealing the limitations of this dualistic, 'state versus market' thinking, we can hopefully shine a little more light onto the root causes of agrarian crisis in India whilst also opening up opportunities for more nuanced thinking about the possible paths of reform.

Such instinctive free market responses typically begin by stating the need to 'get the prices right'. This means deregulating prices so that the market can incentivise firms to improve efficiency and supply the right amount of sugar to meet demand. To achieve the 'right prices' in the Indian case, we can posit two likely sets of reforms. The first would be the extension of the partial measures already undertaken to free up market forces. To date these include the decline of the public distribution system, under which producers had to sell a part of their output at lower prices in order that poorer urban consumers could buy more sugar, and the removal of quantitative ceilings on exports. The extension of these could include a withdrawal of the quota system, allowing inefficient mills to disappear, and a deregulation of prices and establishment of a futures market to 'rationalise' sugar cane pricing. Second, profit sharing arrangements would be encouraged to get farmers and millers working together. The International Sugar Organisation (2003: 26), for example, have argued that the predominant cooperative system in Maharashtra has created a more appropriate business structure by giving farmers an incentive in supplying high-sucrose cane and permitting an effective transport arrangement at harvest to arise through centralised control. By moving to a cooperative system in other states, it is suggested that farmers will become more conducive to introducing cost-saving technology and less willing to jeopardise supply to the mill through collective bargaining.

As suggested above, it is necessary to retain some scepticism against such clear-cut and uniform policy prescriptions. Notwithstanding the normative agenda in the account, which effectively argues for wholesale unemployment in the industry in order to preserve its long-run competitiveness, such analyses also encounter practical problems given their obfuscation of political power, a result of the neo-utilitarian theory on which they draw. As outlined in Chapter 2, a neo-utilitarian approach assumes that institutions are efficient, that is to say, they are capable of being changed in response to exogenous changes in interests and resources. In this case, when we suggest that the relationship between growers and millers should become more cooperative, we underplay the extent to which this change is restricted by prevailing social institutions. Based on fieldwork in Uttar Pradesh for instance, Craig Jeffrey (2002) has noted how cooperative organisation has been stunted by the fact that the rich farmers who possess the social links, education and time to lead and sustain cooperatives are precisely those who benefit the most from the present system, meaning the leadership that is presumed to be imminent is actually co-opted. Reinforcing this institutional logic, Jeffrey also notes how the social tensions between caste and class are much more acute in Uttar Pradesh than in Maharashtra, a factor that adds a further structural layer against the prospect of bottom-up integration between farm and factory.

Not only does the neo-utilitarian approach underplay the difficulties of institutional transformation, it also overlooks the extent to which institutions facilitate unequal outcomes. While the cooperative structure can be praised for offering incentives for cost effective production, it is evident that the economic rewards of this do not always trickle down to the poorer members and employees of the group. In this case, this has much to do with the fact that the cooperatives in both Maharashtra and Gujurat are primarily controlled by state and federal congress politicians, many of whom have enacted legislation to enrich themselves financially and politically by enlarging and consolidating a strong power base in the industry (Lalvani 2008: 1477). This power enables the mill owners to undermine the state-managed system meant to protect the growers through acts such as stopping the transfer of cane to states offering higher prices, securing exemption from labour laws to drive down wage costs, and imposing bans on jaggery, a low-quality artisanal sugar which offers cane growers another market in times of low refined sugar prices. In addition, certain illicit acts have also been reported, namely taking government loans without then carrying on production or refusing to take farmers' cane (Joshi 2005; Johnson 2007). Alongside the burden this places on cane growers in the cooperatives, migrant cane cutters also suffer. Prompted by the 'pull' factor of the cooperatives who refuse to rely on better protected local labour and by the 'push' factors of indebtedness and a lack of agricultural work in the dry and arid plains of their own districts – in part a result of the irrigation subsidy bias toward the thirsty sugar cane crop – hundreds of thousands of temporary cane cutters enter the employment of the cooperatives via labour contractors. These contractors offer cane cutters advances to pay medical bills or marry off children, which are then offset against the amount of sugar cane cut. However, the extortionate interest rates charged often leaves labourers still owing money at the end of the harvest, trapped into coming back year on year (Bunsha 2003).

In sum, what we suggest here is that a neo-utilitarian and free market prescription of price deregulation is compromised by its failure to recognise power relations between industry actors. The instrumental value of price deregulation is said to be smooth functioning markets, which are expected to reduce agrarian suffering by discouraging oversupply and the spiral of indebtedness, leaving only the most efficient producers in business. However, if it is the case that low cost production techniques are themselves *dependent on severe agrarian exploitation*, then as long as they survive, market reform in itself will do little to alleviate poverty and hardship, which is engrained not in the coordination problems of the industry but in its mode of production. When these structures of inequality are recognised, we can denaturalise such calls for market reform and see them for what they really are, not so much a means to an end, but in fact an end in themselves. The flip side of this is that we are then presented with a tricky prospect: instigating policies that recognise that neither heavy regulation *nor* wholesale deregulation offers a pro-poor agenda for change.

Thailand

In Thailand, too, the issue of debt has been at the forefront of industry concerns. The wave of mill expansion and modernisation begun in the 1970s continued into the 1980s due to spikes in world prices and the peculiar incentives of Thailand's quota system, which allocates domestic production allowances based on mill output and has encouraged mill owners to expand capacity. Following capital account deregulation in the early 1990s, it became even easier to acquire cheap credit from abroad, again fuelling investment in mills, leaving them by the middle of the decade as some of the most technologically advanced in the world (Doner and Ramsey 2004: 120). To satisfy the expanded capacity of mills, cane planting increased from 650,000 hectares in the late 1980s to 965,000 hectares in 1997, much of which was acquired through deforestation (NaRanong 2000).

When the economic crisis hit in 1997 and the Thai Baht was floated, the amount of foreign debts doubled and many mills faced repayment problems. In addition, the commercial banks stopped providing loans to the mills, which in turn were unable to provide growers with pre-season credit or even pay for cane already delivered. Taking place within the context of an austere IMF bailout programme that had cut the state agricultural budget by a quarter, irrigation and extension programmes suffering the largest cutbacks, growers thus faced an acute payment problem and were unable to capitalise on the export opportunities presented to them as the Baht devalued *vis-à-vis* the dollar (Goss and Burch 2001: 981). After protests at the lack of payment and state restructuring – one foreign debt-restructuring expert was even murdered in front of a sugar mill – state-led efforts were made to alleviate the crisis. The Thai government pressed the Bank for Agriculture and Agricultural Cooperatives to provide pre-season credit and then borrowed money itself to pay growers an extra amount for their cane through long-term low interest loans (NaRanong 2000: 11). Pushed further by the drop in world prices toward the end of the decade, this state support was formalised in 1999 with the first increase in domestic sugar prices in 17 years.

The financial crisis and attendant dislocation was not the sole cause of change within the national Thai regime. As Jasper Goss and David Burch (2001) have written of Thai agriculture more generally, the 1990s signalled the closing of the land frontier and the end of extensive agricultural expansion as the large agri-business firms that had moved into retailing and offshore investment came to dominate agricultural production, supplying value-added foodstuffs such as chicken, shrimp, and canned and fresh fruits within a regional hub and spoke system centred around Japan. Unable to expand exports in the region due to the trade restrictions described in the first section, the response of the sugar processors to the limits of agriculture has been to invest directly in countries with lower land and labour costs and higher domestic prices. For example, since 1998 Thailand's largest processor, Mitr Phol, has invested in Cambodia, Vietnam and China, where it produced 10 per cent of the entire domestic supply in 2007 (F. O. Lichts 2008a: 473). Along with fellow Thai milling groups Khon Kaen Sugar and Wang Kanai, Mitr Phol has also invested in Laos (where wages are around one quarter of those in Thailand), joining forces with Tate & Lyle to target the duty-free quota-free EU market under the EBA (The Nation 2008). To briefly summate these developments, as opposed to national vertical integration and enmeshment seen in the Japan-centred food import complex, led by Thailand the regionalisation of sugar production in Asia has taken the form of renewed lost-cost production through foreign direct investment and has been targeted more at domestic and non-Asian markets.

China

Although there is little research on politics of the sugar industry in China on which to draw here, we can depict an outline of how the commodity has been managed by the state by piecing together extracts from market studies and newspaper reports. The sketch that results suggests how the entry of foreign firms such as Mitr Phol and British Sugar (which controlled around 5 per cent of supply in 2007, see Chapter 5 for a recap) can be seen as both a solution to, and an aggravation of, the project of agricultural modernisation engineered by the Chinese government. Modernisation in the country has been based on the recognition of the relative paucity of arable land in China compared to its extensive supply of labour, and has been pursued through an intensification of production invoked through the deregulation of prices and formal production quotas, on the one hand, and the promotion of increased yields and improved milling efficiency, on the other (Fang and Beghin 2003). As technologically advanced and market-conscious processors, foreign firms have thus been welcomed by state elites as a solution to achieving this transformation of production toward more efficient land usage.

The consequences of this for the workforce in the industry, though, has been stark 'rationalisation' as many of the 40 million sugar growers who constitute the industry's agricultural base have been unable to sell their output due to the fluctuating prices following deregulation (USDA 2003: 50). For its part, the processing sector too has reduced its number of employees: just four years after deregulation, 150 small, loss-making mills were closed down as prices dropped precipitously, and since then, labour has continued to be shed. Factory employment fell from 470,000 in 1995 to 180,000 by 2003, driven by the introduction of labour-saving machinery as well as price volatility (Wencong 2003). Given that the rural areas where sugar is grown in China are some of its poorest, the national government has attempted to alleviate unemployment by reducing competition from the large artificial sweetener industry in saccharin, which accounts for between 8 and 15 per cent of the total sweetener market, and having nationalised mills stockpile sugar to increase prices (Chan 2008). State governments have followed suit, buying up sugar in order to stop domestic prices falling further, and as a consequence, a considerable 1.1mt was taken off the market in 2008 alone (F. O. Lichts 2009b: 41). Nevertheless, approximately one third of China's remaining sugar mills are still in the red and face bankruptcy, and in a context where the gap between rural and urban wages is ever widening, the imperative to keep unprofitable employers in business has not abated (F. O. Lichts 2008c: 893).

Philippines

Finally, in the Philippines, the relationship between sugar and labour has also been of immense importance in the countryside, though the issue of primary concern has not been the secular decline in employment opportunities offered by the industry but rather the working conditions within it. As opposed to India or China, where a large number of small-scale growers are present, labour relations in the Philippines have been played out between the 'sugar barons', the traditional sugar families that run the haciendas, on the one hand, and their estate workers, who frequently protest over low wages or non-payment and the dismissals of union leaders, on the other. One especially notorious flashpoint in this respect was the massacre at the Hacienda Luisita on 16 November 2004, in which police opened fire on striking workers, killing 14, including two children, and wounding hundreds more (Cook 2004). The International Labor Rights Fund (2007) has even gone as far as to petition the US government to reconsider Philippines' status as a beneficiary country under the TRQ for its failure to take steps to grant its workers freedom of association, freedom of unionisation, and for 'being engaged in the extra-judicial killings and abductions of union leaders, members, organisers, and supporters'.

While the exact form these conflicts take is refracted by the particular history of the Philippines as a colonial plantation economy, that conflicts arise in the first place can be considered symptomatic of the declining profitability of an industry that has been unable to reduce costs of production and maintain its historic export levels. As in the case of India, the economistic prescription has been to change government policy to encourage efficiency gains through exposure to deregulated prices. In their Centre for International Economics study for instance, Borrell *et al.* (1994: 110–112) have suggested that the cane pricing arrangement between planters and millers, known as the *quedan* system, be made more flexible to allow both parties to capture the productivity gains they initiate, and for the land reform programme to reestablish confidence in property rights by concluding redistribution swiftly.

Confounding these changes, Michael Billig (2003: 143) has noted how attempts to initiate an alternative cane pricing institution have been refused, partly because of mutual mistrust within the industry, and partly because of the planters' cultural attachment to the business of trading *quedans,* this despite the fact that it would arguably be beneficial for the industry as a whole were this system introduced. Related to land reform, other authors have commented how the break-up of haciendas has been variously deferred, fudged and evaded by the landowners themselves, meaning the uncertainty over land rights is unlikely to be entirely resolved in the short term (Reidinger 1995; Borras Jr 2001). Debarring a 'rational' transition to a new institutional environment, then, the sugar barons have opted for alternative means to reduce labour tensions, namely, reducing the strength of unions on the estate by hiring children and temporary contract labour (Ombion 2007). Highlighting the prevalence of these practices, the NGO Terres des Hommes (2005) have estimated that, in 2005, between 60,000 and 200,000 children were employed on sugar plantations, predominantly in planting, weeding and applying fertiliser; tasks in which they were frequently exposed to adverse weather conditions, long shifts, and dangerous pesticides.

Protection without permanence: the variegated evolution of Asia's sugar producers

To recap, the aim of this section has been to show that even though the Asian region has been insulated from the liberalisation processes witnessed in many other commodities, the various national sugar industries have not been immune to tensions and transformation. More precisely, through brief studies of four different countries – India, Thailand, China and the Philippines – it has been illustrated how these tensions and transformations have taken different forms depending on the state-society relations within each national regime. For example, at a general level, price instability has been a tension prevalent in all countries yet has manifested itself and been exposed in various ways, including grower indebtedness, renewed exploitation by millers and various acts of rural resistance and submission. The importance of these continued tensions from our perspective lies in the fact that the embedded mercantilism described earlier rests crucially on the ability of states to protect industries such as sugar and thus deliver national equity alongside export-led growth. In failing to do this, architects of the Asian trade project are presented with a stark dilemma: if protection fails to deliver rural growth, to what extent should the state intervene to rectify this?

Related to this point, this section has also offered a second argument about the nature of policy change. As opposed to the economistic analyses that propose *a priori* institutional fixes that gear individuals towards cost-effective production, it has been suggested that many such proposals will be stunted by the reluctance of actors to embrace a whole new way of working, or, to the extent that new institutions do arise, that they will emerge out of the existing (and spatially unique) patterns of state-society relations. For example, the public and private responses to the agrarian crises depicted have been multifaceted, including sporadic government bail-outs in India, overseas investment in Thailand, a clamp down on artificial sweetener production in China, and union-busting in the Philippines. Rather than institutional break, it is again more apposite to describe change as a form of institutional bricolage, as new policies and coalitions are laid over previous ones. In this sense, it can be assumed that, despite the many universal policy solutions to agrarian crises, the type of regime(s) that will arise in the region will retain idiosyncrasy.

The nutrition transition: the causes and consequences of dietary globalisation

In the previous section, some prevalent global 'solutions' to agrarian crisis such as the commercialisation of agricultural credit and the deregulation of state guided prices were highlighted and the extent to which they had been entrenched in Asian sugar regimes discussed. Arguably though, the phenomenon having the biggest impact in Asia is not a universal policy alignment but rather a global dietary shift, as huge numbers of people in developing countries switch to energy dense diets. In particular, there have been marked increases in the contribution to food calories from live-stock products, vegetable oils and sugar, rendering change in both the quantity and quality of dietary intake (de Haen *et al.* 2003). Termed the 'nutrition transition', this shift has had profound consequences for the various national sugar regimes in the region, specifically in pro-duction, commodity prices, and state responses to malnutrition and growing product markets. As such, an explanation of how and why dietary globalisation is emerging is considered essential to understanding the factors shaping our future regime trajectories.

Over the past decade global consumption of sugar has increased at a steady rate of about 2.5 per cent per year (F. O. Lichts 2009b: 28). As Figure 7.2 indicates below, this trend is in large part down to the increasing consumption in Asia, which in fact maps on to even longer periods of continuous growth prior to that. Given this seemingly secular and sizeable trend, countries in Asia have understandably become the focus of industrial sugar users as key growth markets. As a Nestlé executive said of China, 'this is the fastest and most competitive market in the world...Growth in China is up to your imagination'

Figure 7.2   Regional Consumption of Sugar, 1990–2005

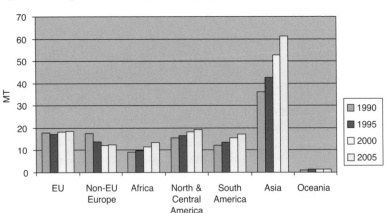

Source: F. O. Lichts *International Sugar and Sweetener Report*. Various Years.
Note: EU data for 1990 and 1995 includes current members' data prior to them joining.

(Weis 2007a: 106). Whereas Chapter 6 examined the political economy of consumption *within* the sweetened foods market (i.e. sugar, HFCS or artificial sweeteners) this section will now focus on the consumption of sweetened foods *themselves*.

The predominant explanations for the increased per capita consumption of sugar in Asia are those that have been derived from the price dynamics of demand (Mitchell 2004: 18; Gudoshnikov *et al.* 2004: 94). Essentially, they argue that as incomes have risen consumers have increased their intake of sweeteners and have done so more rapidly than in developed countries given the higher elasticity of sugar demand at lower levels of income. What is assumed to be an innate human preference for sweetness, catered for by more disposable income, is also said by others to be augmented by urbanisation (OECD 2007: 85). The particular correlation of urbanisation to increased sweetener consumption is that urbanisation equates to better infrastructure and increased access to fast food chains and modern retailers. In this respect it is notable that in 2004, China, India, Thailand and Vietnam all featured in the top ten FDI destinations of global supermarket chains (Hawkes 2005: 360). Thus, through economies of scale in storage, logistics and distribution, a wider and cheaper variety of sweetened products are offered and the 'Westernisation' of food consumption and the acceleration of sugar intake said to follow accordingly. Lending empirical credence to this theoretical model, a longitudinal pooled regression conducted by Barry Popkin and Samara Joy Nielson (2003) on world sweetener consumption between 1962 and 2000 found that 82 per cent of the change in intake could be attributed to changes in national income and urbanisation.

The relationship between income/urbanisation and sweetener consumption is an important but abstract and incomplete one. In light of Popkin and Nielson's findings, two supplementary analyses must be injected into the 'relative prices' account described above. To begin, it is important to recognise that per capita wealth and urbanisation are proxies. In our context, what they really refer to is the creation of a middle class or, more specifically, a consumer society. As Daniel Miller (1995: 17) has argued, the consumer society exists when people have a minimal relationship to production and distribution, such that consumption provides the only arena left in which a relationship with the world can be forged. The creation of this relationship in food and eating therefore requires 'marketising' previously non-market activities such as cooking, and 'segmenting' market demand into niches where none existed before. The aim of this, of course, is to encourage people to desire ever more differentiated, pre-prepared and 'value-added' products.

Thus it is the entry of women into the workforce that should be considered a major factor in the creation of a consumer class, as time constraints push them into buying highly processed foodstuffs to fulfil their obligations as chief food preparers; products which are typically higher in added sweeteners (de Haen *et al.* 2003: 689). And to the extent that the growth of supermarkets has encouraged the uptake of sugar consumption, it is not simply by cheapening the prices and widening availability, but also by enabling bulk buying, which encourages increased consumption at home (think of the large, multipack bottles of fizzy drinks) and introducing the cultural space through which consumers can understand and appreciate new (Western) product lines.

Working in tandem with the substitution of home cooked foods for pre-prepared ones has been the increase in 'snacking', defined here as the ingestion of food and drinks outside meal times.[2] Its rise in urban Asia has been advanced through two avenues: first, the growth of convenience stores, which have targeted modern consumers with ready-to-eat hot and cold snacks; and second, the use of advertising, heightened both by economies of scale, as adverts in urban areas are seen by more potential customers, and economies of agglomeration, as rival brands have developed the processed food market as a whole (Hawkes 2006). Moreover, the ambiguous status of sweetened products as both a food and a non-food has made them particularly receptive to such advertising campaigns. That is to say, products such as soft drinks, chocolates and confectionery can take on meanings relevant to either identity, moving into the realm of non-foods when assigned qualities that go beyond the properties accorded to ordinary sustenance, from whence they can become increasingly desirable (Beardsworth and Keil 1997: 249). Such products do not just satisfy our hunger or slake our thirst; they constitute our very identity. As the President of Coca-Cola, Muhtar Kent makes clear, 'Coca-Cola isn't only a drink. It's an idea, a vision, a feeling. It's a connection and refreshment' (Coca-Cola 2008).

Such ambiguity brings us to the second component of our analysis: the inherent intersubjectivity of consumption. Recall that the Popkin and Nielson study found national income and urbanisation accounted for 82 per cent of change in sweetener consumption, leaving a significant proportion to be explained by cultural shifts in consumer preferences. What this suggests is that the 'consumer' is not simply a universal materialist individual, or, in Robert Lynd's (1936) words, a 'noiseless servant named Demand', but rather a more complex and socially responsive person. In this light, a consumer society should not be seen as emerging *ex nihilo* within developing countries, but instead as emerging out of pre-existing cultures and identities. As a result, the appeals made by corporations to have people participate in the 'ideas, visions and feelings' of sweetened foods must map onto this prevailing social milieu. It is the disjuncture between existing food cultures (or territorial place) and the symbolic and intersubjective qualities of branded Western foods (or deterritorial product) that can help account for the extra 18 per cent of changing consumption in Popkin's model, and which has given dietary globalisation its uneven and uncertain contours.

The remainder of this section presents some examples of these contours and how they emerge from the reciprocal interaction of the local and the global. One influential, local factor in the development of markets for sweetened products in Asia has been the existing level of sugar consumption. In China, what has attracted companies such as Nestlé is the fact that extant consumption of sweetened, processed food is relatively low, thereby making market growth appear both phenomenal and limitless. In the chocolate industry, for example, led by Cadbury-Schweppes, Hershey and Mars, sales in 2007 were already valued at $1.83 billion and were projected to grow by a considerable 37 per cent by 2012 (Leatherhead International 2008: 20). However, the low intake of sweeteners in China has also caused problems for the processed food protagonists. As the export director at luxury Belgian chocolate manufacturer, Guylian, has lamented, most locals in China do not know 'what quality means in terms of chocolate' (Freeman 2007). Given the paucity of a 'chocolate culture' in China, consumers have thus had to be taught what is desirable. Fulfilling this mission, novel exhibitions such as Beijing's 'Salon de Chocolat' hosted in Beijing, a kind of chocolate fashion show featuring models draped in confectionery, have therefore been established to inform cultural entrepreneurs that certain products – in this case those produced by Ferrero Rocher of Italy, Lindt of Switzerland and Leonidas of Belgium – are of a higher quality than others.[3]

To be sure, this educational process runs both ways. To learn about the tastes of local markets, the biggest chocolate manufacturer in the world, Barry Callebaut, has opened training centres for chocolatiers in Shanghai and Mumbai (Simonian 2007). Likewise, Nestlé has established Centres of Excellence in the ASEAN countries, including one in Malaysia which specialises in chocolate and confectionery for export to the rest of the region, in order to draw on the country's cultural knowledge as a relatively high consuming nation (Pritchard 2000: 252). The

Figure 7.3   Annual Sugar Consumption Per Capita in Asia, 1998 and 2008

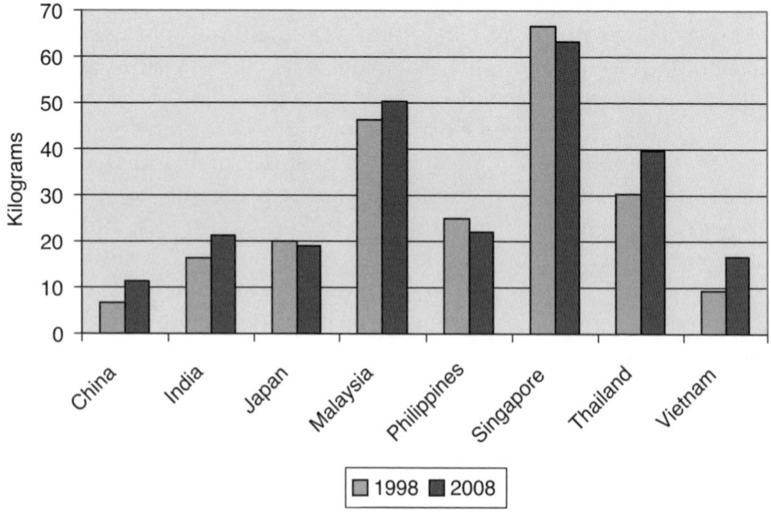

Source: F. O. Lichts *International Sugar and Sweetener Report*. Various years.

successes of these appeals are apparent in the impressive growth of per capita annual intake of sugar in Asia, which rose from 14kg in 1998 to 17kg by 2008 (F. O. Lichts 2008d: 36). The major drivers of this increase were the markets in China and India, which as Figure 7.3 illustrates, recorded relatively impressive growth.

These trends illustrate how food consumerism has had to be cajoled out of people, but still leave the impression that the process is a corporate Western one, imposed on a passive East. In fact, neither sweetener intake nor dietary homogenisation in the region has been a foregone conclusion. For example, we note how the breakfast cereals trialled in Asia by Kellogg's failed to find custom since they were just too alien, leaving the company to focus instead on cereal bars and hot cereals to fit in with the low-milk style of Asian breakfasting (Wei and Cacho 1999: 441). Or how, in China, youngsters have followed the health-conscious habits of the older generation and turned to Wanglaoji, a brand of traditional herbal tea repackaged in cans and cartons, which in 2006 replaced Coca-Cola as the number one soft drink by volume sales (Chung 2007). Indeed, Coca-Cola has since responded by launching a ready-to-drink green tea with herbal ingredients, further highlighting the uncertain and reflexive terrain of consumption. What these examples of marketing success/failure show is that where sweetened foods and drinks find resonance with socially embedded diets, what Sidney Mintz (2002: 284) calls 'real eating' in contrast to 'merely ingesting', their consumption will be less prone to the vagaries of fashion and more likely to become part of the cultural common sense. It is this institutionalisation of consumption that interests us here. For by appending themselves to existing diets or by becoming a habitual snack, the demand for processed food becomes entrenched and, in turn, entrenches the demand for sugar. As a result, it becomes increasingly likely that certain contradictions within the national sugar regimes will begin to escalate, an argument to which we now turn.

Contradictions of consumption: for health, wealth and sugar policy

The shift, albeit an uneven and undecided one, towards diets with a higher sugar content poses a number of challenges to the way the existing regimes of sugar are viewed and regulated. Arguably, the most pressing of these is the impact of sugar on health. As we saw in Chapter 6, the public and private conceptions of the salubriousness or sinfulness of sugar was a key battleground over which various interests overlapped and clashed in respect of the recommended intake of calorific sweeteners and the 'naturalness' of sugar. In Asia, this site can be expected to become more contested as the nutrition transition comes accompanied by an 'epidemiological transition' marking the overhaul of infectious diseases by non-communicable diseases, including heart disease, cancer and diabetes (Pingali 2007: 293).

The links between a high sugar intake and chronic non-communicable diseases are complex and there is insufficient space here to elucidate them all. In the case of heart disease, for instance, one determining factor is the incidence of obesity, which is in turn linked to excess sugar intake because it both it adds calories in itself and is used to make fatty and salty foods more palatable. However, as there are a significant number of additional lifestyle and biological factors that can alter the chance of extra calories manifesting themselves in weight gain, any direct link between sugar and obesity is obfuscated.[4] Nevertheless, the incidence of non-communicable diseases is growing rapidly, taking the lives of 35 million people worldwide in 2005, twice as many as all infectious diseases. Moreover, only a fifth of these deaths attributable to 'diseases of affluence' actually took place in the most affluent nations. Most took place in the developing world (*The Economist* 2007). Apart from the tragic human cost this inflicts, the spread of non-communicable disease has also exacted an acute economic cost on poorer countries. A report from the Indian Council on Economic Relations for example estimated that the loss to India's national income as a result of heart disease, stroke and diabetes in 2005 was $9 billion, and projected that the figure would exceed $200 billion over the following ten years (Yee 2007).

At the level of the state, then, with rising sugar consumption a contradiction begins to manifest itself between the obligation to protect citizens from harm and the political risk of restricting freedom of choice (Mintz 2002: 24). Complicating this ideological contest is the economic complexion of the dietary transition. In the case of increasing consumption of sweetened products, offsetting the increased health bill is the wealth generated by an enhanced food-manufacturing base. The new markets pioneered by Western corporations have not only attracted financial investment and improved infrastructure from overseas investors, but as suggested earlier, in some instances have led to the emergence and renewal of domestic rivals (Wei and Cacho 1999: 441). Hoping to generate such spillover benefits, governments in Asia have been active conduits for Western agri-food capital. By way of example, China's export-import agency has acted as partner to Coca-Cola's operations, while Singapore's strengthened intellectual property protection and access to university research has encouraged companies like Cadbury-Schweppes to establish its regional headquarters there (Singapore Economic Development Board 2006). This helps explain why the 2003 World Health Organisation report which recommended limiting sugar intake was criticised not only by the US, but also by Colombia, on behalf of the Group of 77 developing countries, and China too (Alden and Buckley 2004).

The tension between promoting healthy diets and industrial development is not the only trade-off facing governments as a result of increasing sugar consumption. As demonstrated throughout the book, there is an ever-present friction over the terms of exchange between the sugar-producing and sugar-using industries. As it is being played out in Asia, the majority of sugar-containing products are made for the home market, provided by a mixture of foreign and domestic investment. Increased production of SCPs can thus be expected to boost domestic demand and prices for sugar, which, aside from the pressure placed on low quality producers to modernise or land-limited producers to expand, generally acts as a fillip to the industry. To this extent, the 'ever-present friction' is submerged and the nutrition transition and agricultural expansion can go hand in hand.[5] However, once trade relations are factored in, this friction suddenly resurfaces as maintaining high sugar prices puts domestic food processors at a disadvantage when foreign competitors are able access cheaper inputs.

This challenge to nationally ordered sugar regimes has, somewhat iron-ically, been aided by the embedded mercantilist project that sought to defend such sectors in the first place. As noted by Richard Higgott (1999) an important aspect of the regionalist project in Asia has been the liberal-isation and deregulation of FDI controls, which has reduced barriers of entry to transnational capital. Along with the tariff reductions on 'non-sensitive' products mentioned earlier, this has created the conditions for increased trade in processed foods and drinks. In Japan, for instance, rather than importing the raw sugar ingredient and producing SCPs domestically, a number of manufacturers have moved offshore and now export finished SCPs back to the home market. Between 1985 and 1995, imports of fruit juices, preserved fruit and sugar confectionery registered a growth of 15 per cent, 2 per cent above import growth as a whole. Taking the bigger picture, the trade in SCPs has become one of the fastest growing and most valuable in the entire agri-food sector – far outweigh-ing traditional exports such as sugar – and is worth around $600m in Japan and $15 billion worldwide (Leatherhead International 2008: 38).

The threat this poses for sugar producers is two-fold. Although sugar itself may be subject to protection, the increased import of 'hidden' sugar in SCPs erodes the domestic industrial demand for sugar, thereby acting as a form of indirect agricultural competition and a dampener on prices. In Japan in 1997, imports just of blends – including products like sweet-ened bean paste, cocoa powder and milk powder – contained sugar equiv-alent to nearly a quarter of that year's domestic production (Australian Bureau of Agricultural Economics 1999). In addition, reluctant to see manufacturing jobs escaping their borders and conscious of the gains to their own economy were they to increase exports of SCPs, state elites may reduce domestic sugar prices to help capture these markets for them-selves. In the debate over sugar tariffs in the Philippines, for example, the counterpart to the neo-liberal discourse mentioned earlier has been a nationalist discourse promulgated by the industrial sugar users. These companies have claimed that as long as protection is afforded to the 'out-moded' sugar barons, they can never hope to compete with the food industries in Malaysia, Singapore, Thailand and Vietnam whose govern-ments, in their eyes, bend over backwards to assist value-adding exporters (Billig 2007: 75). As the value of regional markets expands with the nutri-tion transition more generally, the economic weight of export-orientated arguments will only increase.

In sum, increasing sweetener consumption in Asia has not been an automatic process. It has been argued here that demand and, indeed, a consumer society, has had to be actively constructed as price differentials and a general preference for sweetness cannot in themselves deliver continued market growth in sweetened processed foods. More precisely, centred on the younger generation of the urban middle classes, the ambition of (predominantly Western) capital has in fact been to institutionalise consumption of these products so that people *learn* to prefer them and communicate this among themselves, in this way naturalising and hardening brand alliance and growing demand. To the extent that this is successful, industrial markets for sugar will continue to expand and heighten the dilemmas faced by states, chiefly in health policy versus industrial policy, and rural policy versus trade policy. Whatever the outcomes, the important point to note is that, as a result of these antinomies, resolutely *political* choices will have to be made, and it is these decisions (or non-decisions) to which we should pay attention if we are to construct a more telling account of power as it shapes the future sugar regime in this region.

Conclusion

In a special edition of the journal *World Development* that was dedicated to food production in Asia, the lead authors wrote that: 'Food and agricultural commodities are as much globally sourced products as computers, textiles and autos.... In this current era of neo-liberalism, national food and fibre products are increasingly produced via flexible import regimes organised around agro-food and fibre transnationals' (Thompson and Cowan 2000). Given the preceding arguments, it seems difficult to place sugar within this broad trajectory. As opposed to a transnationalisation of production it has been the multinationalisation of sugar processors and domestic sourcing by the majority of industrial sugar users that has prevailed, and it is clear too that states continue to maintain their decisive role in controlling the flow of trade in raw and refined sugars. Nevertheless, while the global changes written about by these authors may not be applicable to this commodity, this chapter has identified a number of significant political economy patterns that are.

Within the domestic market, waves of price instability and instances of credit tightening have caused concrete moments of agrarian crisis and renewed demands on government for the 'rationalisation' of sugar policy. These have manifest themselves in various ways, differentiated according to the group making the call and the country in which they did it, paradoxically creating alternative 'rational' responses to the same types of problems. Another area in which significant change has been taking place, and one which highlights the sinews of an increasingly global regime, relates to consumption. The nutrition transition taking place in Asia was depicted as an active and willed creation of the food sector to instigate a dietary globalisation, albeit one that contained both divergent and convergent aspects. It was found to create divergence *within states* as diets became differentiated more by income, urbanisation and age than national cultural restrictions or the availability of local produce, while it created convergence *between states* as consumer societies were replicated and their nutritional intake more closely aligned, although the form and manner in which sweeteners were ingested retained cultural specificity. In addition, because of the lucrative and mounting opportunities depicted in the processed food sector, dietary globalisation was highlighted, along with commercialised credit and volatile prices, as another non-trade factor propelling demand for change. All this goes to suggest that the embedded mercantilism identified earlier is not a failsafe option capable of equalising wealth and opportunity between the export-oriented and import-sensitive sectors. In light of this, we must continue to recognise the management of the sugar industry as a resolutely political task.

8
The End Game of the Global Regime: A False Promise of Free Markets

To recap our argument thus far, Chapter 4 ended by detailing the embryonic global regime in sugar, inaugurated by the successful conclusion of the Uruguay Round and the inclusion of agriculture into the neo-liberal project as heralded by the WTO. The subsequent three chapters considered the extent to which this project has actually manifested itself in the regimes of three key regions: the EU-ACP, the US, and Asia. Each chapter found that, while the initial attempt at multilateral liberalisation under the Uruguay Round had been variously fudged, in different ways each region had experienced a recalibration of its rules and norms to a more globally orientated regime. The constitutionalism of trade relations, the changing strategies of corporate investment and market development, and the new expressions of capitalist farming each pointed toward the decreased importance of national borders, even if the traditional barometer for measuring their importance, the level of trade barriers, remained fairly constant. This chapter now returns to the issue of multilateral liberalisation and the attempts made over the last decade to take a bigger bite out of these trade barriers and entrench a more liberal, and thus more global, sugar regime. It looks especially at the negotiations in the WTO Doha Round, which began in 2001, as a means of assessing what structures of power underpin the formation of these global rules and what effect they are likely to have on the creation and distribution of wealth in the sugar industry. This latter point is of particular interest given that Doha was launched with the explicit goal of ensuring that 'developing countries, and especially the least-developed among them, secure a share in the growth of world trade commensurate with the needs of their economic development' (Doha Ministerial Declaration 2001).

We begin by charting the emergence of the coalition of developing countries known as the G20 and the rhetoric that suggested this group would be able to overcome the dominance of the EU and the US in the WTO and finally bring about pro-poor liberalisation in the agricultural sector. Following previous arguments about the historic evolution of institutions, however, we offer three sceptical notes on the idea that progressive liberalisation is possible and that it does indeed promote development. First, choosing the right path to liberalisation is confounded by the fact that negotiators are unsure of the value of certain concessions and so may deviate down a 'sub-optimal' route. Second, the belief that the 'uneven playing field' will at least be ultimately levelled as trade-distorting policies are gradually eroded ignores the persistent renewal of government involvement in agriculture as policy instruments evolve over time. Thirdly, to the extent that liberalisation does occur, its benefits are assumed rather than given. By looking at Brazil, a country expected to be one of the prime beneficiaries of a successful rollback in agricultural protection, it is shown how trade expansion is likely to lead to a form of development structured by inequalities. We note how the increased sugar/ethanol exports that Brazil has already managed to achieve have simultaneously excluded the very poor from land and jobs, while helping those middle class employed in the industry toward a more secure and well-paid future. Because of these three factors, we conclude that development through liberalisation remains more an act of ideological faith than a question of willpower, and, further, one in which the state's ability to distribute the fruits of growth may be constrained by its very pursuit of agro-exports.

Agricultural negotiations in the WTO: searching for *El Dorado*

The WTO has experienced a somewhat tumultuous existence since 1994. After a ministerial meeting in Singapore in 1996 to consolidate elements of the post-Uruguay work programme, the organisation members began to gear up for another round of multilateral liberalisation at the Geneva and Seattle ministerials in 1998 and 1999, respectively. Unable to garner the requisite political capital and marred by mass demonstrations outside the events, member states first forestalled, then reflected and ultimately turned toward the Doha ministerial in 2001 to set the WTO process back on track. As a reflection of these previous ministerials, the Doha mandate was framed as a 'Development Agenda' in an attempt to overcome the reluctance of developing countries to ascent to a further round at a time when they were still unconvinced of the benefits of the Uruguay Round's 'Grand Bargain'. This agenda therefore contained commitments, first, to resolve the issue of implementation and, second, to make further reductions in agricultural support, reductions in tariffs affecting the interests of developing countries, greater flexibilities in intellectual property proscriptions, and a strengthening of special and differential treatment integral to any final agreement.

Where Doha set the agenda, the 2003 Cancún ministerial was to increase appetite for a conclusion. Unable to hammer out what the various 'commitments' would actually mean in practice, though, Cancún became the second WTO ministerial to collapse in four years. Angered by what they perceived to be procedural flaws and strong-arm tactics by developed countries, developing countries rallied together as the meeting crystallised into a North-South debate. The breaking point was the attempted inclusion of three of the Singapore issues into the Doha Development Agenda – competition, investment and public procurement – at which the developing countries baulked, feeling that they had no place in the negotiations. But this was only the culmination of dissent. As Amrita Narlikar and Diane Tussie (2004: 953) noted, 'irrespective of the machinations on the final day...agriculture had in fact been the bête noir through most of the conference as well as in the run-up to it.'

Picking up the pieces of Cancún in the July 2004 Package, WTO members brought a technical fix to a political problem, defining the modalities to be negotiated in agriculture, non-agricultural market access (NAMA) and services but leaving the scope of the cuts for another day. This technocratic approach continued into the 2005 Hong Kong ministerial, as ambitions lowered among member states and a mutual expectation arose that they would pick the low-hanging fruit in order to stave off another collapsed round. An end to export subsidies, an Aid for Trade package, and a commitment toward 97 per cent duty-free, quota-free access for LDCs were all confirmed, while the tougher modalities were set aside for their respective negotiations committees, to be ground out in Geneva over the remainder of the ever-lengthening Doha Round.

Given the stakes set out at the initial Doha ministerial, for a meaningful Doha Round to be concluded it became widely acknowledged that agreement on a triangle of issues – market access and domestic support in agriculture and market access in NAMA – was paramount (Lamy 2006). With regards to sugar, since the majority of government support in the industry was derived through border controls, it was negotiations over the market access corner of this triangle that became of principal importance.[1] These negotiations attracted particular attention from proponents of liberalisation as import tariffs were identified as being ten times more distorting than domestic payments (Anderson *et al.* 2005). In addition, it was argued that it was the use of TRQs and safeguards on commodities like sugar, rather than tariff escalation as often cited, that has prevented upgrading on products such as chocolate.[2] So in effect, as one of the commodities to elude extensive liberalisation in the Uruguay Round, sugar was central to the negotiations on agricultural market access, and as one corner of the triangle of key issues requiring resolution, these negotiations were central to the efficacy of the WTO to regulate the world economy as a whole.

Not only were these negotiations important, they were also of a highly technical nature, by now an intrinsic feature of multilateral trade bargaining. The demands on delegates of developing countries to make sense of the complex proposals and forge beneficial market conditions out of this bureaucratic policy minutia were thus considerably heightened. It was in this respect that the G20, led by Brazil and India, was of such significance. In contrast to previous groups that coalesced around broad collective positions or rose only temporarily in response to specific threats, the G20 coalition became what Narlikar (2003) called a 'smart coalition', inheriting characteristics of each. In appealing to the shared weaknesses of developing countries, whilst proposing workable solutions in negotiations, the group effectively bridged the divide between discipline and flexibility required of a credible bargaining identity. As a result, many commentators ascribed to this new grouping the power to shift the balance of negotiation away from the 'Quad' of the US, EU, Japan and Canada and toward the countries traditionally marginalised by the GATT/WTO process: the long sought after *El Dorado* of developmental trade policy (Bergsten 2004; Battisti *et al.* 2006).

It will be recalled that after the Uruguay Round, the base rates in market access resulting from tariffication remained relatively high across the entire commodity spectrum. In the OECD they ranged from 80 per cent to 404 per cent *ad valorem* equivalent (Hoda and Gulati 2004: 364). Countries were able to prevent erosion of these high tariffs by taking advantage of the 'average' stipulation of the required 36 per cent tariff cut, applying the minimum allowable cut of 15 per cent to sensitive industries and making larger cuts in other industries to drag up the average. To address this asymmetry, the G20 pushed during Doha for a 54 per cent average reduction in tariffs for developed countries and 36 per cent for developing countries to make sure that it became harder to hide shallow cuts within the average (G20 Communiqué 2005). Emphasising the importance of these proposals, Agricultural Chair Crawford Falconer later asserted, much to the disapproval of the Quad, that the 'real zone of engagement would have to be around the G-20' (Bridges Newsletter 2006). The February 2008 modalities text later reflected this position, eschewing the deeper, universal cuts promoted by the US and the Cairns Group, as well as the shallow average cut proposed by the G10 group of importers, to propose a tiered tariff reduction for developed countries ranging between 48 per cent on zero or low tariff goods and 73 per cent on high tariff goods. Within this working text, developing countries were to take on the same schedule but at two thirds of the rate cut (World Trade Organisation 2008b).

As the tiered formula went some way to include all products in a meaningful liberalisation process, by the same token special and differential treatment – a centre piece of the Doha agenda – largely boiled down to creating exceptions to these border commitments. As other options such as providing direct compensation for preference erosion faded during the negotiating process, attention converged around the Special Safeguard Mechanism (SSM) and Special Product (SP) policy instruments as the means by which to provide this treatment to developing countries. The concepts of SSM and SP had their origins in the proposals by the Like Minded Group in 2000 and India in 2001 on a Development/Food Security Box intended to operationalise the provisions for special and differential treatment in agriculture. In essence, these proposals intended to protect strategic products linked to rural, food or livelihood security, and to rehabilitate the Special Safeguard policy in a manner applicable for developing countries.[3] As it was, the SSM was designed to enable short-term tariff hikes to be automatically invoked in response to import surges, and the commodities designated as SPs would be permitted lower tariff reduction schedules over a longer implementation period, as well as exemption from minimum access quota provisions. The main proponents of these SSM and SP instruments evolved into the G33 of import sensitive countries, which was supported by the G20 and thus appeared to present a united development front to the WTO membership.[4]

The trouble with opening the door to exceptions in market access commitments, however, was that a stampede of other countries, keen to have their own favoured products excluded, quickly ensued. Unwilling to see tariff exceptions monopolised by the developing countries, developed countries insisted that measurements of security should not be the sole determinant of exclusion and maintained that trade concerns were also a legitimate reason for protecting some agricultural products from the full exposure of the final agreement. Items covered by these trade concerns were to be referred to as Sensitive Products (SSPs – the excessive amount of acronyms bears witness to the technical nature of negotiating mentioned earlier) and, as laid out in the February 2008 modalities, each developed country would be able to designate between 4 and 6 per cent of tariff lines as 'sensitive' and thereby limit the tariff reduction to just one third of the agreed level. The cost of doing this was that they would have to open an expanded TRQ on those same products and thereby import an increased amount under this split tariff system. Given the fairly steep nature of the tariff reductions associated with the G20 position, sugar industries in the US and in the EU both promoted this option. In the case of the EU, it was all-for-one and one-for-all as the farming and processing unions, and the ACP as well, each put aside their differences over the CMO reform and pushed for sugar to be designated as a Sensitive Product and be included on the preference erosion list (Confederation of European Beet Growers and Comité Européen des Fabricants de Sucre 2007). This would have the benefit of creating a shallower tariff reduction and allowing a longer period over which that reduction had to take place, and in this way protect the remaining preferences of the ACP too.

The issue of market exemptions for developed countries, then, was not simply a North-South debate but one that also pitted certain developing countries against others, in this case the ACP against Brazil, Guatemala and Thailand (Stevens *et al.* 2007). In this instance, the latter group of countries were able to fight against the evasion of steep tariff reductions on sugar via the Tropical Products list. As stated in paragraph 43 of the July 2004 Framework, Tropical Products were to be subject to the 'fullest liberalisation' and have all quantitative restrictions on their trade eliminated, meaning SSP protection would be ineffective and preference erosion not an option (WTO General Council 2004). However, two issues served to muddy the initial inclusion of sugar on this list. First, a contradictory paragraph in the July Framework also acknowledged that preferential trade should be taken into account when assigning product status, providing the opportunity for the EU and ACP to challenge the designation of sugar as a Tropical Product. Second, by using their SSP option anyway but counting tariff lines in different ways, developed countries were also able to manipulate the calculation of the obligatory TRQ and could thus minimise the ultimate amount of required market opening.[5]

The specific debates over sugar liberalisation show how it would be too simple to suggest that the agricultural negotiations during the Doha Round were entirely a question of North versus South. Yet despite this latent tension between developing countries, it is fair to say that a deal in agriculture could no longer be presented as a *fait accompli* by the US and EU as it was in the Blair House Accord of 1992. Indeed, the politico-legal machinations of the trade negotiations committees have been increasingly animated, though far from controlled, by the positions of the G20 (Hepburn, interview 2008). As Pascal Lamy, Director-General of the WTO has commented:

> The G20 has encouraged a wider coalition of developing countries to act together within the trading system...The WTO is one of the few places where the geographical and economic changes of the recent past are reflected in changes in the representation around the table (Beattie 2007).

This may be so, but two notes of caution need to be sounded. First, to the extent that Doha has had a Development Agenda, it is one that has attempted to integrate the 'one size *doesn't* fit all' special and differential perspective with the Most Favoured Nation principle of the multilateral trading system. What the G20 offered was a platform where conflicting interests over the extent of this differential treatment could be aggregated and a middle ground among its poles actively sought (Elsig 2006: 28). In short, it did not resolve the tension of who should make what reduction commitments, so much as provided a politically viable route through the negotiations of them (Indian WTO delegate, interview 2008). Second, an active G20 was no guarantor of a 'pro-development' outcome. As Rorden Wilkinson has argued, the emergence of the G20 at Cancún needs to be put in its proper historical and institutional context; as a coalition confronting a system laden with decades of asymmetric trade regulation and centuries of uneven economic growth both skewed in favour of developed countries. When framed in these terms, the emergence of the G20 appears merely as 'a perception of adjustment set against the creation of an environment in which the further extension of the asymmetry of opportunity [is] likely' (Wilkinson 2006: 149). It is to this critique that we now turn.

Perpetuation of asymmetry between sectors

In their account of decision-making in the WTO, Fatama Jawara and Aileen Kwa (2004) suggest that the priorities of the developing countries are held back because flexibilities in the negotiation process and behind the scenes bullying enable developed countries to play 'power politics' in the realist sense and make the organisation the agent of their interests. As such, the G20 countries are seen as a vital counterweight, given that, short of institutional reform, the only hope for developing countries to resist such pressure is to band together and use their collective strength to stand up to the manoeuvrings of the Quad. What led Wilkinson to downplay this rectification of power imbalance and argue that the G20 provides only a perception of adjustment is the structural asymmetry institutionalised in the WTO. That is to say that the rules of the WTO, both formal and informal, have largely reflected the interests of those countries which designed the organisation, and that, as time has passed, those rules have solidified, systematically favouring those same countries despite the piecemeal changes sought by periodic challengers such as the G20.

In terms of agricultural policies, this analysis is borne out by the bargaining dynamics evident over subsidies and tariffs. When the sector was brought into the purview of the GATT after the accession of many developing countries, it did so in accordance with the extensive subsidy programmes of the EU and US. Most developing countries entered the Uruguay Round with minimal agricultural subsidies, as any state support programmes they may have had for agriculture were in the midst of being rolled back by debt and adjustment conditionalities, giving them little to concede on this front. As Tony Weis (2007a: 135) has written:

> The USA and EU argued that they were the ones making the main concessions, pointing especially to their subsidies disciplines, while accusing developing countries of being 'free riders' for getting the competitive benefits of this new discipline while making relatively lighter concessions. So while slower tariff reduction schedules and high tariff ceilings were permitted in the original Agreement on Agriculture it was clear that these would be targeted at future ministerials, with developing countries holding few other bargaining chips, especially after the bilateral policy changes wrought by structural adjustment.

With it being proclaimed the Doha *Development* Round, many countries and commentators have clamoured for the developed states to offer relatively greater concessions in agriculture in an attempt to level the uneven playing field inherited from the Uruguay Round. This discourse about the uneven playing field has conferred a certain moral authority on developing countries – the G20 especially – that the developed countries have found publicly difficult to oppose (Australian WTO delegate, interview 2008). What they have been able to oppose, though, is the abrogation of reciprocity by developing countries when it comes to NAMA and services.

Again and again, the EU and the US in particular have spoken of 'no movement', 'no give and take', and 'no appreciation of the bargaining process' in the context of wider negotiations (Schwab 2006; Mandelson 2007). This is the major dimension of asymmetry about which Wilkinson writes: the fact that opportunities for developing countries to attenuate asymmetries in agriculture are bound with, and made contingent upon, the expansion of multilateral regulation in other areas of trade – the benefits of which are largely captured by the developed countries.

Indefinite postponement of level playing fields within sectors

The brief section above stressed how developing countries have generally been unable to redress the asymmetry in trade regulation and in effect 'gain a round for free' as reforms in the economic sectors of interest to developing countries (agriculture, textiles and other manufacturers) have been structurally linked to incorporation of reforms of interest to developed countries. Recognising this asymmetry, scholars such as S. Javed Maswood (2006: 50) have proposed that:

> The task for developing countries is not to engineer a step-function change in international economic regimes but to make existing liberal regimes more conducive to their developmental interests by removing the many pockets of illiberal practices and securing recognition for special and differential treatment.

The problem with this argument – that developing countries should work through the structures of the WTO to progressively erode existing trade barriers and level the playing field – is that it over-plays the collective ability of developing countries to deliver a pro-development text. Specifically in agriculture, it fails to acknowledge the inherent uncertainties in imposing market order on the agricultural economy that loom over negotiators at the WTO and the persistent renewal of government involvement in farm production. Together, these unknown outcomes thwart the possibility of focused collective action, even in an area like agriculture where many pockets of illiberal practices still persist, and thereby prevent developing countries from gradually shaping the WTO into an institution that could better facilitate their interests.

   In imposing market order on agricultural trade, a primary uncertainty to fall over negotiations is the uncertain value of concessions. Choosing the right path to liberalisation is confounded by the fact that delegates and their national governments cannot envisage exactly how much policies will be worth to other states during negotiations and to their own economy after agreement. For developing countries trying to make the WTO more conducive to their interests, this poses the problem of identifying the 'optimal' route by which to secure welfare gains. Drawing on Robert Wolfe's distinction to explain this problem in more detail, we can set up an heuristic opposition between a negotiating dynamic based on incremental time (corresponding to the efficient view of institutions) and one based on conjunctural time (corresponding to the inefficient view). As Wolfe (2004: 578) puts it:

> In incremental time, analysts think we know what is at stake, whereas conjunctural time is marked by uncertainty about cause and effect relationships... [Thinking in conjunctural time] it is hard, even impossible, for negotiators to know where they are going before they start in this huge diffuse process, one where the goal is never explicit and the means are hard to see.

The ontological premise here is that negotiations are an intersubjective social process in which the means are hard to see because the values of bargaining chips are codified within this process and made mutable over time. Put another way, an inalienable divorce exists between the 'real' economic value of a bargaining chip as a policy tool and its 'use' value as a political concession by virtue of who holds the chip and the context in which it is relinquished. Thus delegates are continually confronted with the complex task of asking 'how much is a tariff cut worth as a domestic subsidy reduction, or an expanded SPs allowance, or a change to rules of origin status?' Economic studies can offer indications of trade flows given specific changes in instruments, but, as the quantity of concessions increases, expected outcomes become too complex to model with confidence and parity impossible to find. This uncertainty is exacerbated by the unknown efficacy of given policies. For example, the bargaining over the SSM, which proved so contentious in the Doha Round, sprang from the fact that it is extremely hard to adjudicate between import surges caused by short-term price depressions and those caused by structural price decline or demand-side changes (International Centre for Trade and Sustainable Development 2005). If the legitimacy of the SSM remained prone to uncertainty, how would it be possible to value its existence?

Under such circumstances, negotiators have learnt to proceed as if 'crossing the river by feeling the stones', learning from each other rather than pursuing exogenously given interests and, over time, slowly constituting the elements out of which a bargain can be constructed (Wolfe

2004: 578). The importance of this for our argument is that, even given an improved negotiating weight of developing countries in the WTO, there is no pre-defined optimal route on which they could embark to make the fullest use of this power. In the negotiating forum, decisions are essentially removed from economic theory as political 'feel' usurps welfare gains in assessing the best course of action, posing an intractable barrier to the unambiguous and instantaneous realisation of a pro-poor round.

Nevertheless, it could still be claimed that, given sufficient time and ambition, agricultural liberalisation will still be achieved as WTO member states slowly relinquish their price and income support policies over time. Moving to our second critique, we respond by arguing that this belief that a sparse and level playing field will ultimately come into being ignores the persistent renewal of government involvement in agriculture as instruments evolve and new industries arise. Theoretically, this assessment is based on our prior reading of the state-market condominium in which private economic activity is seen as inescapably shot through with public authority. Empirically, we can point to the emergence of new measures such as ethanol tariffs and geographical indicators, the protracted survival of supposed temporary instruments such as those contained within the Blue Box, and the range of policies permitted under the Green Box, which contrary to their 'decoupled' designation, are in fact trade distorting (Hennessy and Thorne 2005; Blandford and Josling 2007; UNCTAD 2007). The argument being made is that the WTO can only bring about a level playing field if everyone agrees on what this is, and, quite clearly, different political visions exist about how support should be categorised within the organisation's framework.

It should be stressed that this assessment does not suppose a conspiracy on the part of developed countries to maintain competitive advantage – many developing countries use permissible and/or un-notified state supports also – but more a recognition that it is too simple to consider agricultural negotiations as progressively exhausting interference as governments relinquish their bargaining chips over time. This suggests that there is no perfect market at which to aim, no *El Dorado*, that would foreclose public authority from agricultural production and enable those farmers in weaker and poorer states to compete more favourably with those in the developed world. The danger in ignoring this at the policy-making level is that as the form of state-market authority morphs over time, predicted gains will wax and wane, leaving negotiators to reminisce on what they once thought they had secured in negotiations, the Uruguay Round being the obvious example (Thai WTO delegate, interview 2008). In sum, within the realm of the WTO, the problem for developing countries as a whole cannot be reckoned as a lack of ambition. Rather, the problem is that visions of a successful round typically consider agricultural trade from the ideal and impossible vantage point of totally liberalised world economy. In holding out this false promise of free markets, they therefore provide a misleading imperative animating negotiation politics.

Boom time in Brazil: the 21st century gold rush

One response to these two sceptical notes on progressive liberalisation could be to say that, while the ideal may not be attained, by approximating it significant gains will still be yielded. To return to our metaphor of *El Dorado*, while the search may be futile, the journey may still bear reward. This much will not be denied here. Liberalisation can be expected to create significant, static economic gains for some countries as production is reallocated to where it can be undertaken at lower (monetary) cost. What will be challenged, though, is the argument that this economic gain can be unequivocally equated with development; something that has been assumed throughout the previous discussion of how developing countries can prosper through the WTO.

It is generally acknowledged that, to the extent export gains result from liberalisation in agriculture, these will be captured by the big trading nations of the Cairns Group at the expense of the developed countries reliant upon tariff protection and those developing countries which are simply higher cost producers (Bouët *et al.* 2005). The expected result is that global supply becomes less diverse and a handful of countries begin to dominate certain commodity markets. The interesting thing about sugar in this respect is that since the inauguration of the WTO, despite the lack of significant liberalisation, these intended effects have come about regardless. As UNCTAD (2007: 185) have noted, since 1995, while the structure of the world sugar market on the import side has remained fairly constant at around 0.115 – with 1 representing a perfect monopoly and 0 representing an equal distribution of market share – on the export side there has been significant structural change. In 1995, the concentration index stood at 0.197 but by 2005 it had grown to 0.224, essentially due to expanding Brazilian exports. As Table 8.1 reveals, these exports increased over 500 per cent during the period in question and in this way Brazil provides a suitable 'laboratory' in which to assess development gains *ex post* liberalisation. In other words, if the link

Table 8.1 International Net Sugar Trade, 1994–2005

Largest Exporters, MT			Largest Importers, MT		
1994	2000	2005	1994	2000	2005
Australia 4.52	Brazil 6.50	Brazil 18.40	India 2.63	Russia 5.23	Russia 3.57
Brazil 3.60	Thailand 4.34	EU 4.24	Russia 1.96	Japan 1.61	USA 2.07
EU 3.26	EU 4.30	Australia 4.24	Japan 1.70	Indonesia 1.56	Indonesia 2.00
Cuba 3.19	Australia 3.77	Thailand 3.31	China 1.24	Korea 1.46	Algeria 1.92
Thailand 2.72	Cuba 3.42	Guatemala 1.57	USA 1.13	USA 1.41	Japan 1.35

Source: International Sugar Organisation (2006) *Statistical Bulletin*, 65: 12, p. iii.

between a G20-inspired agriculture text and a pro-development outcome can be severed *even in a country assumed to be a prime beneficiary of such liberalisation*, then the validity of the project must be brought into question.

As noted above, the dominance of Brazil on the world market has come about not because of import liberalisation but rather because of expanding demand for raw sugar by refineries in the Middle East and falling output from the traditional heavyweight exporter, Cuba (and since 2007, the EU too). Furthermore, not only did the volume of exported sugar from Brazil increase but so did its value. Responding to shortages brought on by rising demand for sugar in Asia and crop failure in Thailand and Australia, world sugar prices were bid up sharply during 2005. Another crucial component of this price rise was the increasing diversion of cane into the domestic ethanol market in Brazil, for had this cane been processed into sugar and exported into the world sugar market, it would have significantly dampened prices. While the production of Brazilian ethanol for export arguably received the most press coverage, it was in fact the domestic market, triggered by the introduction of 'flex-fuel' cars in the mid-2000s that can run both ethanol and petroleum, which has driven demand. In fact, so rapid has this sales rise been that the vast majority of new sugar cane now planted is destined for the ethanol market.[6] So in sum, because of supply gaps in sugar and expanding demand in ethanol, the Brazilian sugar cane industry was able to increase production without placing significant amounts of downward pressure on prices. Figure 8.1 shows

Figure 8.1   World Market Price of Sugar, 1945–2008

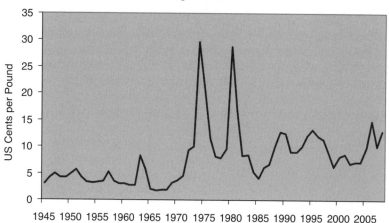

Source: F. O. Lichts *International Sugar and Sweetener Report*. Various years.

the temporary peak in prices that accompanied this boom and its comparability to the two large price spikes in 1974 and 1982 experienced during the first food crisis.

The attention drawn to the previous food crisis is apposite for both sets of spikes took place in the context of price rises across the commodity spectrum as whole. From the mid-2000s onward, sugar, corn, cereals, soybeans, dairy products, meat, and edible oils all jumped in price, promoting incendiary debate about a second global food crisis as the cost of foodstuffs rose beyond the means of many of the world's poorest and most hungry people. Consequently, a U-turn took place in much development commentary, from once suggesting that low agricultural prices were the cause of poverty to now opining that high prices are the problem (Sachs 2008).

While most academic debate has focused on what caused commodity prices to rise, what we focus on here is the impact of these rising prices on development, specifically, the impacts of rising prices in sugar. First, without dismissing the fact that prices in this commodity doubled from 2004 to 2006, it is important to acknowledge that adjusted for inflation, the levels of these prices are considerably lower than those witnessed during the first commodity crisis, and, indeed, lower than those experienced in the mid-1990s. Second, we maintain that it is reduced access to staple crops that is the principal reason for hunger and malnutrition; to the extent that sugar is felt to be a necessity, this is typically the case for people on higher incomes, who are less likely to be affected by rising food costs. And third, it is worth noting that the *indirect* impact of sugar cane production on these staples has also been minimal. Ethanol production from sugar has not taken place at the expense of staple crops (as it has in the US) as Brazilian cane planting has mainly moved into degraded pasture areas occupied by cattle ranchers and, to the extent it has replaced land occupied by soybean, maize and orange growers, the total amount of land dedicated to these crops has grown overall, suggesting that total agricultural production volumes have not been 'squeezed' downward (Nassar *et al.* 2008: 91). Taking these arguments on board, Brazil's President Lula has thus suggested that it was the distribution of food rather than the amount produced that lay at the heart of the food crisis, arguing that 'nobody stops eating because of a shortage of food, people stop eating due to a lack of income' (Mander 2007).

The defence of biofuel production by Lula deserves close attention, for it should not be seen merely as an exercise in development theory but also as a campaign in support of the Brazilian ethanol industry; a campaign indicative of the close relationship that successive governments in the country have had with sugar cane. As in our previous examples of Australia and Thailand, Brazil has obtained, and to an extent retains, its position as a globally competitive sugar producer and exporter through detailed government support. Heavy-handed government intervention was an industry trademark for many years. As mentioned in Chapter 5, production quotas and price controls were all used to govern sugar production – archetypal national regime policies – before fiscal deficits triggered by the 1970s commodity crisis encouraged the state to launch its Proálcool ethanol programme in 1975 to reduce its oil bill. Direct intervention was finally phased out in the early 1990s when the government's Sugar and Alcohol Institute closed and ethanol and petrol prices were freed from state control, though it has maintained its influence through demand-side regulation on ethanol consumption and the provision of subsidised credit.[7] In November 2008, for example, Brazil's Monetary Council asked banks to increase the amount of cheap finance they lent to farmers by $2.6 billion and also submitted requests to the Brazilian Development Bank to create extra credit lines for capital investment (F. O. Lichts 2008c).

In the last decade, the opening of new markets in ethanol has replaced deregulation as the priority of the Brazilian government, with Lula promoting the trade and technology of the industry at every opportunity (Lula 2006). Of particular note in this respect is the Western Hemisphere Energy Compact, signed by Lula and US President George W. Bush in

2008 to coordinate biofuels production, research and infrastructure throughout the region. This pact seeks to wed energy security to economic growth and cement the position of the two countries as the leaders of ethanol and biodiesel providers. Already the US and Brazil have agreed to speed research into 'second generation' cellulosic ethanol and to invest $58 million to create regional and commercial groups to coordinate biofuel policy (Reuters 2008a). In addition – and in contrast to the initial hostility of the company toward rival fuels – Petrobrás, the state-controlled oil company, has secured long-term export markets for Brazilian ethanol, agreeing with Japan's state oil company in 2005 to export 3.5 billion litres per year by 2011 to Japan.

While the state has acted as guarantor and moderator to the sugar/ethanol industry, it is the private sector that is realising its potential. At present the sugar/ethanol industry in Brazil is largely fragmented, with around 350 mills processing cane. However, it is increasingly possible to discern just a few corporations that are coming to control greater numbers of these mills. Following from the last wave of consolidation, which occurred in the 1990s after deregulation forced many smaller mills to subsume themselves within larger entities to protect against price uncertainty, between 2000 and 2005 37 mergers and acquisitions took place within the sugar/ethanol industry (Grain 2007: 17). Chief among these controlling corporations are the recently privatised state-cooperative Copersucar, which groups 33 mills together, Cosan, which groups 18, and Crystalsev, which groups nine. Though they may not yet dominate the market, such is the size of Brazilian production that they constitute huge agro-industrial operations nonetheless. In the 2006/07 harvest for example, Copersucar posted revenues of $2.3 billion and Cosan $2.1 billion (Copersucar 2007; Cosan 2007). Tied to the traditional 'sugar families' of Brazil, these companies have also played their part in nurturing the close relationship the industry has with government. According to Brazil's Superior Electoral Court, the Ometto portfolio of companies, which includes Cosan, contributed $269,000 to Lula's 2006 re-election campaign, and the Biagi family, which owns the majority of Crystalsev, contributed $135,000. In addition, Maurílio Biagi is also a member of Lula's Council for Economic and Social Development and Rubens Ometto is said to frequently accompany Lula on his state visits abroad.

Having mapped out the elite interests at work in the Brazilian cane industry, we now turn to the manner in which they have shaped its recent trajectory. Due to the volumes and values of sugar and ethanol being traded and a number of Initial Public Offerings on the stock exchange, during the mid-2000s the leading Brazilian corporations found themselves awash with capital.[8] This has been further augmented by the huge amounts of foreign investment pouring into the integrated mill-refineries, in expectation of them producing greater amounts of ethanol and generating greater amounts of bioelectricity to sell back to the national grid by recycling the 'bagasse' left over from cane crushing. In short, we can say that Brazil has experienced its very own 'gold rush in green oil'.

Given that raw cane for ethanol cannot be bought in the open market but must be transported from nearby fields, and because of the political power held by traditional elites, for the overseas investors looking to take part in this 21st century gold rush, partnership with existing plantation owners has been a necessary conduit for their capital. Investment funds established by banks like Credit Suisse and Société Générale, oil companies like BP, agro-industrial corporations like Cargill, Tate & Lyle and Tereos, and commodity traders like Czarnikow, ED&F Man, Global Foods, Louis Dreyfus and Sucden have all sought a foothold in Brazilian cane. The big domestic producers have in fact welcomed this 'prospecting', seeing the injection of foreign capital as the means to modernise the industry and consolidate their position at its epicentre. The Chief Commercial Officer of Cosan, for instance, has commented that: 'We have 350 players in Brazil. It would be better to have 20 of those companies expanding in the market because the discipline of those guys is so much better' (Ethanol Statistics 2008a). Although undermined by the high cost of borrowing associated with the global financial crisis, as of November 2008, and accounting for inward as well as foreign direct investment, 92 new plants were expected to come on stream during 2009–2010 (Szwarc 2008). What we are witnessing is thus the conglomeration and concentration of the Brazilian industry, and, reading between the lines of the remarks of the Cosan representative, a trend which is seen as expedient in removing factionalism in the industry and embedding a more coherent coalition of like-minded producers.

For sure, the relationship between these international fractions of capital has not been entirely concordant. Many potential investments have fallen through as Brazilian millers and landowners have quoted exorbitant selling prices, lacked reliable accounts or been plagued by tax disputes or debt. Even the partnerships that have been completed – Cargill investing in Crystalsev, and Tereos and the Kuok Group in Cosan – have constituted double-edged swords for the traditional sugar families. To avoid hostile takeover pressure mounting following its stock market floatation, for example, Cosan had to undergo a complex restructuring to keep its founder at the helm. Indeed, one stock market analyst cautioned that, 'if he [Rubens Ometto and by implication his family] gave up voting control, boom! They would get taken out' (Regalado and Fan 2007). But, despite the differing traditions that are exposed by the meeting of national capitals and management techniques (and the board room bravado that exists in any environment where mergers and acquisitions are rife), the gold rush has continued apace, bearing dramatic consequences for the contemporary patterns of ownership and accumulation in sugar. To give some context to this rush, consider that in August 2007, the sugar consultant DATAGRO reported that overseas groups and investors had more than doubled their control of cane crushed in Brazil, taking the total to 12 per cent of the harvest or 51mt – an amount nearly *twice as big as the entire US cane crop* (Ethanol Statistics 2008b). This must surely constitute the biggest foreign investment in sugar since the colonial era in the Caribbean and suggests a seismic shift in the source of profits for the sugar producers in the developed world that can only further disrupt the national incarnation of state regulation in trade and production – of which more in the concluding chapter.

Brazilian sugar cane: a model of bifurcated development

The growth of the Brazilian sugar/ethanol industry, then, has been truly remarkable. By 2006 it already contributed 2 per cent to national gross domestic product, 17 per cent of agricultural output, and 21 per cent of total agricultural exports (Valdes 2007: 31). On the face of it, our development 'test case' of what would happen under liberalisation appears an unqualified success: as production has gravitated to the most cost effective supplier, the industry in question has acted as an engine to economic growth. Following our research questions and critical intent laid out in the theory chapters, what is needed now is to delve more deeply into these strategies of accumulation prevailing in the industry and interrogate the specific practices on which low-cost production has been dependent – in other words, question the overlap between growth and development. The findings present a mixed picture. Growth in sugar and ethanol production has not translated into an unequivocal boon for development, not least because of its capital intensity and its complex relationship to land and labour.

We begin by noting that for the labour-intensive part of the workforce, physical and structural exploitation has remained prevalent. Most notably, incidences of what the Brazilian Labour and Employment Ministry refers to as contemporary 'slave labour' have been all too common, with over 2,000 cane cutters being freed from forced labour during 2007 alone (Reuters 2008c). This phenomenon has been made possible by the geographic isolation of many production sites and the inflation by overseers of costs incurred by migrant workers, which as we saw in India in the last chapter, are then frequently trapped into working off their indebtedness. The government's 'anti-slavery' programme, instituted largely in response to decades of activism by civil society groups such as the Comissão Pastoral da Terra (the Pastoral Land Commission) has focused increasingly on responding to such abuses in the sugar cane sector, and, by stripping offending companies of access to subsidised credit, has made significant strides in reducing instances of modern slavery. But while the 'ethanol slaves' have dominated the headlines, systematic and quotidian abuse remains endemic. Most notably, alongside the dangerous working conditions and inadequate housing facilities faced by cane cutters, the output expected of them has become increasingly demanding. This is linked to the competition that labourers now face from mechanisation and the piece-rate system of pay that ties the amount they earn to the amount they cut. While there is a minimum wage paid regardless of output, it tends to constitute a small proportion of the final pay packet with the majority still determined by the amount of cane cut (Alves 2008). Thus the average tonnage of cane cut per day in the São Paulo region has doubled from 5–6 tonnes in the 1980s to 10–12 tonnes today; a physical feat that requires around 12,000 strikes of a machete to achieve (Noronha *et al.* 2006: 14).

Despite the arduous nature of the job, if cane cutters are able to match the demands asked of them, they are able to earn a relatively good wage. In the late 1990s for example workers in sugar cane production in São Paulo were receiving total monthly wages that were on average 80 per cent higher than those in other agricultural jobs, 50 per cent higher than those in the service sector, and 40 per cent higher than those in the industrial sector (Smeets *et al.* 2006: 60). This is the major source of attraction for the unemployed and unskilled migrants from the Northeast and Minas Gerais who come in their tens of thousands to work in Brazil's sugar cane heartland in the Centre-South region. Arguably, though, the biggest danger facing these rural workers is not exhaustion or debt but mass redundancy. One of the characteristic facets of the new mode of accumulation in the industry has been the mechanisation of harvesting, which has been encouraged by two dynamics. First, it is simply more cost effective to mechanise as harvesters are estimated to reduce employment expenditure by half, and where once the barrier of high capital outlay stood in the way, now the ready finance available in the industry makes such investments manageable (Noronha *et al.* 2006: 15). Second, manual labour has become more impractical because of changing regulation. When cutting cane by hand, to make the stalks weaker and to rid the area of snakes, the fields are usually burned beforehand. Responding to environmental and health concerns (field burnings are closely linked to local respiratory problems), the Brazilian government has begun to phase this out. In São Paulo, cane burning has gradually decreased from 82 per cent of the harvested area in 1997 to 63 per cent in 2004, and the harvesting done by machine has risen accordingly (Smeets *et al.* 2006: 48). It is worth bearing in mind that the industry has offset this falling labour demand per hectare *to a degree* simply by farming more hectares. However, it has not been enough to tip the scales. By way of illustration, between 1993 and 2003, the area of cane harvested grew from 3.4 million hectares to 4.6 million hectares, while employment on the farm fell from 617,000 to 449,000 (Schmitz *et al.* 2002: 125; Smeets *et al.* 2006: 57). While we do not expect manual cane cutting to entirely disappear in the immediate future – at the very least, labour will serve as the low-risk option for harvest expansion and will also continue to work the hillier areas on which cane is still grown – this general trend is expected to continue. According to figures produced by the Brazilian sugar cane industry association UNICA, between 2010 and 2021 around 114,000 net jobs are expected to be lost in São Paulo alone (Rede Social 2008: 10).

To recap then, the demand for labour within the sugar industry has been steadily scaled back as the shift to capital-intensive production maps on to an existing distribution of holdings skewed in favour of the large and less-labour intensive farms (*latifundio*). Yet the transformation of the Brazilian sugar/ethanol industry cannot be considered unequivocally detrimental for labour. Most notably, while there may be fewer jobs in the field (and fewer overall), the jobs that do remain are more formal, more safe, and, specifically for those in the factory, increasingly well paid (Smeets *et al.* 2006: 57). This change in employment conditions is linked to the knowledge needed to run a modern sugar/ethanol industry and the tight skilled labour markets with which it is confronted. As a result, the industry has had to offer greater incentives to attract and retain employees within the industry. The dynamic effect of this has been that the share of skilled workers in the sugar growing and processing sectors has grown rapidly relative to the rest of the economy, with local universities now even running MBA classes specifically targeted at the industry. Consequently it is the more educated workers that can be expected to capture the biggest percentage of wage increases as the factory owners and independent growers try and attract the human capital necessary to enhance the rate of return on their physical capital. This trend also has the effect of reinforcing racial and gender divisions within the country, as those who possess such qualifications tend to be white, urban males (Krivonos and Olarreaga 2006: 8).

Furthermore, these intellectual and technical demands within the industry are expected to grow as the locus of profit-making strategy increasingly centres on scientific advances and their attendant market creation. Such advances include the breeding of more resilient and ethanol-specific genetically modified variants of cane, the transformation of 'waste' plant matter into cellulosic ethanol, and the development of biodiesel and 'green' plastics from cane-derived ethylene.[9] Feeding back into the state-market relationship mapped out earlier on, we note how this shift has also buttressed the enthusiasm of Brazilian state elites for the sugar/ethanol industry as it is manifest in the Centre-South. No longer are these farms and factories seen merely as a foreign exchange earner or a means to generate rural employment but are now viewed as the vanguard of the country's knowledge economy. Indeed *The Economist* (2005) has gone as far to say that that the sugar-ethanol industry will be a foundation of growth in Brazil just as the wood pulp industry was for Nokia in Finland. In turn, industry owners have been quick to sense the opportunities linked to this material-discursive transformation and have begun to promote the possibilities of patent exports alongside physical commodity exports. In the context of cheap currency for example, Crystalsev shareholder Maurilio Biagi Filho argued that, 'at the current rate of exchange, Brazil should be exporting everything, even ideas' (Johnson 2001).

Bringing the landless back in

Thus far the analysis of poverty reduction and inequality has taken place in the context of the industry itself, investigating how wealth is generated and shared within the sugar/ethanol worker-owner hierarchy. This is a common enough starting point for an account of the development effects of agro-industrial growth, but what is often overlooked, particularly in economic projections, is the effect that growth in the industry has on the people on the margins of production – peasants. Peasants are understood here as those rural dwellers who farm for subsistence or local markets and often do so under informal economic conditions. To say they are on the margins of production is thus to give both a geographical and economic description of their relationship to cane. They reside on the fringes around current cultivation, in the lands into which sugar seeks to spread, and, in cases where land is appropriated, receive dwindling opportunities to re-enter the land as waged employees or service providers.

The issue of land reform in Brazil has a long and contested history that we do not have time to explore in full detail here, suffice to say that opportunities for peasants to gain legal access to existing land has been somewhat limited under the Brazilian agrarian reform programme. This programme has facilitated the sale only of small- and medium-sized farms either under-utilised or abandoned, thereby leaving the redistribution of the *latifundios* to one side; a limitation which has been exacerbated by the expansion of sugar cane planting (Borras Jr 2003). Average prices of cane land in São Paulo state have more than doubled from $1,152 per hectare in 2003 to $2,705 per hectare in 2008, with some of the prime sites actually quadrupling in value (AgraFNP 2008: 14). Thus peasants who might have been able to farm this land profitably are effectively priced out the market. The higher prices offered for land has also encouraged the owners of suspect land deeds to use physical violence against protestors and/or fraud to reassert their right to the land and its attendant value. Further, once expansion has been secured, indigenous people have often been confined by the spreading estates into smaller territories, resulting in eruptions of internal violence as happened amongst the Guaraní people in the Mato Grosso do Sul state (Osava 2008).

It is in this environment that the Movimento dos Trabalhadores Rurais Sem Terra (MST) – translated as the Landless Rural Workers Movement – has attempted to redress the unequal access to land. The organisation's history is closely bound with sugar cane. It was established in the mid-1980s and traces its ideological roots back to the *quilombos* communities of runaway slaves from sugar mills and the Peasant League societies that sprang from the waged sugar cane workers in Northeast Brazil (Wolford 2003: 505). More recently, it has been in the face of expansion by Brazilian agro-industry, and sugar cane and soy in particular, that MST has become increasingly radical, switching its target from the occupation of unproductive land to the occupation of commercial cropland (Branford and Rocha 2002: 10). By way of example, in 1999 more than 5,000 MST families took over 41 sugar plantations in the Pernambuco state, and, in 2007, MST invaded the Cevasa ethanol mill in São Paulo (owned in part by Cargill) to disrupt production and a month later invaded 6,000 hectares of land, also in São Paulo, torching 30 tonnes of unplanted sugar cane in the process (Reuters 2007b).

This 'democratisation by appropriation' approach of the MST has tested its relations with both state elites and rural waged labour, two sets of agents with which it has sought to work to effect change. In respect to the former, MST has presented itself to the rural populace as an effective counsellor to a corruptible and predatory state. The ambition of the movement has not been to replace the state, but rather to work through it, cajoling its leaders into making the rule of law compatible with greater territorial autonomy (Wolford 2003: 517). Geraldo Fontes (2004) an MST coordinator, has suggested how this is possible:

> When we occupy *latifundio*, large landholding, it is not because we are against Lula's government. We are occupying to help Lula's government to apply what the constitution says in order to change this model, which they are using now.

The constitution to which Fontes refers is the 1988 ruling on agrarian reform, which affirms that only 'rural property that is not performing its social function' should be expropriated. To reconcile this stipulation with the occupation of working farms, MST (2006) have argued that the function of land is to provide jobs and improve living standards, something the *latifundios* prevent and which can only be provided through the democratisation of property and the sharing of natural resources. When MST uses the concept 'jobs', it does so with a particular type of job in mind, namely, those linked to smallholder production and food sovereignty, emphasising choice over the way in which food is produced and traded and incorporating such issues as land rights, biodiversity and seed-saving. In binding itself to this notion of agrarian citizenship, MST has thus risked antagonism with those non-farming rural workers who depend on the *latifundios* for waged jobs. To overcome this, the concept of *Sem Terra* (landlessness) has been used to make a connection between the two social groups based not on modes of production but on similar experiences of poverty and exploitation (Fanelli and Sarzynski 2003: 334). So while the growth of the sugar industry has been met by resistance, it has been a resistance dependent on the marginalisation of certain voices and the willed construction of a unified alternative to the expansion of agro-industry.

For its part, the government has defended its record on creating access to land but noted as well that the rising labour productivity on the *latifundio* has lowered the cost of food domestically and so reduced the very need for land reform (Downie 2008). As Guilherme Cassel, the Minister of Agrarian Development, has reasoned:

> In Brazil we have two models: agribusiness, based on large exten-sions of land and monoculture farming, and the family farm model, based on land reform settlements, crop diversification and protec-tion of the environment. [Lula has] supported both models, and both were very effective (Frayssinet 2007).

Yet to the extent that the family farm model has been supported, it has been by resettling landless farmers away from the borders of agro-industry and into the Amazonian region: 65 per cent of new settle-ments have taken place here according to the MST (Frayssinet 2007). Further, while the supply of food in Brazil has indeed been augmented, it has not necessarily resulted in more being available for the rural poor, who lack the resources to acquire it. In fact, the hungry in Brazil have become increasingly dependent on state programmes such as the 'Family Fund', which transfers direct cash payments to families as a reward for attending school or medical clinics, and the national school meals project, which constitutes the second main source of food for poor families. Chronic malnutrition in children nearly halved from 1996 to 2006 as a result of these programmes but 20 per cent (2.3 million) of the recipients of the Family Fund hand-outs still went without food once every three days (Osava 2008). With this in mind, the argument made by Lula that 'lack of income not biofuels causes hunger' takes on a depressing irony. Biofuels should be linked to hunger, but not because the land used to produce cane ethanol could otherwise have supplied cash crops for needy mouths, but because the way they have been produced – indeed, the way most export commod-ities are produced in Brazil – has denied people in Lula's own country the land or wage labour to feed themselves. As Fred Magdoff (2004) has argued, though the conditions of the countryside may be harsh, having land on which to grow food does at least provide a degree of protection against hunger.

In sum, to equate the vanguard rural economy with a pro-poor form of development in Brazil, the state must begin to harness this growth to rectify the huge inequalities that mark its society. Yet its ability to redistribute through growth in sugar/ethanol production is constrained on two fronts. First, the model of growth is one that discounts the poor from employment and channels revenues to his-torically wealthy landowner-industrialists, thereby impeding a natural dispersal of income. Second, it is evident that the institutional make-up of the state itself is such that it lacks the ability to challenge and change this relationship. Brazil is the only country in the world with two agricultural ministries, but the one that deals with agrarian reform is notably weaker than the one that deals with agricultural trade and commerce (Reis 1998; Welch 2006). The model of development evident in Brazil's sugar cane industry is one that is bifurcating the beneficiaries of its boom.

Conclusion

Despite the small share of agriculture as a proportion of global GDP, the sector continues to assume a status of supreme significance in multilateral trade negotiations. As pointed out in this chapter, a central debate animating this status has been the entitlement of developing countries to adhere to different rules in order to bring about a historical corrective to erstwhile patterns of international trade. In an environment where this tension remains unresolved (and arguably will remain so), the prevailing norm has been to carry on as normal, or, as one of the key guiding metaphors of the WTO has it, 'keep riding the bicycle'. This suggests that, despite any wobbles, states have to keep riding and strive to liberalise their economies else fall off and descend into protectionism and recession. The problem we have raised in this chapter is that states are not fully cognisant of *where they are riding to*. If the path that WTO member states have found themselves negotiating along is paved with trouble, or even just bordered by doubt, then the journey needs to be rethought. Nevertheless, many statesmen, commentators and NGOs continue to assume that as long as developing countries can evade political 'arm twisting' in the WTO, then a regulatory environment can be built that will stimulate development in these parts of the world (Khor 2002; Panagariya 2002a; Oxfam 2005).

This chapter has sounded three sceptical notes on this claim. First, there is no known route through the WTO negotiating process out of which a 'sure fire' pro-developing country text could emerge, given both the differences between developing countries, notably on Tropical Products like sugar, and the future uncertainties looming over intended outcomes. Second, the notion that developing countries will benefit some time in the future as playing fields are successively levelled downward ignores the constant renewal of state-support in agriculture, as governments find loopholes in, create policies compatible with, or exclude commodities from, WTO regulation. Third, to approve unhesitatingly a regulatory environment inspired by developing countries is to conflate the choices of those countries in greatest need of development with development itself. As the case of Brazil showed, rural development has bifurcated under the export-led agricultural model; a model that the country's elites wish to push even further through multilateral liberalisation. The conclusion to draw from all of this is that while the neoliberal rules entrenched in the WTO gain increasing momentum, the logic that unfailingly links the emergence of these to development contains a chunk of ideological faith and host of unquestioned assumptions. While not denying the probability that *some* fractions of capital and labour in *some* developing countries will benefit from the ongoing removal of government policies in agriculture, it is argued here that these initial benefits and their intended knock-on effects (multiplier effect, redistributive taxation, etc.) are contingent and circumscribed, and that, as a consequence, the pursuit of liberalisation may represent a developmental dead end. In the case of sugar, this leaves the purpose at the heart of the global regime both under-theorised and over-hyped.

9
Conclusions

Motivated by a critical agenda and with a theory grounded in post-states and markets IPE, this book has sought to investigate the changing nature of sugar production and the distributive consequences therein. It has done so with reference to three specific research questions outlined in the introductory chapter. These concerned: 1) the terms of competition for sugar producers; 2) the ascendant strategies of accumulation within these terms of competition; and 3) how these terms of competition are remade. In addressing these questions, it has also aimed to develop and operationalise a mode of analysis, namely, an industrial regimes approach, by which to enhance the conceptual and critical purchase on the exercise of power within the international political economy. Methodologically, the book proceeded with a comparative study of four regions of sugar production – the EU-ACP, the US, Asia and Brazil – and attempted to delineate the patterns of convergence and contestation by which they were characterised. This final chapter brings together the different arguments highlighted in each study and, referring back to our initial research questions, ties them together to offer some broader conclusions about the contemporary nature of the sugar regime and a consideration of the theoretical implications of this book for the study of IPE more generally.

Empirical observations, 1995–2008

Regulating the terms of competition

It has been argued throughout this book that the significance of a regime lies in the extent to which it guides behaviour and conditions outcomes in a given industry, creating such structures through regulatory rules and behavioural norms. Of increasing importance in this respect has been the move to a rules-based trade system, which has incorporated agriculture, industry and service sectors within the realm of the WTO and its legalistic framework. Many scholars have argued that the 'judicialisation' of trade relations augured by the WTO, and in particular, its Dispute Settlement Mechanism, have in a sense depoliticised trade policy, marking a shift toward jurisprudence and inclusion that have lessened the discriminatory treatment historically accorded to dissonant regimes, sugar being one of the most notable (Esserman and Howse 2003). From this point, it could be concluded that as the regulation of the international terms of competition has passed to a supranational governing body, and given the overall welfare gains to be had from liberalisation, production will begin to gravitate toward its respective sources of comparative advantage. Moreover, it could also be argued that this regulation will be increasingly self-policing, given that WTO member states now have an equalised ability to impose free-trade rules on others while encountering more difficulty in preserving their own protectionist practices. The conclusions for state elites to draw from such accounts appear equally ineluctable: remove all trade-distorting barriers and, for the industries that can survive, promote specialisation so as to develop a niche in the global marketplace, and, for the ones that cannot, soften the adjustment costs through short-term transfer payments.

In the case of sugar, a number of developments appear to vindicate this reading. The constitutionalisation of trade agreements, the withering of preferences incompatible with WTO rules, and the winding down of the most egregious state supports, namely, export subsidies, have all suggested the universalisation of liberal, multilateral rules. Furthermore, as both negotiations and disputes over these rules have been shaped to a significant degree by the role of developing countries, thereby ending the duopoly of the EU and US in agricultural policy-making, one could also make the argument that a de-politicisation of traditional power broking is now apparent.

Probing a little deeper, however, our reading of international regulation has led us to view this account as analytically incomplete and normatively injurious. To begin, what has been noticeable in our study is the way in which the Dispute Settlement Body has not emptied trade of politics, but rather, by placing increased emphasis on application of the law, has heightened the need for states to 'get the rules right' in the first place. By this we mean that those states likely to be affected by a slated tariff reduction or production support discipline have gone to extra lengths to ensure that their domestic industries will be able to abide by them with relative ease, in the knowledge that the exercise of economic, military or diplomatic power is a depleted way of escaping these rules should the need arise later on. Arguably, this is more pronounced in sugar than in other industries because of the fact that the biggest economies – the US, the EU and Japan – all have 'defensive' negotiating positions over the commodity and thus have the incentives as well as the resources to engage in the exclusion and eluding of discipline.

The most common practice in this regard has been to dodge and defer tariff reductions (this goes too for the myriad FTAs concluded under WTO auspices). In the Uruguay Round this took the form of hiding tariff peaks in the average reduction, while in the Doha Round it has manifested itself in the use of Sensitive Products and preference erosion allowances to create exceptions to liberalisation and delay implementation. Another prevalent practice has been the transfer of government support into new policy instruments, such as domestic supports and government compensation (recall the novel US FTA policy mentioned in Chapter 6), which has been constructed within WTO discourse as non-trade distorting and therefore legitimate, despite the many arguments to the contrary. Finally, in more sporadic instances, state intervention has been marginalised from the WTO remit entirely, if only temporarily; the most notable in this respect being the US ethanol tariff and the Japanese state trading body that places a mark up on all sugar imports.

To flesh this point out theoretically, we can refer to Linda Weiss's (1998: 197) argument that to read off policy instruments made anachronistic by the WTO overstates the decline of the state in the economy as novel policy instruments become apparent under qualitatively novel conditions. Going further, our case study of sugar also showed how traditional policy instruments such as tariffs may be reinvigorated as qualitatively novel products like ethanol become apparent. This 'reinvention' reading of the state suggests that, while trade policy has become *constrained in law*, in the sense that practices must be legal, or at least not inconsistent with extant WTO rules, there is room for national markets to remain *deviant in spirit*. An important part of such reinvention has been the mobilisation of 'discursive vehicles' that interpret commodities as goods of special social or strategic interest and thereby worthy of exclusion. In the case of Sensitive Products for instance, the ACP, LDC and EU sugar industries all stressed the need to protect the margin on what remains of the preferential access to the European market for the sake of development, notwithstanding the fact that it was the interests of dominant EU processors that previously undermined the ACP and LDC sugar interests during CMO reform. In the US, meanwhile, the priority to provide fuel security through ethanol production has entered the agricultural lexicon as a popular justification for protection, acting also as a somewhat hypocritical counterpoint to the priority of food security, which as we saw in Chapter 4, the US itself has done so much to malign.

Moving now to the nature of this world trade in sugar, it is evident that, over the *longue durée*, the sugar market has continued to be characterised by price volatility. Two things are important to note here. The first is that when price fluctuations are subsequently described in the press or policy circles as temporary oscillations around 'market fundamentals', i.e. the cost of production and the rate of demand, a significant misreading takes place. Describing world prices in this manner overlooks the extent to which instability is endemic, and, indeed, constitutive of, competitive commodity markets. We have been at pains to point out in this book that stable prices result from barriers to entry and *controlled* competition; the sugar-using industry being our prime example in its abatement of price war through brand alliance and market segmentation. The case is no different at the international level for sugar production – as long as supply is left indeterminate, few cast iron guarantees can be made about the movement of the world price. To give a quick example, take the world price graph shown earlier in Chapter 8 but this time highlighted with the Cuban and EU supply shocks. According to the economistic prescriptions for international sugar policy, these types of supply shocks – where significant state-subsidised producers reduce exports following a cut in support – are desirable because they raise the world market price and act as a fillip to exporters holding comparative advantage. As Figure 9.1 reveals, the price actually dropped on both occasions; the reason being that Brazil happened to increase its supply at the same time. The point here is not that support programmes have no effect on world prices, nor that they are defensible in all cases, but to show that the world market is predicated on an uncertainty that should not be theorised away.

The second point to note is that efforts to liberalise trade through the WTO in effect seek to institutionalise this volatility in international sugar trade. Rather than managing trade, the WTO is above all an organisation imbued with a project to *de*-regulate trade (reduce tariff and non-tariff barriers) and *re*-regulate production (permit only certain types of domestic supports). On this point, many authors have noted the increasing enclosure of policy space within the WTO to ensure this productive

Figure 9.1   Impact of Supply Shocks on the World Market Price of Sugar, 1945–2008

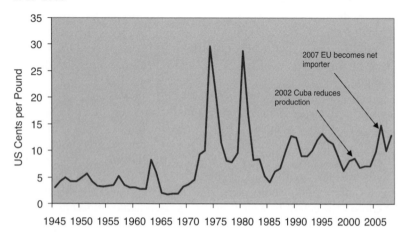

Source: F. O. Lichts *International Sugar and Sweetener Report*. Various years.

regulation is progressively extended, the inclusion of intellectual property protection serving as a good example. What is equally striking in our case has been the expulsion of policies deemed inconsistent with the prerogative of deregulating trade, the failed attempts by developing countries to insert compensatory mechanisms into WTO texts to mitigate fluctuating prices being among the most notable. There is an important contradiction to consider here, then, in that rules-based trade actually augments unruly markets. This is an especially pressing concern for farmers in that their supply schedules are far from smooth. In other words, once farmers are exposed to low prices and forced to reduce supply, it is extremely difficult to switch back into production as many factories and growers, certainly in sugar, exit for good. Likewise, without access to stable markets, countries that do have a comparative advantage in sugar production will not be able to utilise it – even when market conditions become (temporarily) favourable – as good harvests must be built up slowly over time and cannot be conjured up in response to sudden shifts in demand. As illustrated in Figure 9.2, given the fluctuations already endemic in world production, it is no surprise that the majority of sugar producers are reluctant to move to a system where further supply uncertainty is encouraged.

In sum, the reluctance of the major sugar-producing and consuming states to liberalise their sugar markets, in response to farmer concerns about the typically low and unstable nature of the world market, has meant that the proportion of sugar crossing borders has remained rela-

Figure 9.2   World Sugar Production, 1950–2008

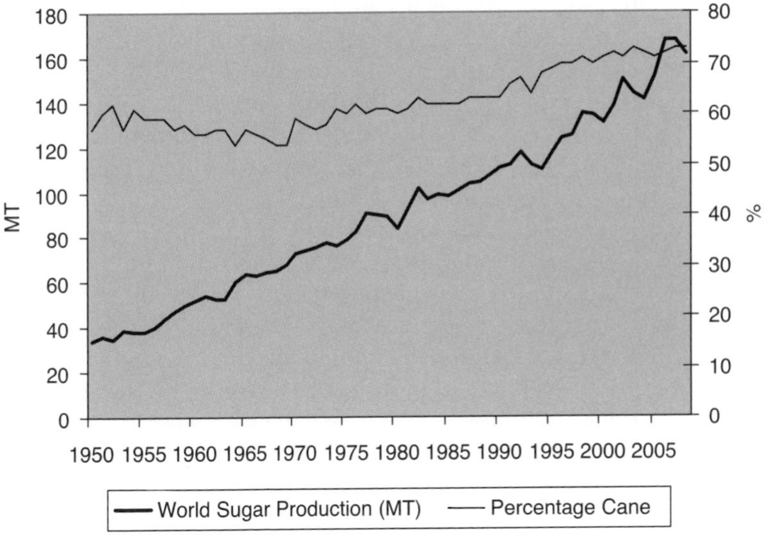

Source: F. O. Lichts *International Sugar and Sweetener Report*. Various Years.

tively unchanged in the post-Uruguay period. In 1996 imports of sugar as a percentage of consumption were 32.7 per cent; by 2007 they were 33 per cent, just 0.3 per cent higher (F. O. Lichts 2008d: 4). Developing this point further, we can also comment on the globalisation of liberal rules in their causal capacity. In much development and agri-food literature there seems a reflexive impulse to identify the elimination of small producers and alternative agricultures as a result of WTO-led liberalisation. This is not a plausible explanation in sugar, demanding that an alternative account be generated. As such, what has been stressed in this book is that, while trade relations are important to the structure and purpose of the sugar industries, as an explanatory variable they are not exhaustive. In order to better explain the general trends of reduced employment, intensification of farming and development of new markets across the international spectrum, we have thus laid focus on the strategies of accumulation by corporations themselves, suggesting that, within the general international terms of competition, corporations are key actors in deciding outcomes.

The ascendant strategies of accumulation

A key commitment of the industrial regimes approach outlined in Chapter 2 was to recognise economic activity as taking place within a state-market condominium and to widen the array of actors able to exercise power across this space. Corporations were identified as central agents in this process, making accumulation – the transformation of capital into privatised wealth – possible, and influencing the distribution of existing and future income streams within this. Under the national regime, which generally insulated national economies from world market prices, we noted how differential accumulation (or winning market share) was deferred as these import sensitive, highly regulated regimes encouraged market sharing. Not only was international trade off the agenda, there was also little international investment between national markets not least because competition was politically and economically stunted and what penetration was possible was dependent on privileged access to political elites. There was, however, a simulacrum of market competition manifest in these regimes in the form of falling real prices. As prices in most markets were set by the state and then institutionalised in policy that frequently lagged behind inflation, sugar producers had to cut costs in order to defend profit margins just to maintain static levels of accumulation. Broadly speaking, this took place through intensified production, which involved mechanisation and modernisation in the field and the factory, and mergers and acquisitions, which generated further economies of scale and shed labour costs.

As we picked up the threads of accumulation in the 1990s, these strategies were becoming increasingly limited. Discounting fringe improvements, such as improving the sucrose content of plants through better breeding or milling through the night to increase factory throughput, there appeared few remaining technological frontiers to push back. The one obvious option was to introduce GM crops, though hesitant consumers and lengthy regulatory approval had made this somewhat impractical. Not only that, but from the point of view of dominant capital, these types of cost cutting measures were no way to institutionalise competitive advantage; as innovations and fringe improvements spread through the industry – as the POJ cane developed in Java did in the early 20th century – the initial gains from investment were quickly eroded. Mergers and acquisitions, on the other hand, provided a more appropriate means by which to institutionalise advantage as they allowed firms to increase their profits relative to the average, redistributing control over existing capacity and employment. But, again, this strategy became limited as the availability of suitable national takeovers reached a threshold. In most markets, industry concentration actually took place through (typically smaller) companies exiting the business, unable to make a profit.

These strategies of accumulation soon began to evolve, however, as the terms of competition were rewritten. Specifically, the changing rules of the game heralded by the EBA and EPAs in the EU, by NAFTA in the US, by growing consumption in Asia and by the ethanol boom in Brazil all prompted the pre-existing dominant sugar processors to begin to break the national envelope of ownership and invest abroad. Most prominently, British Sugar and Tate & Lyle invested in EBA eligible countries, Flo-Sun purchased refineries in Canada and Mexico, Mitr Phol and other Thai processors moved into growing regional markets, and Tereos and the Kuok Group became part of the Brazilian conglomerates. There remains huge potential for this concentration in global ownership to continue. To illustrate, in 2007 the ten biggest sugar corporations accounted for 25.6mt of production, or just 15 per cent of the entire world total (F. O. Lichts 2008a: 471). Allied to this, trading groups also began entering the industry on an increasing scale. Contrary to many other agricultural sectors, sugar traders – those intermediary logistics and risk management firms that arrange the storage, transport and sale of the commodity – had been constrained in the amount of value they could capture in the industry by virtue of the strict controls on trade and the national orientation of ownership. Now, the biggest among these, including Sucden, Louis Dreyfus, Cargill, ED & F Man, Czarnikow and Bunge, have each invested in infrastructure and productive capacity in Brazil. According to Eduardo Carmona (2008), Managing Director of ED & F Man, the task for trading houses, like sugar processors, is also to pursue vertical integration and diversification, in this case moving from delivery service to supply chain manager and offering assurances on commodity quality and providence as well as the traditional logistic service.

After decades of ownership and land holding concentration in mature markets, the ethanol boom has also precipitated a sudden rush to Greenfield investment, which has presented dominant capital with the opportunity to achieve differential accumulation by building new capacity faster than average, as well as by establishing a tight rein over new biofuel policy. As former Brazilian Agriculture Minister, Roberto Rodrigues, has exuded, 'agroenergy is a new civilisation, a new geography for the agriculture of the world' (Smith and Caminada 2007). What we have been at pains to point out is the extent to which this new geography has been mapped by governments, which have created biofuel markets *de novo* by demonstrating their intent to underwrite investments. In other words, through an expansive complex of tariff protection, standards setting, mandatory targets, R&D funds, tax breaks and more, states have acted as first mover for biofuel investment, effecting an upward spiral of mutual confidence among farmers, processors, refiners, retailers and consumers.

In terms of its international dimension, the political management of ethanol production has in many ways replicated the national regime seen in sugar, primarily because of the suppression of liberal trade in favour of preferential trade. For example, Dominican Republic and Mozambique have availed themselves of the ethanol import licenses available under the EPAs, while in Guyana, Ecuador, El Salvador and Jamaica, investments have already been made in plants and equipment to take advantage of the countries' status as preferential importers into the US and act as trans-shipment points for dehydrated Brazilian ethanol.[1] Compare this to the general trend in ethanol trade, which declined from 10 per cent of production traded in 2005 to 5 per cent by 2008 (Carmona 2008).

Placing the ethanol boom and the nascent sugar cellulose and diesel developments in the context of sugar production, the central dynamic at work has been for processors to use sugar as a platform on which to open up horizontal synergies onto new planes of accumulation. This is evident too in the sugar beet industry, albeit on a much smaller scale, as biofuel and bioplastic markets have been targeted here too. Extrapolating from these trends, we can posit that it may become more appropriate in the future to speak of cane and beet *biomass regimes* rather than *sugar* or *ethanol regimes*, especially in cane given how easily modern refineries are able to switch between the two outputs. It may be more appropriate, too, to append these biomass regimes to the oil regime, given that transport fuel and plastics are both substitutable for oil-based products (though, in that sense, the rationale for a regimes approach to biomass would attenuate given its derivative status).

Returning to our assessment of accumulation in the sugar industry, we can also identify some emergent trends in the way capital is likely to relate to land and labour in this field of production – in short, how it will affect development. Undertaken by the larger, well-capitalised sugar processors, the shift to mechanised and integrated production of refined sugars, ethanol and artificial sweeteners has tended to promote a narrow band of relatively well-paid and increasingly technical jobs in the factory and on the farm. We say narrow because, agronomically at least, under this trajectory the sugar industry has become significantly deskilled and certainly depopulated. There has been a marked disappearance of farmers on smaller holdings, and, for the farmers that do remain, it is becoming ever more apt to see them as businessmen rather than cultivators. Arguably growing sugar in this environment now has much more to do with managing complex finances than about taking decisions as to how the crop will be grown.

For the mass of smaller sugar processors located in developing countries, accumulation has taken a more vivid form of exploitation as farmers have in many instances found themselves trapped in liquidity crises and cane cutters have been exposed to unremunerative, hard physical labour. Thus structural violence and physical violence can still be found in the sugar-growing countryside: the former referring to the endemic existence of malnutrition and the need to sell labour under dangerous and exploitative conditions; the latter to the practices of modern slavery and expulsion that exist on the fringes of contemporary capitalist production. At the margin, this can be expected to change under the multinationalisation of production described above. Based on our analysis, we can point to two emerging trends. First, that more bulk production is likely to take place in developing countries as developed country processors, especially in Europe, move to refine raw imports from the ACP/LDCs and invest directly in foreign production. Second, as illustrated with reference to sub-Saharan Africa in Chapter 5 and Brazil in Chapter 8, it is likely that these new supply chains will impart the kind of system encapsulated in our 'bifurcated' model: better labour conditions but less labour intensive.

Contesting practice and changing policy

Around a century ago, corporate influence over trade policy in sugar began to mutate, contested as it was between the colonial grouping of refiners, sugar-using industries and foreign sugar interests, on the one hand, and the newer national grouping of domestic cane and/or beet growers, on the other. As policy preferences slowly coalesced around the latter group, the national regime began to seep into view, reaching its zenith in the post-war protectionist trading arrangements permitted under the US-led GATT. The third research question attempted to take this story of change into the 21st century by asking how the terms of competition are remade today. It was also couched with a particular concern for how marginalised groups might come to challenge the 'inertias' characteristic of contemporary policy and thereby reshape existing patterns of wealth distribution. To put it simply, we considered the democratic opportunities contained in the structures of the global sugar regime and how these might facilitate change.

Within the academic and popular discourse on sugar policy, most attention has focused on how the *international* terms of competition can be remade in order to give sugar exporters from developing countries a better deal within the global economy. Under the national sugar regime, decisions over preferential trade were firmly within the hands of the (developed) importing states and so the International Sugar Agreements were seen as the best opportunity for weaker states to influence the terms of trade by negotiating over the price boundaries and withholding supply as appropriate. Ultimately, these proved to be ineffectual as the rules governing supply management were weak and there was too much vested interest in breaking them. Under the embryonic global regime, it was therefore expected that developing countries would gain more meaningful opportunity to shape their regulatory environment, namely, by offering concessions on industrial and service sectors in exchange for deregulating trade barriers and disciplining the terms of production.

Unfortunately, for advocates of this perspective, the Uruguay Round reinforced the international relations maxim that just because incentives for mutual cooperation exist they are no guarantee that benign engagement will actually happen. The intended 'Grand Bargain' instead turned out to be a 'Bum Deal' as protectionist practices were maintained in sugar and other commodities besides (Ostry 2002). It was clear that, apart from the right economic conditions, developing countries would also need the diplomatic and technocratic acumen to get their agenda heard and acted upon. Renewing their efforts to influence policy, developing countries have learnt considerably about the dynamics of WTO process. In our case, the most prominent culminations of this have been the defeat of the EU by Australia, Brazil and Thailand in the DSB sugar case, and the emergence of the G20 in the Doha Round. The former acted as an impetus (and subsequent justification) for the biggest overhaul in EU policy since 1973, while the latter has promoted workable proposals for deeper and more disciplined cuts to tariffs and market support biased in favour of developing countries.

Whilst not denying the agency hitherto exhibited, this book has cast a sceptical eye on the 'successes' of developing countries in the global regime. For one, it has tried to shed light on the interests within developed countries that have supported challenges made by developing countries to existing practices; the best example being the independent interests of the European Commission, and through them the export-orientated EU industries and sugar-using firms, which wanted to bring sugar policy in line with WTO protocol anyway. Another point worthy of reiteration is the difficulty of constructing a unified agenda for developing countries to pursue, given the uncertainties of trade negotiation twinned with the fact that some are low cost exporters while others are tied to the protected markets of the EU and US or else are sugar importers themselves. To repeat the point made in the previous chapter, the G20 has not resolved the differences between developing countries in the WTO, but rather provided a political route through it. And, on a separate note, it has been consistently stated that preferable international terms of competition are no guarantors of development if the intra-national terms of competition are set to privilege or permit continued exploitation. Whether under protectionist *or* export-orientated policy, we have noted instances of social degradation caused by the modes of production fostered in the industry. It is resistance toward these that we now turn.

The theoretical underpinnings of the regime concept led us initially to the quotidian, 'everyday' challenges that might exist below the rarefied air of global meetings between state actors and civil society. In Chapter 2, one such source of agency was identified in consumer movements, which, borne on the back of concerns about the natural, social and ethical conditions of food production, have created a space for select producers to buck the logic of the market. However, the conclusion that must be presented here is that the politicisation of sugar through consumption remains a parasitic and partial phenomenon. Take, for example, the organic market, which we highlighted in the theory chapter as a potential challenge to, and contradiction within, the capitalist agri-food system. A market for organic sugars certainly exists, but compared to fruit and vegetables, there has been limited uptake. In 2007 in the US, organic sugars comprised just 0.9 per cent of total sugar demand (Willerton 2008). This is in large part because of the nature of the product and the way we have come to consume it. As the majority of sugar is ingested invisibly in processed goods, and because, in its common refined state, it is a pure and undifferentiated chemical compound, organic sugar is both inconspicuous and incapable of generating quality appeals to its superior taste. As such, sales of the product have had to 'piggyback' on the trend for organic products more generally, hence the characterisation of the movement as parasitic.

The fair trade phenomenon would seem to illustrate a more concerted effort to change the distributive patterns of the contemporary sugar regime, not least because, in February 2008, Tate & Lyle announced it would sell its entire retail sugar range under the 'Fairtrade' label, so excluding the 'invisible' sugar sent to food manufacturers but transferring millions of pounds in premiums to sugar cane farmers nonetheless (Wearden 2008). Although there was not time to discuss this, following on from our research on the restructuring of the EU sugar regime we are able to place this decision within its wider context. This context concerns the demise of the ACP Sugar Protocol, in which millions of pounds to millers have already been cut, and future uncertainty over the EU guaranteed price, because of which Tate & Lyle has limited its contracted import obligation to 2013. Tentatively, we could thus conclude that the move has less to do with consumer awareness, certainly not to the degree seen in the colonial abolition movement anyway, and more do with an opportunistic fit between corporate greening and ethical entrepreneurship.

An element of consumer politicisation over the mode of production in sugar that *was* successfully located concerned the take-up of GM crops in the US. It is quite an anomaly that GM sugar has yet to take off in the US, and, for the time being, in Brazil – both big sugar-producing states that have approved genetic modification in crops such as rice and wheat – especially as sugar is refined down to chemical sucrose and so the genetically altered DNA is not even ingested. Given that legalisation of GM crops would dramatically alter the landscape of production, in particular by leveraging the influence of biotechnology firms over the management of inputs, the ability to resist new rules must too be considered a demonstration of power, if only in negation.

Arguably the most important everyday activity to influence the profitability of global agri-food companies and their sugar suppliers during the period in question has been the construction of the consumer in Asia and the subsequent shifts to diets high in added sugar. Potential consumers have become the subject of powerful acts of interpellation on the part of the processed food industry, though, as demonstrated in Chapter 7, these acts have been reflexive, and sometimes even rejected, as societies have retained a certain autonomy over their spending habits. Regarding our ambition to make consumption endogenous to our analysis, two points can be gleaned from this. First, to gain a fuller understanding of the ways in which power affects and underpins economic activity, it has been necessary to extend the politics of consumption beyond advocacy and boycotts to include the actual act in itself. However, contrary to the self-conscious agency evident in the organic or fair trade movements for example, and, because of the efforts of corporations to make consumption an instantaneous and unthinking act, it remains the case that in most instances of food and beverage purchase people are less inclined to recognise the political backdrop to their actions. In turn, they will then be less inclined to politicise the mode of production and exchange by which such goods are brought to market. Second, it can be posited that, just as the supply of sugar is not smooth (the point made above in relation to farmers and volatile prices) neither is demand for sugar latent. Contrary to the common economic assumption in which demand rises as price falls in some kind of mechanical materialist interplay, demand schedules should also be considered contingent rather than constant, open to moral, cultural and social persuasion as well as plain economic incentive.

Alongside the agency of consumers, the theory chapter also took from recent agri-food literature the agency identified in peasant movements such as *Via Campesina*, which sprang from a commitment to inject progressive resistance into communities often marginalised in IPE discourse. The key demand of these movements has been for food sovereignty in place of food security, given that the latter has been equated with export-orientated agriculture, cash cropping and resource appropriation. Hence sugar provided us with another anomaly in that, as one of these cash crops peasants are meant to stand against, it confounds agrarian solidarity and eludes comprehension within this mode of analysis. For example, we have noted how small-scale cane growers in India and China have acted as a bulwark to the mass concentration of land holdings but, by the same token, have in some cases also ruthlessly exploited landless workers. In our study on Brazil, meanwhile, we noted how attempts by the MST to redistribute land by reclaiming plantation territory have risked undermining waged employment and further fissure among the rural poor.

Within our account, the bottom-up agency of the rural poor became easier to recognise, if not to characterise, when a class-based Manichean reading of rural society – i.e. 'Good' peasants versus 'Evil' agri-business – was eschewed in favour of one that emphasised the complex fractions of people that exist in and around the sugar industry. Moreover, it proved necessary again and again to recognise the centrality of the state in their demands, not just as the focus of demands for policy change, but also because of the proclivity of the state to take a Janus-faced approach to agrarian crisis. Variously compromised by the involvement of state officials in the industry, the inability to extend itself into the rural polity and its patchwork of local authoritarian enclaves, or by the need to raise foreign exchange and therefore support commercial land claims, the state has in many developing countries been unable or unwilling to make the prevailing regime of sugar production work for the poor. Nevertheless, we maintain that it will remain the essential mediator of this relationship.

One final point about the remaking of regulation concerns the changing preferences of corporations. This represents a shift away from an agency of resistance, but, as suggested in the opening to this section, it was in large part the battle between domestic and foreign-oriented capital in the capitalist core that determined the successor to the colonial regime. What is more, the argument can plausibly be made that the same is likely to take place today. Essentially, as powerful processors see the share of domestic sugar production in their profits dwindle and take concomitant steps to invest abroad and benefit from freer trade – in this way both reacting to existing WTO and FTA legislation and preparing for more – they will have decreasing incentives to defend the protectionism redolent of the national sugar regime. Further, as previously argued, it has been the agri*culture* of sugar production in developed countries that has been vital in upholding protection, a resource which has since been systematically degraded under industrial farming and concentrated ownership. In this path dependent way, the sugar industry may have sown the seeds of its own demise in the developed world, though its dominant fractions of capital will arguably retain an influence over its settlement in the developing world.

The global regime in sugar

Having proffered answers to our three research questions, one final line of enquiry still needs to be cleared up. That is to ask what kind of regime now exists in sugar? Can we say that the global has finally triumphed over the national? And if we can, should we also proclaim the end of the state in this particular industry? The first step in addressing this issue is to clarify how the regime concept has been used, and the claims being made when we speak of regime shifts. During this book, the concept has been used as both an analytical approach and a term of description. In its latter guise, we have applied the prefix 'colonial', 'national' or 'global' to mark the ways in which the industry has functioned on a worldwide scale. In doing so, we have not intended to impart a teleology onto this order, suggesting that the global regime was an inevitable terminus in our journey, and nor have we argued that the prevailing regime moves from one discreet type to the next (as mentioned in the conclusion to Chapter 5, so entrenched were the legacies of the colonial regime that took 400 years for them to disappear). Rather, the evolution of regimes toward ideal-types has been our preoccupation. Given this, we have not merely been interested in the spatial delineation of markets, though this has certainly been an important component in our choice of prefix, but also in finding a conceptual frame that adequately characterises the nature of the power being used to exercise control over production. It is for these reasons that we can speak of a global regime, in spite of the continued existence of policies and practices redolent of its national predecessor.

What our findings indicate is that in the sugar industry it is those policies that are consonant with contemporary neo-liberalism that are gaining ascendancy, and, to the degree that policies entrenched in the national regime era remain, they do so only insofar as they can be justified as supportive of, or viable exceptions to, this vision. The best example of the former is the FDI strategies of dominant sugar capital; the best example of the latter is the WTO compatibility engineered by states as they defend their market regulation in new and complex ways. However, it does not follow from this point that the end of state in the industry is nigh. In the tradition of post-states and markets theory, we should speak not of the end of public authority under globalisation but rather its (differentiated) metamorphosis: from nation states to global states. Thus, just how multiple national regimes – depicted as different instances of the same phenomenon – existed alongside one another, so too are multiple global regimes coming into view. To reiterate, the use of the term 'global' is not used here in contradistinction to the 'state'. It is fully expected that the global regime will develop with uneven geographical contours as state authority contends with and facilitates this order in ways appropriate to the domestic industry it inherits. The crucial point is that it is globally orientated policy that is perceived as most plausible, and which, in practice, is increasingly gathering the most momentum.

Theoretical observations: refined power and the study of regimes

Having discussed the descriptive connotations of our favoured concept, in this final section we turn to the analytical value in using an industrial regimes approach for practitioners and scholars of IPE. In the case of extant commentary on sugar, it is fair to say that what motivates most coverage are the instances of explicit, crude and coercive forms of power that emanate from the industry: modern forms of slavery and the lobbying of governments over health policy are two that instantly spring to mind. In short, what might be characterised as 'raw' power. However, what we have consistently advocated is an approach that looks beyond these notorious expressions of power or the landmark ruptures in world markets and instead seeks to examine the day-to-day recurrence of patterns of accumulation and the power structures that underpin them. The key to doing this was said to be in identifying forms of refined power, defined as institutionalised power embedded in regulatory structures, actor coalitions and economic identities, in order that we might better conceive of and critique the actions of agents in the international political economy. It is hoped that this perspective will be useful in unearthing power structures in many other sectors too, but, before we discuss the potential insights generated by the industrial regime approach, it is worth asking whether such an approach is even amenable to other areas of production. In more technical terms, we need to ask about its external validity.

This question is especially important given the argument made throughout the book regarding the *specificity* of the regime in sugar, stating how its unique evolution had to be appreciated and how it had to be delinked, if only temporarily and analytically, from developments in the wider agri-food sector. This would suggest that our industrial regime approach perhaps has purchase only for the case study in question. However, within our study, the sugar regime was in fact conceptualised as a historically mutable and dynamic arrangement of rule and norm-driven practices, thereby creating the theoretical space to recognise different constellations of these practices, even if they happen to be in other sectors. In addition, once the sugar regime had been conceptualised on its own terms, it was then resituated in the broader trends of the agri-food sector, such as agricultural liberalisation or consumerism, in order to show how this industry-specific regime related to these developments. By highlighting the interstitial nature of regimes, it was implicitly acknowledged that a multitude of other regimes exist in other sectors, and it is argued that the techniques used to nest the sugar regime in its overarching order can be applied to these also.

Having made the case for the wider applicability of the industrial regimes approach, we now turn to the analytical insights offered by the concept and how they may be useful in illuminating power and agency in other areas of the international political economy. It was noted in Chapter 2 how our approach was designed to 'interrogate the inertias of accumulation' by exposing the asymmetrical and embedded nature of different forms of power. In tracing the evolution of production within a given industry, this provides an alternative perspective to arguably the two most popular theories of contemporary capitalism: liberalism and Marxism. The former tends to see firms as atomistic profit-maximisers and thus emphasises the competitive nature of production, whereas the latter sees firms as inherently exploitative and thus has a tendency to emphasise the coherent (even conspiratorial) nature of production. Using the regime concept, we have tried to steer a course between these two poles and focus instead on the multiple contests and coalitions between firms that compose the shifting sands of corporate alliance. For example, while at loggerheads over trade policy, sugar producers and sugar-using industries were found to quickly put their differences aside to lobby jointly when an attack was made on sugar consumption as a whole. For another, while farmers and processors would join forces to support trade barriers and high internal prices, they would just as quickly fall out over how that price is divided. Many more fault lines can be found that split the industry in different ways, and it has been one of the most notable regularities of this research how easily firms have been able to submerge latent conflict and previous high profile conflicts in order to present a united front to policy makers.

In effect, what we are arguing here is that when a direct and identifiable challenge is posed, firms are willing to reach across the table and join hands with erstwhile rivals in order to shape policy conducive to the growth of all. So far, so materialist. But what the regime approach has also made paramount is the need to take institutionalised behaviour seriously to help to illuminate the hidden structures of power. In the case of sugar this has been extremely notable when challenges are vague and reform just a possibility, as is often the case. In these instances, rather than reading off their economic interests and forming coalitions accordingly (which in any case is hindered when the future business environment is indeterminate), firms are much happier to avoid uncertainty and commit instead to the *status quo* – even if there was a chance that they could have otherwise instigated policy reform in their favour. The long-standing deference of the sugar-using industry to sugar producers in the EU and US, in part bought off by export refunds, is testament to this type of path dependency. Teasing this account out a little, we conclude with three insights in particular that suggest tenable ways of exploring this process in other sectors of production.

The first is the importance that industry actors place on separating themselves from broader political economy trends and demands. In the theory chapter it was suggested how capital can create an 'imprisoned zone' of policy-making by virtue of network advantages held by businesses in policy dialogue. This point now has to be broadened out and the argument made that the interests of dominant capital lie not just in influencing policy when the need to reform organically arises in their area of business but also in insulating themselves from (potentially detrimental) reform being foisted upon them from 'outside'. Bob Jessop's (1998) concept of heterarchy or self-organisation, in which differentiated institutional orders assume their own complex operational logic such that it becomes impossible to exercise effective overall control of their development from outside that system, captures this insulation well. One of the biggest challenges posed by the inclusion of sugar into the WTO, as we saw in the EU case, is precisely the ties it makes between different institutional orders, or regimes, and which thereby threaten their sovereignty.

Second, building on the notion of heterarchy, when change does occur it usually manifests itself as a form of institutional bricolage, where new rules are assembled out of pre-existing policy ideas and then internalised by actors into intelligible practices. Together with the idiosyncrasies embodied in the product itself – in our case the refined and largely invisible consumption of the cash crop sugar – they make regimes something more than simple derivatives of the wider neo-liberal economic order and suggest that, analytically, we place as much emphasis on the historical paths that actors find themselves walking along as much as the political economy vistas that currently confront them. In making this claim, we also provide a rationale for looking beyond global governance or food regimes as a conceptual approach, which both tend to emphasise a grand, broad-brush take on theorising production, and promote instead a mode of analysis that encourages us to ask 'who or what actually exercises authority, and how it is done' (Cohen 2008: 117).

Lastly, in relation to the global trajectory of production, looking at sectors through an industrial regimes prism suggests that globalisation is a destination untold. Not only does the internal contestation within regimes, existing or potential, suggest that capital itself is riven with fissures, but it also highlights the point that the images of collective order that do prevail, neo-liberal free trade being one of the most powerful currently, are in themselves poorly constructed utopias. In much existing IPE literature, to create a role for agency, globalisation is often conceptualised as a 'Project', meaning that it is a process that is not yet finished and as such open to alteration. The space for agency created within an industrial regimes approach is different because it emphasises in contrast that there is no fully conceptualised End Game, Project or Terminus in mind, at least not one free of contradiction and within which 'alternative' practices could be viably eliminated. In short, it suggests that choice and contingency are intrinsic elements of globalisation and that we do not need to put all our faith in one grand challenge to the prevailing order, but rather retain sensitivity to the multitude of reform possibilities that are continually renewed within capitalism, and remain alert as to how these could be seized upon.

Notes

Chapter 2

1 As well as many academics, some NGOs, most prominently Oxfam, also follow this take on trade inequality. For example, 'The problem is not that international trade is inherently opposed to the needs and interests of the poor, but that the rules that govern it are rigged in favour of the rich'. Oxfam International, *Rigged Rules and Double Standards: Trade, Globalization and the Fight Against Poverty* (Oxford: Oxfam, 2002b), p. 5.

Chapter 3

1 Brazilian competition was also aided by political developments in Europe. In 1580, Brazil and Portugal came under Spanish control meaning Brazilian sugar could enter Spanish Mediterranean dominions and reach new markets.
2 British slave trade was further aided by the 1713 Treaty of Utrecht, which granted Britain monopoly rights on supplying the Spanish colonies with African slaves for 30 years.
3 Refining took place near the point of consumption, initially because of the nature of sugar, which tended to coalesce during the long and humid early sea-voyages and so needed re-processing upon arrival. When the technology became available to refine abroad, governments still preferred to refine at home because of the jobs it created.
4 As the European immigration to the sugar colonies was largely male, many naturally turned to the black women for wives and mistresses with the result that there emerged a segment of the population that was of mixed racial descent.
5 In the 1920s, around 70 per cent of Cuban cane was grown by *colonos* (traditional sugar planters) whereas by 1950 this had increased to almost 90 per cent (Pollitt: 1988: 105).
6 The signatories included Belgium, Cuba, Czechoslovakia, Germany, Hungary, Java, Peru, Poland and Yugoslavia.

Chapter 4

1 In the case of Chad, Uganda, Ghana, Nigeria, Sierra Leone, Somalia and Sudan sugar constituted one of the largest items in the food bill.
2 Alternatives to industrial mass production in sugar were sought out. Kenya was able to cooperate with Booker to instigate a sugar estate that avoided costly labour-saving devices and maintained extra smallholdings for its 5,000 off-estate growers, while, in Rwanda, Gabon and Liberia, the technicians and labour-intensive technology of Taiwan were brought in to start up sugar mills in a number of successful self-reliance projects.

3 Per capita income growth has a proportionately greater impact on demand for sugar, i.e. demand is more elastic, at lower incomes, and so economic development in poorer countries is more significant for world demand than development in mature economies.

Chapter 5

1 In Finland, Denmark, Sweden, Greece, Austria, Ireland and UK there was just one processor. In Portugal, Spain, Netherlands and Belgium there was either two or three. Only in Italy, Germany and France were quotas more fragmented.
2 The other two commodities were rice and bananas. For sugar, a quota was opened from 2001 and import duties fell from 2006, gradually removing barriers until complete quota-free duty-free access comes into force in 2009.
3 The waiver was required for the Cotonou Agreement, which replaced the Lomé Conventions, because the non-reciprocal and discriminatory preferences that it enshrined ran counter to the GATT principle of Most Favoured Nation and its Enabling Clause. Although the Sugar Protocol had a separate legal identity, it was included in the Cotonou text and its survival as an independent agreement was closely bound with the evolution of the broader preferential trade regime.
4 It is notable, too, that while generous amounts of aid for sugar restructuring were promised after reform, threats were also been made by the Commission to reduce the amount should the EPAs not be 'negotiated' in time (Cronin 2007).
5 Based on author's calculations. According to DEFRA, the reduction in the intervention price will be imperfectly transmitted to consumers, who gain 60 to 70 per cent of a price fall in sugar, the remainder being captured by food processors and/or retailers. Thus the price of kilo bag, taken as 72p, multiplied by intervention price reduction (36 per cent) * consumer capture (65 per cent), gives a saving of 16p.
6 World price based on author's calculations: average world price across 2002–2006 (9.16 cents per pound) * pounds in a metric tonne (2,204) converted into Euros at the exchange rate \$1 = €0.643.
7 In July 2007, however, both European Commission President, José Manuel Barroso, and EU Trade Commissioner, Peter Mandelson, agreed that tariffs on Brazilian ethanol, which then stood at around 70 per cent, would have to be slashed. This is likely be used as a bargaining chip in any EU-Mercosur Free Trade Agreement or Doha Round agreement.
8 The phrase comes from Judges 14:8, in which Samson returns to a lion that he tore in half to find a swarm of bees in there producing honey. Samson took the honey home to feed his mother and father.
9 The volume safeguard is known as a double trigger. Trigger 1 is pulled if ACP imports exceed 1.3mt. Trigger 2 is pulled if ACP plus LDC imports exceed 3.5mt. If both are pulled, then non-LDC ACP sugar is guillotined.
10 After 2009, there can be no quantitative limits on imports from sugar produced in EBA countries. Further, due to the liberal rules of origin stipulations in the EBA, these countries are also allowed to import sugar to meet their domestic needs, and export the remainder to the EU. However, a

Declaration added to the 2005 EU reform bill stipulated that if imports from a third country under the EBA increase by more than 25 per cent in comparison with the previous year, then market access can be suspended. The EU farming and processing lobbies have pushed for this to be reiterated to EBA suppliers to maintain their supply cartel within the region (Confederation of European Beet Growers and Comité Européen des Fabricants de Sucre 2007).

Chapter 6

1   The TRQ was enacted in 1990 as a slight of hand response to a trade complaint made by Australia that the absolute import quotas operated by the US were in violation of GATT. The US changed to a dual tariff system, but the 'over-quota' tariff was so high that the TRQ remains an absolute import quota in all but name.
2   Between 2000 and 2008 the US signed bilateral trade agreements with 14 countries but many of these had little interest in negotiating on sugar access (i.e. Bahrain, Chile, Jordan, Oman, Morocco and Singapore).
3   Sugar beet is often grown on mixed crop farms and so the size of the beet holding may not account for the entirety of the farm size. In 2002 the average farm size of sugar beet farms was 1,700 acres, of which three-fourths were cropland. Sugar beet accounted for nearly one-fourth of the total harvested acreage and contributed to about 40 per cent of the total value of production (Haley and Ali 2007: 54).
4   Stevia is a herb that can produce a compound which is up to 300 times sweeter than sugar and naturally calorie free. Despite being passed fit as a dietary supplement in the US, and even being used by companies such as Coca-Cola and Nestlé in Japan, it has failed to attain status as a legal food additive largely due to the efforts of aspartame producers (Hawke 2003).
5   There are allegations, too, that the corn refiners benefited from price fixing HFCS. In 2004 Archer Daniels Midland agreed to pay $400 million, Cargill and American Maize to pay $24 million and Tate & Lyle (who own AE Staley) £55 million to end their role in a class action lawsuit led by PepsiCo and Coca Cola, who alleged that they had conspired to fix fructose prices from the late 1980s through 1995 (Jones 2004).
6   The top recipients of sugar funds between 2001 and 2007 have been Charles Melancon ($95,000), Thomas Harkin ($84,000), Hilary Clinton ($77,000), Saxby Chambliss ($76,000), Mel Martinez ($71,000), Max Baucus ($69,000) and Colin Peterson ($67,000). All are either from sugar growing states and/or involved in Agricultural, Energy or Finance committees at the top level (Map Light 2008).
7   The USDA does not carry statistics of farm employment but it seems fair to assume that because larger farms tend to be more capital- and less labour-intensive, a reduction in the number of farms would translate into a reduction in farm employment.
8   In this way, the US and Mexican re-export programmes actually act to undermine each others' sugar industry by allowing third market sugar to enter North America: the bulk of the US cane refinery re-export makes its way as refined sugar to Mexico, which swiftly returns to the US in sugar-containing products.

9 In 2004 the US sugar crop was worth nearly $2 billion while wheat was $7 billion, soybeans were $17 billion and corn grain was $24 billion (Haley and Ali 2007: 3).

Chapter 7

1 As the likely beneficiary of sugar liberalisation, Thailand sought compensation in the ASEAN FTA Council for what it considered an abrogation of the terms of the agreement, and in response, received a guarantee from the Philippines to import 0.2mt of Thai rice over three years and to assure the country 33 per cent of the its eventual import requirement (Asian Economic News 2002).
2 The importance to sweetener consumption of snacking can be illustrated by data from the US, which show that since the late 1970s around half the increased sweetener intake came from this type of ingestion (Popkin and Nielson 2003: 1328).
3 Many promotional activities are sponsored by the exporting states. The US Market Access Program, for example, uses funds from the USDA to pay for consumer promotions, market research, technical assistance and trade servicing. Almost $1 million has been made available for the US confectionery industry alone to help offset the costs of promotions in the international marketplace.
4 One direct causal link that the sugar industry will acknowledge is that between the frequency of sugar consumption and the incidence of tooth decay. Note, though, that this does not presuppose limits on the ultimate quantity of sugar consumed (Sugar Association 2008).
5 A notable exception is the 'no/low calorie' sweetener market that can come to challenge sugar production. For example, the stevia-based sweetener developed by Coca-Cola and Cargill to be used in products in Asia and South America can replace sugar production at the ratio of 1 hectare of stevia to 5 hectares of sugar cane (in terms of sweetness). Should production shift to stevia, sugar industries would come under increasing pressure, as happened to the US industry when HFCS entered the market.

Chapter 8

1 Only the EU used substantial export subsidies on sugar and had begun to phase them out under CMO reform. As for domestic support, as sugar typically constitutes only a small percentage of the total allowance, restrictions are only a concern to the extent they include product specific caps.
2 In many OECD countries there is actually de-escalation on sugar tariffs, meaning that the tariff of raw sugar is less than that for refined sugar/sugar-containing products. But tariff de-escalation does not necessarily result in negative protection to the processing industry and encourage foreign suppliers to upgrade. Effective protection (the excess in domestic value added created by a tariff divided by the domestic value added available under free trade) still exists as long as the tariff on the raw materials is less than the ratio of the tariff on the processed good over the share of the price of the processed good made up of raw material costs.

3 Only countries to undergo tariffication in the Uruguay Round have this option. Of the 22 developing countries this applied to, few have used it, in part because of difficulties reforming domestic legislation to enable the safeguard to be successfully triggered. Specifically on sugar, only Chile and Slovakia have invoked the safeguard between 1995 and 2003.

4 As with many of these coalitions in the WTO, the G20 and the G33 have some overlapping members, notably China, Cuba, Guatemala, India, Pakistan and Tanzania.

5 Counting tariff lines at the HS Customs Classification 8-digit level allows importers to: a) pinpoint protection over a more diverse range of products given that only 4–6 per cent of tariff lines can be designated as sensitive, and b) if more products, especially processed products, can be accounted for as containing sugar, then the consumption figures on the raw product will be reduced, reducing in turn the size of the TRQ that has to be opened up. The EU, Japan, and the US have been proponents of using 8-digit level data (Bridges Newsletter 2008).

6 In 2006 3.1 million ha were dedicated to sugar production and 3.1 million ha to ethanol. By 2018, this is projected to increase to 4.1 million ha to sugar production and 7.7 million ha to ethanol (Nassar *et al.* 2008).

7 This influence includes altering the required ratio of ethanol-to-petrol to be sold at the pump, setting lower tax levies on ethanol than petrol, and using auctions where the state-owned oil company Petrobras can buy up ethanol.

8 For example, after listing on the São Paulo stock exchange in November 2005, raising about $400 million, Cosan then filed for Wall Street listing on the NYSE in 2007 raising $2 billion. In 2007, São Martinho (part of the Copersucar group) followed Cosan's lead and launched an initial public offering on the Brazilian stock exchange raising $176 million (Wheatley 2007).

9 No GM organisms are used at present in Brazil (they have yet to be submitted to the federal biosafety council) but UNICA have acknowledged that they will be 'necessary in the future'. Cellulosic ethanol is thought to be a commercial possibility within 5–10 years (Szwarc 2008).

Chapter 9

1 In the US the equivalent of up to 7 per cent of annual production could be imported tax-free in 2009 via the 19 Caribbean Basin Initiative countries, thereby avoiding the 54 cents per gallon tariff. Around 1.3 billion litres was to be exported through the Caribbean in 2008 (Reuters 2008a).

Bibliography

Alves, Francisco (2008) 'Work Processes and Damage to the Health of Sugarcane Cutters', *Interfacehs: Journal on Integrated Management of Occupational Health and the Environment,* 3: 2, 1–22.

Australian Bureau of Agricultural and Resource Economics (1999) 'Sugar: International Policies Affecting Market Expansion', *ABARE Research Report,* 99: 14.

Australian diplomat (2008) interviewed in Washington D.C., 5 March 2008.

Australian WTO lawyer (2008) interviewed in Geneva, 1 February 2008.

Australian WTO delegate (2008) interviewed in Geneva, 1 February 2008.

Abbott, George C (1990) *Sugar* (London: Routledge).

ACP Sugar Group (2005a) 'Joint Declaration by the ACP Ministerial Delegation and Representatives of the LDCs and the Spanish Ministry of Agriculture, Fisheries and Food on the Reform of CMO Sugar', Press Release, 21 January 2005. http://www.acpsugar.org/docs/ACP-LDCCOMMON%20PLATFORMFINAL% 20150905.pdf (Accessed 10 August 2007).

ACP Sugar Group (2005b) 'The Outcome of Last Week's EU Budget Negotiations has been Greeted with Deep Concern by African, Caribbean and Pacific Sugar Supplying States', Press Release, 21 December 2005. http://www.acpsugar.org/ docs/ACP%20Press%20Release%20-%20211205.pdf (Accessed 5 June 2007).

Adamson, Martin (2007) 'Chairman's Statement' in *Associated British Foods Interim Report 2007* (London: Associated British Foods).

Adler, Emanuel and Haas, Peter (1992) 'Conclusion: Epistemic Communities, World Order, and the Creation of a Reflective Research Program', *International Organization,* 46: 1, 367–390.

AgraFNP (2008) *Biofuels Brazil,* 37, 21 October 2008.

Agritrade News (2007) 'Tate & Lyle invest in Laos', 2 March 2007.

Albert, Bill and Graves, Adrian (1988) 'Introduction', in Bill Albert and Adrian Graves (eds) *The World Sugar Economy in War and Depression 1914–1940* (London: Routledge).

Alden, Edward and Buckley, Neil (2004) 'Big Sugar Fights Threats from Free Trade and Dieticians', *Financial Times,* 26 February 2004.

Alvarez, José (2005) 'Sweetening the US Legislature: The Remarkable Success of the Sugar Lobby', *The Political Quarterly,* 76: 1, 92–99.

American Sugar Association (2008) interviewed in Washington D.C., 28 February 2008.

Anderson, Kym, Martin, Wil, and Van Der Mensbrugghe, D. (2005) 'Market and Welfare Implications of Doha Reform Scenarios', in Kym Anderson and Wil Martin (eds) *Agricultural Trade Reform and the Doha Development Agenda* (Basingstoke: Palgrave Macmillan).

Asian Economic News (2000) 'Indonesia to Unveil 2000 Budget, Sign IMF Accord', 24 January 2000.

Asian Economic News (2002) 'Bangkok to Discuss Sugar Tariffs with Jakarta, Manila', 24 January 2002.

Asian Economic News (2004) 'ASEAN-China FTA Pledges to Phase Out Most Tariffs by 2010', 13 December 2004.

Austen, Ralph A. and Smith, Woodruff D. (1990) 'Private Tooth Decay as Public Economic Virtue: The Slave-Sugar Triangle, Consumerism, and Economic Industrialization', *Social Science History*, 14: 1, 95–115.

Bair, Jennifer (2005) 'Global Capitalism and Commodity Chains: Looking Back, Going Forward', *Competition and Change*, 9: 2, 153–180.

Balfour, Sebastian (1995) *Castro*, 2nd ed. (London: Pearson Education Ltd).

Baru, Sanjaya (1987) 'Structural Changes in the International Sugar Economy', *Social Scientist*, 15: 4/5, 58–76.

Battisti, Jolanda E. Ygosse, von Maltzan Pacheco, Julia and D'Arti, Fabiana (2006) 'The Role of the G20' in Pitou van Dijck and Gerrit Faber (eds) *Developing Countries and the Doha Development Agenda* (London: Routledge).

Beardsworth, Alan and Keil, Teresa (1997) *Sociology on the Menu: An Invitation to the Study of Food and Society* (London: Routledge).

Beattie, Alan (2007) 'Troubled Talks Threaten WTO's Credibility', *Financial Times*, 23 January 2007.

Bergsten, C. Fred (2004) 'The G-20 and the World Economy', 4 March 2004 http://www.iie.com/publications/papers/paper.cfm?ResearchID=196 (Accessed 10 June 2008).

Better Sugarcane Initiative (2005) 'Meeting Report', Sugar Quay, London, 23–24 June 2005. http://www.wwf.org (Accessed 8 July 2008).

Billig, Michael (2003) *Barons, Brokers and Buyers: The Institutions and Cultures of Philippine Sugar* (Honolulu: University of Hawaii Press).

Billig, Michael (2007) 'The Interests of Competing Elites: Fighting Over Protectionism and 'Free Markets' in Philippine Sugar', *Culture and Agriculture*, 29: 2, 70–77.

Birchall, Jonathon (2008) 'Gene Modified Sugar Beets Spurs Investor Revolt', *Financial Times*, 5 March 2008.

Blackburn, Robin (1997) *The Making of New World Slavery: From the Baroque to the Modern, 1492–1800* (London: Verso).

Blandford, David and Josling, Timothy (2007) 'Should the Green Box Be Modified?' *International Food & Agricultural Trade Policy Council Discussion Paper*, April 2007.

Boomgaard, Peter (1988) 'Treacherous Cane: The Java Sugar Industry between 1914 and 1940', in Bill Albert and Adrian Graves (eds) *The World Sugar Economy in War and Depression 1914–1940* (London: Routledge).

Borras Jr., Saturnino (2001) 'State-Society Relations in Land Reform Implementation in the Philippines', *Development and Change*, 32: 3, 545–575.

Borras Jr., Saturnino (2003) 'Questioning Market-Led Agrarian Reform', *Journal of Agrarian Change*, 3: 3, 367–394.

Borrell, Brent, de la Peña, Beulah, Noveno, Lourdes and Quirke, Derek (1994) *Philippine Sugar: An Industry Finding its Feet* (Canberra: Centre for International Economics).

Borrell, Brent and Duncan, Ronald C. (1990) 'A Survey of the Costs of World Sugar Policies', *World Bank Working Paper*, WPS 522, October 1990.

Borrell, Brent and Pearce, David (1999) 'Sugar: the Taste Test of Liberalisation', Paper prepared for the Conference on Agriculture and New Trade Agenda, Geneva, September 1999.

Bouët, Antoine, Bureau, Jean-Christophe, Decreux, Yvan and Jean, Sébastien, (2005) 'Multilateral Agricultural Liberalisation: The Contrasting Fortunes of Developing Countries in the Doha Round', *The World Economy*, 28: 9, 1329–1354.

Branford, Sue and Rocha, Jan (2002) *Cutting the Wire: The Story of the Landless Movement in Brazil* (London: Latin American Bureau).

Braudel, Fernand (1981) *Civilization and Capitalism. Volume 1: The Structures of Everyday Life* (London: William Collins).

Brenner, Marie (2001) 'Kingdom of Sugar', *Vanity Fair*, February 2001.

Bridges Newsletter (2006) 'Chair's Ag Market Access Paper Sparks Fierce Debate on Tariff Cuts', *International Centre for Trade and Sustainable Development*, 10: 21, no page numbers.

Bridges Newsletter (2008) 'Revised Ag Text Reflects Progress, But Final Deal Still Elusive', *International Centre for Trade and Sustainable Development*, 12: 42, no page numbers.

Brooks, J., Cameron, A. and Carter, C. (1998) 'Political Action Committee Contributions and U.S. Congressional Voting on Sugar Legislation', *American Journal of Agricultural Economics*, 80: 3, 441–454.

Bunsha, Dionne (2003) 'Sugar Daddies', *New Internationalist*, 363, 11–14.

Burbach, Roger and Flynn, Patricia (1980) *Agribusiness in the Americas* (London: Monthly Review Press).

Bush, George W. (2008) 'Statement by the President on the Farm Bill', *White House* Press Release, 13 May 2008. http://blog.nam.org/farm%20bill%20SBTP.pdf (Accessed 16 June 2008).

Business Standard (2007) 'Sugar Mills to Get Interest Free Loan', 11 December 2007.

Carmona, Eduardo (2008) 'New Developments and Patterns in Sugar and Ethanol Trade', Presentation to International Sugar Organisation, London, 19 November 2008.

Cardoso, Fernando Henrique (1972) 'Dependency and Development in Latin America', *New Left Review*, 74, 83–95.

Carrington, Selwyn (2002) *The Sugar Industry and the Abolition of the Slave Trade, 1775–1810* (Florida: University Press of Florida).

Center for Food Safety, 'Farmers, Consumer Advocates, Conservationists Challenge Federal Approval of Genetically Engineered Beets', Press Release, 23 January 2008. http://www.centerforfoodsafety.com (Accessed 21 March 2008).

Cerny, Phil (ed.) (1993) *Finance and World Politics* (Aldershot: Elgar).

Chait, Jonathan (2005) 'John Breaux: Hero or Hack?', *Los Angeles Times*, 14 January 2005.

Chan, Jackson (2008) 'Where is China's Sweetener and Ethanol Market Heading?', Presentation to International Sugar Organisation, London, 19 November 2008.

Chand, Satish (2005) 'Globalisation or Self-Inflicted Wounds in the Fiji Sugar and Garment Industries?', *Pacific Economic Bulletin*, 20: 3, 124–129.

Chaplin, Hannah and Matthews, Alan (2006) 'Coping with the Fallout for Preference-receiving Countries from EU Sugar Reform', *The Estey Centre Journal of International Law and Trade Policy*, 7: 1, 15–31.

Chiang, Chang-Chou (2003) 'Can Money Buy Votes? A Case Study of U.S. Sugar Policy', *Agriculture and Economics*, 31, 79–101.

Chorev, Nitsan (2007) 'A Fluid Divide: Domestic and International Factors in US Trade Policy', *Review of International Political Economy*, 14: 4, 653–689.

Christensen, Cheryl (1978) 'World Hunger: A Structural Approach', *International Organization*, 32: 3, 745–774.

Christian Aid (2005) *The Damage Done: Aid, Death and Dogma* (London: Christian Aid).

Chung, Olivia (2007) 'After the Coke Craze, it's Tea Time in China', *China Business*, 11 May 2007.

Clapp, Jennifer (2003) 'Transnational Corporate Interests and Global Environmental Governance: Negotiating Rules for Agricultural Biotechnology and Chemicals', *Environmental Politics*, 12: 4, 1–23.

Cliffe, Lionel (2000) 'Land Reform in South Africa', *Review of African Political Economy*, 27: 84, 273–286.

Coca-Cola (2008) *Annual Review, 2007* (Atlanta: Coca-Cola Company).

Coen, David and Grant, Wyn (2005) 'Business and Government in Policy-making', in Dominic Kelly and Wyn Grant (eds) *The Politics of International Trade in the 21ˢᵗ Century: Actors, Issues and Regional Dynamics* (Basingstoke: Palgrave Macmillan).

Cohen, Benjamin (2008) *International Political Economy: An Intellectual History* (Princeton, NJ: Princeton University Press).

Comité Européen des Fabricants de Sucre, 'CEFS Communiqué on the Sugar Reform', 11 June 2004. http://www.subel.be/myDocuments/01/001/004/cefs_press_release_040611_e.doc (Accessed 17 May 2007).

Committee of Industrial Users of Sugar (2005) 'The Point of View of Europe's Sugar-Using Industry', Speech at the European Parliament Hearing on CMO Sugar Reform, 13 July 2005. http://www.europarl.europa.eu/hearings/20050713/agri/beaumont_zimmer_en.pdf (Accessed 24 February 2007).

Comor, Edward (ed.) (1994) *The Global Political Economy of Communication* (London: Macmillan).

Confederation of European Beet Growers and Comité Européen des Fabricants de Sucre, 'The Success of EU Sugar Regime Reform is Being Undermined by its External Trade Policy', Joint Position Paper, 19 December 2007. http://www.comitesucre.org/userfiles/CIBE%20CEFS-CIBE%20PositionPaper%2019th%20December%20full%20version.pdf (Accessed 22 May 2008).

Cook, Terry (2004) 'Outrage in the Philippines over Killing of Plantation Workers', *World Socialist*, 24 December 2004. http://www.wsws.org (Accessed 10 June 2008).

Coote, Belinda (1987) *The Hunger Crop* (Oxford: Oxfam).

Copersucar (2007) *Management Report: 2003/04, 2004/05, 2005/06* (São Paulo: Copersucar).

Corn Refiners Association (2006) Letter Sent to the FDA Regarding the Definition of the term Natural, 14 November 2006. Obtained privately.

Corn Refiners Association (2008) interviewed in Washington D.C., 5 March 2008.

Cosan (2007) *Annual Report 2007* (São Paulo: Cosan).

Cox, Robert (1981) 'Social Forces, States and World Orders: Beyond International Relations Theory', *Millennium*, 10: 2, 126–155.

Cox, Robert (1987) *Production, Power and World Order* (New York: Colombia University Press).

Cox, Robert (1993) 'Structural Issues of Global Governance: Implications for Europe', in Stephen Gill (ed.) *Gramsci, Historical Materialism and International Relations* (Cambridge: Cambridge University Press).

Crespo, Horacio (1988) 'The Cartelization of the Mexican Sugar Industry, 1924–1940', in Bill Albert and Adrian Graves (eds) *The World Sugar Economy in War and Depression 1914–1940* (London: Routledge).

Cronin, David (2007) 'Small Island States Stand Up to EU', *Inter Press Service*, 3 August 2007.

Dalmeny, Kath (2003) 'Sugar Spin', *The Ecologist*, 1 November 2003.

de Haen, Hartwig, Stamoulis, Kostas, Shetty, Prakesh and Pingali, Prabhu (2003) 'The World Food Economy in the Twenty-first Century: Challenges for International Cooperation', *Development Policy Review*, 21: 5–6, 683–696.

Denemark, R. and O'Brien, Robert (1997) 'Contesting the Canon: International Political Economy at UK and US Universities', *Review of International Political Economy*, 4: 1, 214–238.

Department for the Environment, Food and Rural Affairs (2006) *Regulatory Impact Assessment of Options for Reform of the EU Sugar Regime* (London: DEFRA).

Digges, Cheryl (2008) Vice President of Public Policy and Education, Sugar Association, interviewed in Washington D.C., 3 March 2008.

Dinham, Barbara (1983) *Agribusiness in Africa* (London: Earth Resources Research).

Doha Ministerial Declaration, WT/MIN(01)/DEC/1, 20 November 2001. http://www.wto.org/English/thewto_e/minist_e/min01_e/mindecl_e.htm (Accessed 12 May 2008).

Dolan, D., Humphrey, J. and Harris-Pascal, C. (1999) 'Horticulture Commodity Chains: The Impact of the UK Market on the African Fresh Vegetable Industry', *IDS Working Paper*, 96: 1–39.

Doner, Richard and Ramsey, Ansil (2004) 'Growing into Trouble: Institutions and Politics in the Thai Sugar Industry', *Journal of East Asian Studies*, 4: 1, 97–138.

Downie, Andrew (2008) 'As Food Prices Soar, Brazil and Argentina React in Opposite Ways', *New York Times*, 27 August 2008.

Drummond, Ian and Marsden, Terry (1999) *The Condition of Sustainability* (London: Routledge).

Earley, Thomas and Westfall, Donald (1996) *International Dynamics of National Sugar Policies* (Rome: Food and Agricultural Organisation).

Elsig, Manfred (2006) 'Different Facets of Power in Decision-Making in the WTO', *Swiss National Centre for Competence in Research Trade Regulation Working Paper*, 2006/23.

Esserman, Susan and Howse, Robert (2003) 'The WTO on Trial', *Foreign Affairs*, 82: 1, 130–140.

Ethanol Statistics (2008a) 'Cosan's Strategy for Future Growth', Expert Opinions. http://www.ethanolstatistics.com (Accessed 16 April 2008).

Ethanol Statistics (2008b), 'Top 10 Ethanol News Items, 2007'. http://www. ethanolstatistics. com (Accessed 16 April 2008).

European Bioethanol Fuel Association, 'Bioethanol Fuel Production Data 2007', Press Release, 7 April 2008. http://www.ebio.org/uploads/080407PRbioethanol-production2007.pdf (Accessed 12 August 2008).

European Commission (2003) 'Reforming the European Union's Sugar Policy', *Commission of the European Communities Staff Working Paper*, Brussels, Belgium.

European Commission (2004) 'EU Sugar Sector: Facts and Figures', Press Release, 14 July 2004. http://europa.eu/rapid/pressReleasesAction.do?reference=MEMO/04/177&format=HTML&aged=0&language=EN&guiLanguage=fr (Accessed 20 September 2007).

European Commission (2005) 'The Commission Outlines its Support to ACP Protocol Countries', Press Release, 24 January 2005. http://europa.eu/rapid/press-ReleasesAction.do?reference=IP/05/85&format=HTML&aged=0&language=EN&guiLanguage=en (Accessed 10 March 2007).

European Court of Auditors (2000) 'Special Report No. 20/2000 Concerning the Management of the Common Market Organisation of the Market for Sugar, together with the Commission's Replies', *Official Journal of the European Communities*, 2001/C50/01.

European Parliament (2005) 'Sour Reaction to Sugar Reform', News Report, Brussels, 14 July 2005.

European Union (2003) *Sugar: International Analysis – Production Structures in the EU* (Brussels: Agriculture and Rural Development Department).

Evenson, Robert (1974) 'International Diffusion of Agrarian Technology', *The Journal of Economic History*, 34: 1, 51–73.

Fairtrade (2007) 'Fairtrade FAQ', no date. http://www.fairtrade.net (Accessed April 2007).

Fanelli, Luca and Sarzynski, Sarah (2003) 'The Concept of Sem Terra and the Peasantry in Brazil', *Journal of Developing Societies*, 19: 2–3, 2003, 334–364.

Fang, Cheng and Beghin, John C. (2003) 'Protection and Comparative Advantage of Chinese Agriculture: Implications for Regional and National Specialisation', in Scott Rozelle and Daniel Sumner (eds) *Agricultural Trade and Policy in China: Issues, Analysis and Implications* (Ashgate: Aldershot).

Farley, Miriam (1935) 'Sugar – A Commodity in Chaos', *Far Eastern Survey*, 4: 22, 172–178.

Fine, Ben, Heasman, Michael and Wright, Judith (1996) *Consumption in the Age of Affluence: The World of Food* (Routledge: London).

Fischer Boel, Mariann (2005) 'Reform of Sugar CMO', Speech for the European Parliament Committee on Agriculture and Rural Development, Brussels, 13 September 2005. http://europa.eu/rapid/pressReleasesAction.do?reference=SPEECH/05/504&format=HTML&aged=0&language=EN&guiLanguage=en (Accessed 26 August 2007).

Fischer Boel, Mariann (2007) 'EU Agriculture in a Globalised World', Speech at the Carnegie Endowment for International Peace, Washington DC, United States, 9 February 2007. http://www.europa-eu-un.org/articles/en/article_6757_en.htm (Accessed 26 August 2007).

Fischler, Franz (2004) 'The Future of the Community Sugar Regime', Speech at NGG Sugar Conference, Oberjosbach, Germany, 19 May 2004. http://europa.eu/rapid/ pressReleasesAction.do?reference=SPEECH/04/257&format=PDF&aged=1&language=EN&guiLanguage=en (Accessed 25 August 2007).

Fitter, R. and Kaplinsky, Raphael (2001) 'Who Gains from Product Rents as the Coffee Market becomes More Differentiated?', *IDS Bulletin*, 32: 3, 69–82.

Fletcher, Anthony (2006) 'Südzucker Confident in Long-term Sugar Viability', 31 January 2006. http://www.foodnavigator.com/Financial-Industry/Suedzucker-confident-in-longterm-sugar-viability (Accessed 12 May 2008).

Fold, Niels (2002) 'Lead Firms and Competition in 'Bi-polar' Commodity Chains: Grinders and Branders in the Global Cocoa-chocolate Industry', *Journal of Agrarian Change*, 2: 2, 228–247.

Fontes, Geraldo (2004) 'Interview with Nic Paget-Clarke', *In Motion Magazine*, 2 September 2004.

Frayssinet, Fabiana (2007) 'Brazil: David, Goliath and Land Reform', *Inter Press Service,* 13 June 2007.

Freeman, Duncan (2007) 'EU Chocolatiers Chase Chinese Market', *Asia Times,* 20 November 2007.

Friedmann, Harriet (1982) 'The Political Economy of Food: The Rise and Fall of the Postwar International Food Order', *The American Journal of Sociology,* 88, S248–S286.

G20 Communiqué (2005) 'G20 Proposal on Market Access', 12 October 2005. http://ww.agtradepolicy.org (Accessed 4 April 2008).

Gale, Fred (1998) *'Cave 'Cave! Hic Dragones'*: a Neo-Gramscian Deconstruction and Reconstruction of International Regime Theory', *Review of International Political Economy,* 5: 2, 252–283.

Gallagher, Kevin (2008) 'Trade Politics and Economic Development in the Americas', *New Political Economy,* 13: 1, 37–59.

Galloway, J. H. (1989) *The Sugar Cane Industry* (Cambridge: Cambridge University Press).

Garrett, Geoffrey and Lange, Peter (1996) 'Internationalization, Institutions and Political Change', in Robert Keohane and Helen Milner (eds) *Internationalization and Domestic Politics* (Cambridge: Cambridge University Press).

General Secretariat of the ACP Group (2005) 'The ACP Countries and the Reform of the EU Sugar Regime', Background Document for the Press, Brussels, 22 June 2005.

Gereffi, Gary, Korzeniewicz, M. and Korzeniewicz, R. P. (1994) 'Introduction: Global Commodity Chains', in G. Gereffi and M Korzeniewicz (eds) *Commodity Chains and Global Capitalism* (London: Praeger).

Gereffi, Gary, Humphrey, John and Sturgeon, Timothy (2005) 'The Governance of Global Value Chains', *Review of International Political Economy,* 12: 1, 78–104.

George, Susan (1976) *How the Other Half Dies* (Harmondsworth: Penguin).

Gibb, Richard (2004) 'Developing Countries and Market Access: The Bitter-Sweet Taste of the European Union's Sugar Policy in Southern Africa', *Journal of Modern African Studies,* 42: 4, 563–588.

Gibbon, Peter (2001) 'Upgrading Primary Production: A Global Commodity Chain Approach', *World Development,* 29: 2, 345–363.

Gilbert, Christopher (1996) 'International Commodity Agreements: An Obituary Notice', *World Development,* 24: 1, 1–19.

Gill, Stephen (1990) *American Hegemony and the Trilateral Commission* (Cambridge: Cambridge University Press).

Gilpin, Robert (1971) 'The Politics of Transnational Economic Relations', *International Organization,* 25: 3, 398–419.

Gilpin, Robert (1987) *The Political Economy of International Relations* (Princeton: Princeton University Press).

Gokcekus, Omer, Knowles, Justin and Tower, Edward (2004) 'Sweetening the Pot: How American Sugar Buys Protection', in Devashish Mitra and Arvind Panagariya (eds) *The Political Economy of Trade, Aid and Foreign Investment Policies* (New York: Elsevier).

Goldstein, Judith (1989) 'The Impact of Ideas on Trade Policy: The Origins of U.S. Agricultural and Manufacturing Policies', *International Organization,* 43: 1, 31–71.

Goss, Jasper and Burch, David (2001) 'From Agricultural Modernisation to Agri-Food Globalisation: The Waning of National Development in Thailand', *Third World Quarterly,* 22: 6, 969–986.

Gourevitch, Peter (1986) *Politics in Hard Times* (London: Cornell University Press).

Grain, *Seedling Newsletter*, July 2007.

Green, William (1976) *British Slave Emancipation: The Sugar Colonies and the Great Experiment, 1830–1865* (Oxford: Oxford University Press).

Grocery Manufacturers Association (2008), interviewed in Washington D.C., 6 March 2008.

Gudoshnikov, Sergey, Jolly, Lindsay and Spence, Donald (2004) *The World Sugar Market* (London: CRC Press).

Haas, Ernst (1975) 'Is There a Hole in the Whole? Knowledge, Technology, Interdependence, and the Construction of International Regimes' *International Organization*, 29: 3, 827–876.

Hagelberg, G. B. and Hannah, A. C. (1994) 'The Quest for Order: A Review of International Sugar Agreements', *Food Policy*, 19: 1, 17–29.

Haley, Stephen and Ali, Mir (2007) 'Sugar Backgrounder', *USDA Economic Research Service Report*, SSS-249-01.

Hall, Peter and Rosemary, C. R. T. (1996) 'Political Science and the Three New Institutionalisms', *Political Studies*, 44: 4, 936–957.

Hannah, A. C. (2000) 'Early History', in Jonathon Kingsman (ed.) *Sugar Trading Manual* (Cambridge: Woodhead Publishing Limited).

Hannah, A. C. and Spence, Donald (1997) *The International Sugar Trade* (Cambridge: Woodhead Publishing).

Harris, Simon (1987) 'Some Current Issues in the World Sugar Economy', *Food Policy*, 12: 2, 127–145.

Harrison, Michelle (2001) *King Sugar: Jamaica, the Caribbean and the World Sugar Economy* (London: Latin American Bureau).

Hasenclever, Andreas, Mayer, Peter and Rittberger, Volker (1997) *Theories of International Regimes* (Cambridge: Cambridge University Press).

Hathaway, Dale (1987) *Agriculture and the GATT: Rewriting the Rules* (Washington DC: Institute for International Economics).

Hathaway, Dale and Ingco, Melinda (1995) 'Agricultural Liberalization and the Uruguay Round', in Will Martin and L. Alan Winters (eds) *The Uruguay Round and Developing Economies* (Washington DC: World Bank).

Hawke, Jenny (2003) 'The Bittersweet Story of the Stevia Herb', *Nexus Magazine*, 10: 2.

Hawkes, Corinna (2005) 'The Role of Foreign Direct Investment in the Nutrition Transition', *Public Health Nutrition*, 8: 4, 357–365.

Hawkes, Corinna (2006) 'Uneven Dietary Development: Linking the Policies and Processes of Globalization with the Nutrition Transition, Obesity and Diet-Related Chronic Diseases', *Globalization and Health*, 2: 4, no page numbers.

Hawkins, Tony (2008) 'Sugar: Learning to Live Without Preferential Treatment', *Financial Times*, 11 March 2008.

Held, David and McGrew, Anthony (2002) 'Introduction', in David Held and Anthony McGrew (eds) *Governing Globalization* (Oxford: Polity Press).

Hemsted, Anthony (1991) 'Bittersweet: US Sugar Import Quotas and the Caribbean Basin', in Scott McDonald and Georges Fauriol (eds) *The Politics of the Caribbean Basin Sugar Trade* (New York: Praeger).

Hennessy, Thia and Thorne, Fiona (2005) 'How Decoupled are Decoupled Payments?: The Evidence from Ireland', *EuroChoices*, 4: 3, 30–35.

Hepburn, Jonathon (2008) Programme Officer for Agriculture at International Centre for Trade and Sustainable Development, interviewed in Geneva, 24 January 2008.

Heron, Tony and Richardson, Ben (2008) 'Path Dependency and the Politics of Liberalisation in the Textile and Clothing Industry', *New Political Economy*, 13: 1, 1–18.

Hewson, Martin and Sinclair, Timothy J. (eds) (1999) *Approaches to Global Governance Theory* (New York: State University of New York Press).

Higgott, Richard (1999) 'The Political Economy of Globalisation in East Asia: The Salience of Region Building', in Kris Olds, Phillip Kelly, Peter Dicken, Lily Kong and Henry Wai-chung Yeung (eds) *Globalisation and the Asia-Pacific: Contested Territories* (Routledge: London).

Hirst, Paul and Thompson, Grahame (1996) *Globalization in Question* (Cambridge: Polity Press).

Hoda, Anwural and Gulati, Ashok (2004) 'Special and Differential Treatment in Agricultural Negotiations', in Giovanni Anania, Mary Bohman, Colin Carter and Alex McCalla (eds) *Agricultural Policy Reform and the WTO: Where Are We Heading?* (Northampton, MA: Edward Elgar).

Hollander, Gail (2004) 'Agricultural Trade Liberalization, Multifunctionality, and Sugar in the South Florida Landscape', *Geoforum*, 35: 2, 299–312.

Hopkins, Raymond and Puchala, Donald (1979) 'Perspectives on the International Relations of Food', in Hopkins and Puchala (eds) *The Global Political Economy of Food* (London: University of Wisconsin Press).

Houbert, J. (1981) 'Mauritius: Independence and Dependence', *Journal of Modern Africa Studies*, 19: 1, 75–105.

House of Commons Select Committee on Environment, Food and Rural Affairs (2006) *Reform of the Sugar Regime*, Second Report Session 2005–06 (London: House of Commons).

Hurt, Stephen (2003) 'Cooperation and Coercion? The Cotonou Agreement between the European Union and ACP States and the End of the Lomé Convention', *Third World Quarterly*, 24: 1, 161–176.

Indian WTO delegate (2008), interviewed in Geneva, 25 January 2008.

Insanally, Riyad (2005) 'EU Sugar Regime: The ACP Perspective', Speech at Conference on Trade, Agriculture and Intellectual Property, Helsinki, Finland, 19 April 2005. http://www.acpsugar.org/docs/RInsanally.pdf (Accessed 12 May 2008).

International Centre for Trade and Sustainable Development (2005) 'Special Products and the Safeguard Mechanism: Strategic Options for Developing Countries', ICTSD Issue Paper 6.

International Fund for Agricultural Development, 'Rural Poverty in Ethiopia'. http://www.ruralpovertyportal.org/web/guest/country/home/tags/ethiopia (Accessed 12 July 2007).

International Labor Rights Fund (2007) 'Request for Review of the GSP Status of the Republic of the Philippines for Violations of Worker Rights', Country Practice Petition submitted to the Office of the United States Trade Representative, 22 June 2007.

International Labour Organisation (1994) *Recent Developments in the Plantations Sector* (ILO: Geneva).

International Labour Organisation (2005) *World Employment Report 2004–05* (Geneva: ILO).

International Sugar Organisation (2000) 'Developing Country Perspectives on the 1994 GATT Uruguay Round Agreement on Agriculture and the World Sugar Market', *MECAS Study*, 00: 09.

International Sugar Organisation (2001) *Statistical Bulletin*, 60: 1.

International Sugar Organisation (2003) 'Deregulation of India's Sugar Sector: Status: Prospects and Impacts', *MECAS Study*, 03: 19.

International Sugar Organisation (2006) *Statistical Bulletin*, 65: 12.

International Sugar Organisation (2008) *Statistical Bulletin*, 67: 4.

International Trade Administration (2004) *Employment Changes in U.S. Food Manufacturing: The Impact of Sugar Prices* (Washington DC: US Department of Commerce).

Jabara, Cathy and Valdés, Alberto (1993) 'World Sugar Policies and Developing Countries', in Stephen Marks and Keith Maskus (eds) *The Economics and Politics of World Sugar Policies* (Ann Arbor: University of Michigan Press).

Jain, S. L. (2008) 'India – A Sustainable Exporter or Back to the Cycle?', Presentation to International Sugar Organisation, London, 19 November 2008.

James, C. L. R. (1938) *The Black Jacobins* (Harmondsworth: Penguin).

Jawara, Fatoumata and Kwa, Aileen (2004) *Behind the Scenes at the WTO: The Real World of International Trade Negotiations* (London: Zed Books).

Jayasuriya, Kanishka (2003) 'Embedded Mercantilism and Open Regionalism: The Crisis of a Regional Political Project', *Third World Quarterly*, 24: 2, 339–355.

Jeffrey, Craig (2002) 'Caste, Class and Clientelism: A Political Economy of Everyday Corruption in Rural North India', *Economic Geography*, 78: 1, 21–42.

Jeffrey, Henry (2007) 'Is This Partnership, or What?', Guyana Ministry of Foreign Trade and International Cooperation Press Release, 30 July 2007. http://www.moftic.gov.gy/PressReleases/PR-Is_this_partnership.htm (Accessed 1 November 2008).

Jessop, Bob (1998) 'The Rise of Governance and the Risks of Failure: The Case of Economic Development', *International Social Science Journal*, 50: 155, 29–45.

Johnson, Elizabeth (2001) 'Sugar Rush', *Latin CEO: Executive Strategies for the Americas*, October 2001.

Johnson, T. A. (2007) 'Sugarcane Piles Driving Bidar Farmers to Suicide', *The Indian Express*, 18 May 2007.

Jolly, Lindsay (2007) Senior Economist, International Sugar Organisation, interviewed in London, 29 August 2007.

Jones, Adam (2004) 'Tate & Lyle in Bid to Settle Price Fixing Case', *Financial Times*, 22 June 2004.

Joshi, Sharad (2005) 'Maharashtra Sugarcane Farmers: Bitter Deal from the Weather and Government', *The Hindu Business Line*, 21 September 2005.

Josling, Timothy, Tangermann, Stefan and Warley, T. K. (1996) *Agriculture in the GATT* (Basingstoke: Macmillan).

Jurenas, Remy (2007) 'Sugar Policy Issues', *Congressional Research Service Report for Congress*, RL33541, 26 February 2007.

Kaplinsky, Raphael (1983) *Sugar Processing: The Development of a Third-World Technology* (London: Intermediate Technology Publications Ltd).

Kaplinsky, Raphael (2005) *Globalization, Inequality and Poverty: Between a Rock and a Hard Place* (Cambridge: Polity Press).

Keohane, Robert (1983) 'The Demand for International Regimes', in Stephen Krasner (ed.) *International Regimes* (London: Cornell University Press).

Keohane, Robert (1984) *After Hegemony* (Princeton: Princeton University Press).

Keohane, Robert and Nye, Joseph (1977) *Power and Interdependence* (New York: Longman).

Khor, Martin (2002) 'The WTO, the Post-Doha Agenda and the Future Trade System: A Development Perspective', Paper prepared for the Asian Development Bank, May 2002.

Kindleberger, Charles (1973) *The World in Depression* (London: Allen).

Koo, Won W. (2002) 'Alternative US and EU Trade Liberalization Policies and Their Implications', *Review of Agricultural Economics*, 24: 2, 336–352.

Koon, Heng Pek (1997) 'Robert Kuok and the Chinese Business Network in Eastern Asia: A Study in Sino-Capitalism', in Timothy Brook and Hy Long (eds) *Culture and Economy: The Shaping of Capitalism in Eastern Asia* (Ann Arbor: University of Michigan).

Krasner, Stephen (1983a) 'Structural Causes and Regime Consequences: Regimes as Intervening Variables' in Stephen Krasner (ed.) *International Regimes* (Ithaca: Cornell University Press).

Krasner, Stephen (1983b) 'Regimes and the Limits of Realism: Regimes as Autonomous Variables', in Stephen Krasner (ed.) *International Regimes* (Ithaca and London: Cornell University Press).

Kratochwil, Friedrich (1989) *Rules, Norms and Decisions* (Cambridge: Cambridge University Press).

Kreuger, Anne (1990) 'The Political Economy of Controls: American Sugar' in Maurice Scott and Deepak Lal (eds) *Public Policy and Economic Development: Essays in Honour of Ian Little* (Oxford: Clarendon Press).

Krivonos, Ekaterina and Olarreaga, Marcelo (2006) 'Sugar Prices, Labour Income, and Poverty in Brazil', *World Bank Policy Research Paper*, 3874.

Krugman, Paul (1996) *Pop Internationalism* (Massachusetts: MIT Press).

Lalvani, Mala (2008) 'Sugar Co-operatives in Maharashtra: A Political Economy Perspective', *Journal of Development Studies*, 44: 10, 1474–1505.

Laming, Richard (2007) Public Affairs Manager, UK Industrial Sugar Users Group, interviewed in London, 20 July 2007.

Lamy, Pascal (2001) 'From Doha to Dhaka: EU-Bangladesh Cooperation for Sustainable Development', Speech given at Seminar on Everything But Arms Agreement, Dhaka, 21 November 2001. http://europa.eu/rapid/pressReleases-Action.do?reference=SPEECH/01/561&format=DOC&aged=1&language=EN&gui Language=en (Accessed 25 May 2006).

Lamy, Pascal (2006) 'The WTO and the Doha Round: The Way Forward', Speech given to Indian Council for Research on International Economic Relations, New Delhi, 6 April 2006. http://www.wto.org/english/news_e/sppl_e/sppl23_e.htm (Accessed 19 March 2007).

Larson, Donald F. and Borrell, Brent (2001) 'Sugar Policy and Reform', *World Bank Policy Research Working Paper*, 2602.

Latham, Robert (1999) 'Politics in a Floating World', in Martin Hewson and Timothy J. Sinclair (eds) *Approaches to Global Governance Theory* (New York: State University of New York Press).

LDC Sugar Group (2007) 'Deliveries of EBA Sugar to the EU', 2 March 2007. http://www.ldcsugar.org (Accessed 22 May 2008).

Leatherhead International (2008) *Food Industry Updates: Confectionery*, 143.

Lee, Donna (2007) 'The Cotton Club: The Africa Group in the Doha Development Agenda', in Donna Lee and Rorden Wilkinson (eds) *The WTO After Hong Kong: Progress In, and Prospects For, the Doha Development Agenda* (London: Routledge).

Levitt, Theodore (1983) 'The Globalization of Markets', *Harvard Business Review*, May–June, 92–102.

Lewis, Arthur (1955) *The Theory of Economic Growth* (London: Allen and Unwin).

Lewis, Arthur (1970) *Tropical Development, 1880–1913: Studies in Economic Progress* (London: Allen and Unwin).

Leys, Colin (1997) *The Rise and Fall of Development Theory* (Oxford: James Currey).

Lichts F. O. (2008a) *International Sugar and Sweetener Report*, 140: 15.

Lichts F. O. (2008b) *International Sugar and Sweetener Report*, 140: 33.

Lichts F. O. (2008c) *International Sugar and Sweetener Report*, 140: 35.

Lichts F. O. (2008d) *International Sugar and Sweetener Report, 1998/99–2007/08* (Ratzeburg: F. O. Lichts).

Lichts F. O. (2009a) *International Sugar and Sweetener Report*, 141: 1.

Lichts F. O. (2009b) *International Sugar and Sweetener Report*, 141: 2.

Ling, Lilly (1996) 'Hegemony and the Internationalisation of the State: A Post-Colonial Analysis of China's Integration into Asian Corporatism', *Review of International Political Economy*, 3: 1, 1–26.

Lipschutz, Ronnie (1992) 'Reconstructing World Politics: The Emergence of Global Civil Society', *Millennium*, 21: 3, 389–420.

LMC International (2004) *EU Sugar Reform: The Implications for the Development of LDCs* (Oxford: LMC International).

LMC International (2006) *Review of Sugar Policies in Major Sugar Industries* (Oxford: LMC International).

London Sugar Trader (2007) interviewed in London, 1 August 2007.

Lula da Silva, Luiz Inácio (2006) 'Join Brazil in Planting Oil', *The Guardian*, 7 March 2006.

Lynd, Robert (1936) 'Democracy's Third Estate: The Consumer', *Political Science Quarterly*, 51: 4, 481–515.

Macinnis, Peter (2002) *Bittersweet: The Story of Sugar* (Australia: Allen and Unwin).

Mackintosh, James (2006) 'Elusive Cornucopia: Why it Will be Hard to Reap the Benefit of Biofuel', *Financial Times*, 21 June 2006.

Madeley, John (2002) *Food for All: The Need for a New Agriculture* (London: Zed Books).

Magdoff, Fred (2004) 'A Precarious Existence: The Fate of Billions', *Monthly Review*, 55: 9, no page numbers.

Mahler, Vincent A. (1981) 'Britain, the European Community, and the Developing Commonwealth: Dependence, Interdependence, and the Political Economy of Sugar', *International Organization*, 35: 3, 467–492.

Mandelson, Peter (2006) 'EU Agriculture and the World Trade Talks', Speech at the National Farmers Union Annual Conference, Birmingham, UK, 27 February 2006. http://europa.eu/rapid/pressReleasesAction.do?reference=SPEECH/06/130&type=HTML&aged=0&language=EN&guiLanguage=en (Accessed 28 November 2007).

Mandelson, Peter (2007) 'Doha Clock is Ticking', Speech given at International Trademark Association Committee, Brussels, 11 September 2007. http://trade.ec.europa.eu/doclib/ html/135909.htm (Accessed 2 March 2008).

Mandelson, Peter, Michel, Louis and Fischer Boel, Mariann (2007) 'Why has the EU proposed to end the EU-ACP Sugar Protocol?', *Guyana Chronicle*, 25 July 2007.

Mander, Benedict (2007) 'Chávez seeks to Defuse Brazil Rift on Ethanol', *Financial Times*, 18 April 2007.

Mann, Michael (1997) 'Has Globalization Ended the Rise and Rise of the Nation-State?', *Review of International Political Economy*, 4: 3, 472–496.

Map Light, 'Political Donations Database'. www.maplight.org (Accessed 2 April 2008).

March, James and Olsen, Johan (1998) 'The Institutional Dynamics of International Political Orders', *International Organization*, 52: 4, 943–969.

Marsden, Sandra (2002) 'Managing Canada-US Sugar Trade in the North American Context', in Andrew Schmitz, Thomas H. Spreen, William A. Messian and Charles B. Moss (eds) *Sugar and Related Sweetener Markets* (New York: CABI Publishing).

Marsden, T. and Arce, A. (1995) 'Constructing Quality: Emerging Food Networks in the Rural Transition', *Environment and Planning A*, 27: 8, 1261–1279.

Martin, Lisa and Simmons, Beth (1998) 'Theories and Empirical Studies of International Institutions', *International Organization*, 52: 4, 729–757.

Maswood, S. Javed (2005) *The South in International Economic Regimes: Whose Globalization?* (Basingstoke: Palgrave Macmillan).

Mazumdar, Sucheta (1998) *Sugar and Society in China: Peasants, Technology and the World Market* (Cambridge, MA: Harvard University Press).

McCusker, John J. and Menard, Russell R. (2004) 'The Sugar Industry in the Seventeenth Century: A New Perspective on the Barbadian "Sugar Revolution"', in Stuart B. Schwartz (ed.) *Tropical Babylons* (London: The University of North Carolina Press).

McMichael, Philip (1996) *Development and Social Change: A Global Perspective* (California: Thousand Oaks).

McMichael, Philip (2006) 'Peasant Prospects in the Neoliberal Age', *New Political Economy*, 11: 3, 407–418.

Miller, Daniel (1995) 'Consumption as the Vanguard of History', in Daniel Miller (ed.) *Acknowledging Consumption* (London: Routledge), 1–57.

Milner, Chris, Morgan, Wyn and Zgovu, Evious (2004) 'Would All ACP Sugar Protocol Exporters Lose from Sugar Liberalisation?', *The European Journal of Development Research*, 16: 4, 790–808.

Milner, Helen (1988) *Resisting Protection: Global Industries and the Politics of International Coalitions* (Princeton: Princeton University Press).

Mintz, Sidney (1985) *Sweetness and Power: The Place of Sugar in Modern History* (London: Penguin).

Mintz, Sidney (2002) 'Food and Eating: Some Persisting Questions', in W. Belasco and P. Scranton (eds) *Food Nations: Selling Taste in Consumer Societies* (New York: Routledge).

Mitchell, Donald (2004) 'Sugar Policies: Opportunity for Change', *World Bank Policy Research Working Paper*, 3222.

Morgan, Dan (2007) 'Sugar Industry Expands Influence', *The Washington Post*, 3 November 2007.

Morgan, Dan (2008) 'A Sweeter Farm Bill for Sugar', *The Washington Post*, 18 January 2008.

Morton, Adam David (2006) 'The Grimly Comic Riddle of Hegemony in IPE: Where is Class Struggle?', *Politics*, 26: 1, 62–72.

Movimento dos Trabalhadores Rurais Sem Terra, 'The Perverse Nature of Agribusiness for Brazilian Society', *MST Informa 109*, February 2006.

Moynagh, Michael (1973) *Brown or White? A History of the Fiji Sugar Industry 1873–1973* (Canberra: Australia National University).

Moyo, Sam (2000) 'The Political Economy of Land Acquisition and Redistribution in Zimbabwe, 1990–1999', *Journal of Southern African Studies*, 26: 1, 5–28.

Mulgan, Aurelia George (2005) 'Japan's Interventionist State: Bringing Agriculture Back In', *Japanese Journal of Political Science*, 6: 1, 29–61.

Mulgan, Aurelia George (2006) 'Agriculture and Political Reform in Japan: The Koizumi Legacy', *Pacific Economic Papers*, 360, 1–23.

Murphy, Craig (1994) *International Organization and Industrial Change: Global Governance since 1850* (Oxford: Oxford University Press).

Murphy, Craig (2002) 'Foreword', in Rorden Wilkinson and Steve Hughes (eds) *Global Governance: Critical Perspectives* (London: Routledge).

Murphy, Craig and Nelson, Douglas (2001) 'International Political Economy: A Tale of Two Heterodoxies', *British Journal of Politics and International Relations*, 3: 3, 393–412.

NaRanong, Viroj (2000) 'The Thai Sugar Industry: Crisis and Opportunities', *Thailand Development Research Institute Quarterly Review*, 15: 3, 8–16.

Narlikar, Amrita (2003) *International Trade and Developing Countries: Bargaining Coalitions in the GATT and WTO* (London: Routledge).

Narlikar, Amrita and Tussie, Diane (2004) 'The G20 and the Cancún Ministerial: Developing Countries and Their Evolving Coalitions in the WTO', *The World Economy*, 27: 7, 947–966.

Nassar, Andre Meloni, Rudorff, Bernardo, Antoniazzi, Laura Barcellos, de Augiar, Daniel Alves, Bacchi, Miriam Rumenos Piedade, and Adami, Marcos (2008) 'Prospects of the Sugarcane Expansion in Brazil: Impacts on Direct and Indirect Land Use Changes', in Peter Zuurbler and Jos van de Vooren (eds) *Sugarcane Ethanol: Contributions to Climate Change Mitigation and the Environment* (The Netherlands: Wageningen Academic Publishers).

National Confectioners Association (2008) *Annual Report 2007*. http://www.ecandy.com (Accessed 12 March 2008).

Nestle, Marion (2002) *Food Politics: How the Food Industry Influences Nutrition and Health* (Berkeley, California: University of California Press).

Nitzan, Jonathan and Bichler, Shimson (2000) 'Capital Accumulation: Breaking the Dualism of 'Economics' and 'Politics'' in Ronen Palan (ed.) *Global Political Economy: Contemporary Theories* (London: Routledge).

Noronha, Silvia, Ortiz, Lúcia and Schlesinger, Sergio (2006) *Agribusiness and Biofuels: An Explosive Mixture* (Rio de Janeiro: Friends of the Earth Brazil).

Nwokeji, G. Ugo (2001) 'African Conceptions of Gender and the Slave Traffic', *The William and Mary Quarterly*, 58: 1, 47–68.

O'Brien, Robert, Goetz, Anne Marie, Scholte, Jan Aart and Williams, Marc (2000) *Contesting Global Governance: Multilateral Economic Institutions and Global Social Movements* (Cambridge: Cambridge University Press).

OECD (2002) *Agricultural Policies in OECD Countries Monitoring and Evaluation 2002* (Geneva: OECD).

OECD (2007) *OECD-FAO Agricultural Outlook, 2007–2016* (Geneva: OECD).

Ohmae, Kenichi (1990) *Borderless World* (New York: HarperCollins).

Olson, R. Dennis (2008) 'Farmer Agreement Offers Alternative to NAFTA's Failures', Commentary, Institute for Agriculture and Trade Policy, 4 February 2008. http://www.iatp.org (Accessed 14 March 2008).

Ombion, Karl G. (2007) 'Sugar Crisis Worse than the 1970s Looms; Workers Suffer Most', *Butalat*, 7: 25, no page numbers.

Onuf, Nicholas (1989) *World of Our Making: Rules and Rule in Social Theory and International Relations* (Columbia: University of Southern California Press).

Orbie, Jan (2007) 'The European Union and the Commodity Debate: From Trade to Aid', *Review of African Political Economy*, 34: 112, 297–311.

Orden, David (2008) 'The Pending 2008 U.S. Farm Bill in Perspective', Presentation given at the International Agricultural Trade Research Consortium, Washington DC, 8 January 2008.

Orden, David, Paarlberg, Robert and Roe, Terry (1999) *Policy Reform in American Agriculture: Analysis and Prognosis* (Chicago: University of Chicago Press).

Organic Monitor (2007) 'The Global Market for Organic Food and Drink'. http://www.organicmonitor.com (Accessed 14 April 2007).

Osava, Mario (2008) 'Brazil: Land Shortage Provokes Murders of Indigenous People', *Inter Press Service*, 14 January 2008.

Ostry, Sylvia (2002) 'The Uruguay Round North-South Grand Bargain', in Daniel Kennedy and James Southwick (eds) *The Political Economy of International Trade Law: Essays in Honour of Robert E. Hudec* (Cambridge: Cambridge University Press).

Oxfam (2002a) 'The Great EU Sugar Scam', *Oxfam Briefing Paper*, 27.

Oxfam International (2002b) *Rigged Rules and Double Standards: Trade, Globalization and the Fight Against Poverty* (Oxford: Oxfam).

Oxfam (2004) 'Dumping on the World: How EU Sugar Policies Hurt Poor Countries', *Oxfam Briefing Paper*, 61.

Oxfam, 'Show of Unity and Strength by G20 Countries', Press Release, 21 March 2005. http://www.oxfam.org/en/pressroom/pressreleases?page=65 (Accessed 21 April 2006).

Panagariya, Arvind (2002a) 'Developing Countries at Doha: A Political Economy Analysis', *The World Economy*, 25: 9, 1205–1233.

Panagariya, Arvind (2002b) 'EU Preferential Trade Arrangements and Developing Countries', *The World Economy*, 25: 10, 1415–1432.

Payne, Anthony (2005) *The Global Politics of Unequal Development* (Basingstoke: Palgrave Macmillan).

Pearson, Daniel R. (1993) 'Commentary', in Stephen V. Marks and Keith E. Maskus, (eds) *The Economics and Politics of World Sugar Policies* (Michigan: University of Michigan).

Peter Buzzanell & Associates (2003) 'North America's Confectionery Industries: Structure, Trade and Costs and Trends in Sugar Demand', Report prepared for the American Sugar Alliance, 24 March 2003.

Peterson, V. Spike (2003) *A Critical Rewriting of the Global Political Economy: Integrating Reproductive, Productive and Virtual Economies* (London: Routledge).

Phillips, Nicola (2004) 'U.S. Power and the Politics of Economic Governance in the Americas', *Latin American Politics and Society*, 47: 4, 1–25.

Phillips, Nicola (2005a) 'State Debates in IPE', in Nicola Phillips (ed.) *Globalizing International Political Economy* (Basingstoke: Palgrave Macmillan).

Phillips, Nicola (2005b) 'Whither IPE', in Nicola Phillips (ed.) *Globalizing International Political Economy* (Basingstoke: Palgrave Macmillan).

Pigman, Geoffrey Allen (1997) 'Hegemony and Trade Liberalization Policy: Britain and the Brussels Sugar Convention of 1902', *Review of International Studies,* 23, 185–210.

Pingali, Prabhu (2007) 'Westernization of Asian Diets and the Transformation of Food Systems: Implications for Research and Policy', *Food Policy,* 32: 3, 281–298.

Polanyi, Karl (1944) *The Great Transformation* (Boston: Beacon Press).

Pollack, Andrew (2007) 'Round 2 for Biotech Beets', *New York Times,* 27 November 2007.

Pollitt, Brian (1988) 'The Cuban Sugar Economy in the 1930s', in Bill Albert and Adrian Graves (eds) *The World Sugar Economy in War and Depression 1914–1940* (London: Routledge).

Pollitt, Brian (2004) 'The Rise and Fall of the Cuban Sugar Economy', *Journal of Latin American Studies,* 36: 2, 319–348.

Polopolus, Leo C. (2002) 'World Sugar Markets and Entangled Government Programs', in Andrew Schmitz, Thomas H. Spreen, William A. Messian and Charles B. Moss (eds) *Sugar and Related Sweetener Markets* (New York: CABI Publishing).

Pomeranz, Kenneth and Topik, Steven (1999) *The World that Trade Created* (London: M. E. Sharpe).

Ponte, Stefano and Gibbon, Peter (2005) *Trading Down: Africa, Value Chains, and the Global Economy* (Philadelphia, PA: Temple University Press).

Popkin, Barry and Nielson, Samara Joy (2003) 'The Sweetening of the World's Diet', *Obesity Research,* 11: 11, 1325–1332.

Prebisch, Raul (1950) 'The Economic Development of Latin America and its Principal Problems', *United Nations Document E/CN.12/89/Rev.1.*

Price, David E. (1971) 'The Politics of Sugar', *The Review of Politics,* 33: 2, 212–232.

Pritchard, Bill (2000) 'Geographies of the Firm and Transnational Agro-Food Corporations in East Asia', *Singapore Journal of Tropical Geography,* 21: 3, 246–262.

Promar International (2008) 'Farm Bill Sugar Provisions Move Program from Bad to Worse', Promar Consultancy Report, 19 February 2008.

Putnam, Judith Jones and Allshouse, Jane E. (1999) 'Food Consumption, Prices and Expenditures, 1970–97', *USDA Economic Research Service Statistical Bulletin,* SB-965.

Quinlan, Paul (2009) 'Florida Crystals Steps Up Attack on Proposed Land Deal', *Palm Beach Post,* 7 January 2009.

Raikes, P., Friis Jensen, M. and Ponte, Stefano (2000) Global Commodity Chain Analysis and the French Filière Approach: Comparison and Critique, *Economy and Society,* 29: 3, 390–417.

Ransom, David (2003) 'The Sugar Trap', *New Internationalist,* 363, 3–6.

Ravenhill, John (2003) 'The New Bilateralism in the Asia Pacific', *Third World Quarterly,* 24: 2, 299–317.

Rede Social (2008) 'Direitos Humanos e a Indústria da Cana' (São Paulo: Rede Social).

Regalado, Antonio and Fan, Grace (2007) 'Ethanol Giants Struggle to Crack Brazil Market', *Wall Street Journal,* 10 September 2007.

Reidinger, J. M. (1995) 'Land System and its Reform in India', *Indian Journal of Agricultural Economics,* 51: 1–2, 218–237.

Reis, Elisa (1998) 'Brazil: One Hundred Years of the Agrarian Question', *International Social Science Journal,* 50: 157, 419–432.

Reuters (2007a) 'Brazil Peasants Storm Farms, Torch Sugar Plants', 13 April 2007.

Reuters (2007b) 'Sudan Aims for 10 mln tonne Sugar Output by 2015', 31 May 2007.

Reuters (2008a) 'Brazil's Ethanol Exports Expected to Rise in 2008: F.O. Lichts', 5 March 2008.

Reuters (2008b) 'Highlights of $289 billion US Farm Bill', 15 May 2008.

Reuters (2008c) 'Amnesty Condemns Forced Cane Labour in Brazil', 28 May 2008.

Riley, Anne (2007) 'Crops Compete for Scarce Resources', *Capital Eye Newsletter*, Centre for Responsive Politics, 12 July 2007.

Risse-Kappen, Thomas (2004) 'Ideas Do Not Float Freely: Transnational Coalitions, Domestic Structures, and the End of the Cold War', in Timothy Sinclair (ed.) *Global Governance: Critical Concepts in Political Science, Vol. 2* (London: Routledge).

Rogowski, Ronald (1989) *Commerce and Coalitions* (Princeton: Princeton University Press).

Roney, Jack (2008) 'NAFTA 2008 and Beyond – What Does it Mean for Sugar and HFCS?', Presentation to International Sugar Organisation, London, 19 November 2008.

Rosenau, James (1992) 'Governance, Order, and Change in World Politics', in James Rosenau and Ernst-Otto Czempiel (eds) *Governance without Government: Order and Change in World Politics* (Cambridge: Cambridge University Press).

Rosenau, James (1997) *The Domestic-Foreign Frontier* (Cambridge: Cambridge University Press).

Rothstein, Robert L. (1984) 'Regime-Creation by a Coalition of the Weak: Lessons from the NIEO and the Integrated Program for Commodities', *International Studies Quarterly*, 28, 307–328.

Roxborough, Ian (1979) *Theories of Underdevelopment* (Basingstoke: Macmillan).

Ruggie, John (1975) 'International Responses to Technology: Concepts and Trends', *International Organization*, 29: 3, 557–583.

Ruggie, John (1983) 'International Regimes, Transactions and Change: Embedded Liberalism in the Post-War Economic Order', in Stephen Krasner (ed.) *International Regimes* (London: Cornell University Press).

Ruggie, John (1998) *Constructing the World Polity: Essays on International Institutionalization* (London: Routledge).

Rural Payments Agency, 'CAP Payments to the Sugar Industry 2003–2004'. http://www.rpa.gov.uk/rpa/index.nsf/vContentByTaxonomy/0E02AC44E9EC8282802570520046FF75?OpenDocument (Accessed 12 June 2007).

Saca, Elias Antonio (2005) 'El Salvador's CAFTA Imperative', *Business Week*, 20 June 2005.

Sachs, Jeffrey (2008) 'G8 Leaders are Able but Unwilling to Act', *The Guardian*, 24 July 2008.

Santamarina, Juan C. (2000) 'The Cuba Company and the Expansion of American Business in Cuba, 1898–1915', *Business History Review*, 74: 1, 41–83.

Scheper-Hughes, Nancy (1992) *Death without Weeping* (Berkeley: University of California).

Schmidt, Vivian (2005) 'Institutionalism' in Colin Hay, David Marsh and Marjorie Lister (eds) *The State: Theories and Issues* (Basingstoke: Palgrave Macmillan).

Schmitz, Troy, Searle, James and Buzzanell, Peter (2002) 'Brazil's Domination of the World Sugar Market', in Andrew Schmitz, Thomas Spreen, William Messina and Charles Moss (eds) *Sugar and Related Sweetener Markets: International Perspectives* (New York: CABI Publishing).

Schwab, Susan (2006) 'Op-Ed: Still Ready to Talk', *Wall Street Journal*, 11 September 2006.

Secretariat of the Association of Southeast Asian Nations (2002) *Southeast Asia: A Free Trade Area* (Jakarta: ASEAN Secretariat).

Sell, Susan K. (2002) 'Intellectual Property Rights', in David Held and Anthony McGrew (eds) *Governing Globalization* (Oxford: Polity Press).

Shadlen, Kenneth (2005) 'Exchanging Development for Market Access? Deep Integration and Industrial Policy under Multilateral and Regional-Bilateral Trade Agreements', *Review of International Political Economy*, 12: 5, 750–775.

Sheridan, Richard (2000) *Sugar and Slavery: An Economic History of the British West Indies* (Trinidad: University of West Indies).

Simonian, Haig (2007) 'Asia Finds a Taste for Swiss Chocolate', *Financial Times*, 26 December 2007.

Singapore Economic Development Board (2006) 'Cadbury-Schweppes Asia Pacific Ramps up Investment', News Room, 1 August 2006. http://www.sedb.com (Accessed 21 June 2008).

Singer, Hans (1949) 'Economic Progress in Underdeveloped Countries', *Social Research: An International Quarterly of Political and Social Science*, 16: 1, 1–11.

Smeets, Edward, Junginger, Martin, Faaij, Andre, Walter, Arnaldo and Dolzan, Paulo (2006) 'Sustainability of Brazilian Bio-Ethanol', Commissioned Study by Netherlands Agency for Sustainable Development and Innovation, Report NWS-E-2006-110, Utrecht, The Netherlands.

Smith, Alan K. (1991) *Creating a World Economy: Merchant Capital, Colonialism and World Trade, 1400–1825* (Boulder: CO: Westview Press).

Smith, James (2004) 'Inequality in International Trade? Developing Countries and Institutional Change in WTO Dispute Settlement', *Review of International Political Economy*, 11: 3, 542–573.

Smith, Michael and Caminada, Carlos (2007) 'Ethanol's Deadly Brew', *Bloomberg Markets News Report*, 4 October 2007.

Söderbaum, Frederick (2005) 'Regionalism', in Nicola Phillips (ed.) *Globalizing International Political Economy* (Basingstoke: Palgrave Macmillan).

Soederberg, Susanne (2006) *Global Governance in Question: Empire, Class and the New Common Sense in Managing North-South Relations* (Ann Arbor, Michigan: Pluto Press).

Stabroek News (2007) 'Sugar Protocol Scrapped by EU in Midst of Talks', 29 September 2007.

Starr, Kenneth (1998) *Report Relating to the Impeachment of President William Jefferson Clinton*, Referral to the US House of Representatives pursuant to Title 28, Office of the Independent Counsel, 9 September 1998. http://icreport.access.gpo.gov/report/6narrit.htm#L36 (Accessed 10 February 2008).

Stevens, Christopher and Webb, Carole (1983) 'The Political Economy of Sugar: A Window on the CAP', in Helen Wallace, William Wallace and Carole Webb (eds) *Policy Making in the European Community* 2nd ed. (Chichester: John Wiley and Sons, Chichester).

Stevens, Christopher, Kennan, Jane and Meyn, Mareike (2007) 'South-South Trade in Special Products', *International Centre for Trade and Sustainable Development Issue Paper*, 8.

Stols, Eddy (2004) 'The Expansion of the Sugar Market in Western Europe', in Stuart B. Schwartz (ed.) *Tropical Babylons* (London: The University of North Carolina Press).

Strange, Susan (1983) *'Cave! Hic dragones*: A Critique of Regime Analysis', in Stephen Krasner (ed.) *International Regimes* (London: Cornell University Press).

Strange, Susan (1988) *States and Markets: An Introduction to International Political Economy* (London: Pinter).

Sugar Cane League (2008) interviewed in Washington D.C., 17 March 2008.

Sunkel, Osvaldo (1972) 'Big Business and 'Dependencia': A Latin American View', *Foreign Affairs*, 50, 517–531.

Sussman, Charlotte (2000) *Consuming Anxieties: Consumer Protest, Gender and British Slavery, 1713–1833* (Stanford: Stanford University Press).

Swedish Competition Authority (2002) *Sweet Fifteen: The Competition on the EU Sugar Market* (Stockholm: Court of Auditors).

Swinbank, Alan (2005) 'Developments in the Doha Round and WTO Dispute Settlement: Some Implications for EU Agricultural Policy', *European Review of Agricultural Economics*, 32: 4, 551–561.

Szwarc, Alfred (2008) 'Brazil's Future Road Map', Speech at the International Sugar Organisation Conference, London, 19 November 2008.

Talbot, John M. (2004) *Grounds for Agreement: The Political Economy of the Coffee Commodity Chain* (Lanham MD: Rowman and Littlefield).

Tate, Merze (1968) *Hawaii: Reciprocity or Annexation* (East Lansing: Michigan State University Press).

Tereos (2006) 'Tereos dévoile sa stratégie face au nouveau Règlement Sucre', Press Release, Lille, 27 January 2006.

Terres des Hommes (2005) *Sweet Hazards: Child Labor on Sugarcane Plantations in the Philippines* (Den Haag: Terres des Hommes).

Thai WTO delegate (2008), interviewed in Geneva, 28 January 2008.

The Associated Press (2007) 'Watchdog Investigates Alleged Canadian Chocolate Cartel', 28 November 2007.

The Economist (2007) 'Globalisation and Health: The Maladies of Affluence', 11 August 2007.

The Economist (2005) 'The Harnessing of Nature's Bounty: Brazilian Agriculture', 5 November 2005.

The Nation (2008) 'Mitr Phol to Launch Bt150m Silo: Facility Part of Deal with Tate & Lyle', 30 May 2008.

The Sugar Association (2006) 'Food and Drug Administration Citizen Petition Re: Definition of the term "Natural"', Docket Number 2006P-0094, 28 February 2006. Obtained privately.

The Sugar Association, 'Sugar Intake: What Does Science Say?', Promotional Leaflet. http://www.sugar.org (Accessed 20 June 2008).

Thelen, Kathleen (1999) 'Historical Institutionalism in Comparative Politics', *Annual Review of Political Science*, 2, 369–404.

Thomas, R. P. and McCloskey, Deidre (1981) 'Overseas Trade and Empire, 1700–1860' in Roderick Floud and Deidre McCloskey (eds) *The Economic History of Britain since 1700: Volume 1* (Cambridge: Cambridge University Press).

Thompson, Susan and Cowan, J. Tadlock (2000) 'Globalizing Agro-Food Systems in Asia: Introduction', *World Development*, 28: 3, 401–407.

Toussaint, Eric and Millet, Damien (2005) 'Indonesia: History of a Bankruptcy Orchestrated by IMF and World Bank', Committee for the Abolition of Third World Debt, 2005. http://www.cadtm.org/article.php3?id_article=1529 (Accessed 14 April 2007).

Trentmann, Frank (1998) 'Political Culture and Political Economy: Interest, Ideology and Free Trade', *Review of International Political Economy*, 5: 2, pp. 217–251.

UNCTAD India (2007) *Green Box Subsidies: A Theoretical and Empirical Assessment* (New Delhi: UNCTAD India).

Underhill, Geoffrey (2000) 'State, Market, and Global Political Economy: Genealogy of an (Inter-?) Discipline', *International Affairs*, 76: 4, 805–824.

United Nations Commission for Global Governance (1995) *Our Global Neighbourhood* (Oxford: Oxford University Press).

United States Department of Agriculture (2003) 'World Sugar Policy Review', *USDA Economic Research Service Report*, SSS-236, 31 January 2003.

United States Department of Agriculture (2007) 'Agricultural Advisory Committees for Trade', Departmental Regulation, No. 142–068, 22 May 2007. http://www.ocio.usda.gov/directives/doc/DR1042-068.htm (Accessed 3 May 2008).

United States International Trade Commission civil servant (2008), interviewed in Washington D.C., 17 March 2008.

Valdes, Constanza (2007) 'Ethanol Demand Driving the Expansion of Brazil's Sugar Industry', *USDA Economic Research Service Report*, SSS–249.

van Campen, Jos (2008) 'Ray of Hope After Reform?', Presentation to International Sugar Organisation, London, 18 November 2008.

van der Pijl, Kees (1984) *The Making of an Atlantic Ruling Class* (London: Verso).

Ward, Neil and Alma[o]s, Reidar (1997) 'Explaining Change in the International Agro-Food System', *Review of International Political Economy*, 4: 4, 611–629.

Warwick-Ching, Lucy (2007) 'ABF in £100m Mali Investment', *Financial Times*, 23 November 2007.

Warwick-Ching, Lucy and Shelley, Toby (2007) 'Splenda Leaves a Sour Taste for Tate & Lyle', *Financial Times*, 23 January 2007.

Watson, Matthew (2005) *Foundations of International Political Economy* (Basingstoke: Palgrave Macmillan).

Wearden, Graeme (2008) 'Tate & Lyle Hopes Fairtrade will Sweeten Results', *The Guardian*, 23 May 2008.

Wei, Anning and Cacho, Joyce (1999) 'Competition Among Foreign and Chinese Agro-Food Enterprises in the Process of Globalisation', *International Food and Agribusiness Management Review*, 2: 3, 437–451.

Weis, Tony (2004) 'Restructuring and Redundancy: The Impacts and Illogic of Neoliberal Agricultural Reforms in Jamaica', *Journal of Agricultural Change*, 4: 4, 461–491.

Weis, Tony (2007a) *The Global Food Economy: The Battle for the Future of Farming* (London: Zed Books).

Weis, Tony (2007b) 'Small Farming and Radical Imaginations in the Caribbean Today', *Race and Class*, 49: 2, 112–117.

Weiss, Linda (1998) *The Myth of the Powerless State: Governing the Economy in a Global Era* (Cambridge: Polity Press).

Weiss, Linda (2005) 'Global Governance, National Strategies: How Industrialized States Make Room to Move under the WTO', *Review of International Political Economy*, 12: 5, 723–749.

Welch, Cliff (2006) 'Globalization and the Transformation of Work in Rural Brazil: Agribusiness, Rural Labour Unions, and Peasant Mobilization', *International Labor and Working-Class History*, 70, 2006.

Wencong, Lu (2003) 'Trade and Environment Dimensions of the Food and Food-Processing Industries: A Case Study of China', Chinese Ministry of Commerce.

Wendt, Alexander (1992) 'Anarchy is What States Make Of It: The Social Construction of Power Politics', *International Organization*, 46: 2, 391–425.

Whatmore, Sarah (1994) 'Global Agro-Food Complexes and the Refashioning of the Rural in Europe', in N. Thrift and A. Amin (eds) *Holding Down the Global* (Oxford: Oxford University Press).

Wheatley, Jonathan (2007) 'Brazil's Cosan files for Wall Street Listing', *Financial Times*, 25 June 2007.

Williams, Marc (2001) 'Trade and Environment in the World Trading System: A Decade of Stalemate?', *Global Environmental Politics*, 1: 4, 1–9.

Williams Walsh, Mary (2008) 'Florida Deal for Everglades May Help Big Sugar', *New York Times*, 14 September 2008.

Wilkinson, Rorden (2000) *Multilateralism and the World Trade Organisation: The Architecture and Extension of International Trade Regulation* (London: Routledge).

Wilkinson, Rorden (2001) 'The WTO in Crisis: Exploring the Dimensions of Institutional Inertia', *Journal of World Trade*, 35: 3, 397–419.

Wilkinson, Rorden (2006) *The World Trade Organisation: Crisis and the Governance of Global Trade* (London: Routledge).

Willerton, Nigel (2008) 'US Organic Food and Organic Sugar Market', *USDA Agricultural Farm Outlook*, 21 February 2008.

Wolfe, Robert (2004) 'Crossing the River by Feeling the Stones: Where the WTO is going after Seattle, Doha and Cancún', *Review of International Political Economy*, 11: 3, 574–596.

Wolford, Wendy (2003) 'Producing Community: The MST and the Land Reform Settlements in Brazil', *Journal of Agrarian Change*, 3: 4, 500–520.

World Bank (1986) *World Development Report 1986* (Washington DC: IBRD).

World Trade Organisation (2008a) 'Regional Trade Agreements Notified to the GATT/WTO and in Force'. http://www.wto.org (Accessed 10 June 2008).

World Trade Organisation (2008b) 'Revised Draft Modalities', Committee on Agriculture Special Session, TN/AG/W/4/Rev. 1, 8 February 2008.

WTO General Council (2004) 'Text of the "July Package"', 1 August 2004. http://www.wto.org/english/tratop_e/dda_e/draft_text_gc_dg_31july04_e.htm (Accessed 21 June 2008).

Yancey, Dalton (2003) Representative of Florida Sugar Cane League, Rio Grande Valley Sugar Growers and Hawaii Sugar Farmers, Testimony to Farm Service Agency of the USDA Regarding the Granting of Cane Sugar Marketing Allotments to New Entrants, 29 January 2003.

Yee, Amy (2007) 'India's Over-Weight and Over-Stressed Rich', *Financial Times*, 29 October 2007.

Young, Oran (1980) 'International Regimes: Problems of Concept Formation', *World Politics*, 32: 3, 331–356.

Young, Oran (1999) *Governance in World Affairs* (Ithaca, NY: Cornell University Press).

Zacher, Mark (1987) 'Trade Gaps, Analytical Gaps: Regime Analysis and International Commodity Trade Regulation', *International Organization*, 41: 2, 173–202.

Zysman, John (1996) 'The Myth of the Global Economy: Enduring National Foundations and Emerging Regional Realities', *New Political Economy*, 1: 2, 157–184.

Index